HOW TO READ A LATIN POEM

PRAISE FOR *HOW TO READ A LATIN POEM*

'This book helps remind one of how poetry can be incredibly rich without being incomprehensible.'

Charles Moore, *Daily Telegraph*

'It deserves strong support from all classicists, who should consult it themselves (for personal stimulation and as a way of enlivening their lectures) and recommend it warmly to others who will benefit from it. This book will do much for the popularity of the Latin language and Roman verse and will do much to help them survive and stay healthy.'

Paul Murgatroyd, *Latomus*

'In this book William Fitzgerald acts as an expert guide through a carefully arranged selection of examples... the spirit of rediscovery which Fitzgerald invokes in his introduction will enchant the previously initiated.'

Astrid Voigt, *Museum Helveticum*

'William Fitzgerald's book on Latin poetry for those who "can't read Latin yet" takes us right to the heart of Latin literature... Fitzgerald's book makes demands, but the dividends are immense.'

Michael Kerrigan, *The Scotsman*

'mercurial and bold... Fitzgerald animates the dead language, covering acres but often highlighting details, such as the expressive power of word order, or English derivations... This attempt to return to Latin without being elitist and stuffy highlights a fault line in our discipline. The glass ceiling is still there; this book helps to demonstrate how we might smash it and why we should.'

Roger Rees, *Times Higher Education*

'can be warmly recommended to all curious about Roman poetry, even to those who have no intention of learning (or remembering) Latin any time soon.'

Roy Gibson, *Times Literary Supplement*

HOW TO READ
A LATIN POEM

If You Can't Read Latin **Yet**

WILLIAM FITZGERALD

OXFORD
UNIVERSITY PRESS

OXFORD
UNIVERSITY PRESS

Great Clarendon Street, Oxford, OX2 6DP,
United Kingdom

Oxford University Press is a department of the University of Oxford.
It furthers the University's objective of excellence in research, scholarship,
and education by publishing worldwide. Oxford is a registered trade mark of
Oxford University Press in the UK and in certain other countries

Published in the United States of America by Oxford University Press
198 Madison Avenue, New York, NY 10016, United States of America

British Library Cataloguing in Publication Data
Data available

Library of Congress Cataloging in Publication Data
Data available

ISBN 978–0–19–965786–5 (Hbk.)
ISBN 978–0–19–878812–6 (Pbk.)

To the next generation:
Patrick, Tom, and Beatrice

ACKNOWLEDGEMENTS

My greatest debt in the writing of this book is to my colleagues. Latin studies have flourished in recent decades, and I have drawn freely on the work of other scholars, though the need to keep footnotes to a minimum has meant that they have not all been acknowledged by name. I began writing this book while teaching at Cambridge, inspired by the example of others in the Faculty of Classics who had written books reaching out to a broader audience than that of professional classicists. They, and others like them, have done much to keep Classics on the agenda beyond the university, and I am grateful for their inspiration and example. My thanks go to the three readers for OUP, who made some helpful suggestions and saved me from a number of embarrassing errors; also to my copy editors, Sylvia Jaffrey and, especially, Richard Abram, who, with cheering good humour, went far beyond the call of duty in the final stages. Hilary O' Shea and Desiree Kellerman have been encouraging and efficient in seeing this book through from conception to publication.

CONTENTS

INTRODUCTION

Latin poetry takes us to a distant place, both alien and familiar. It can seem a long way from the concerns and the pleasures of the modern world, and in many ways it is. And yet it still speaks to us. It speaks to us, paradoxically, in a language that is no longer spoken. A dead language? We call it that, but there are many ways in which a language can live, and nowhere is a language more alive than in its poetry. We can still read this poetry, and encounter ways of thinking, feeling, and sensing that are different from our own, and yet accessible to us. In this book, I want to give the reader, and especially the reader who has little or no knowledge of the ancient world, or of ancient languages, a feeling for different possibilities of expression, different ways of feeling and thinking through language. I also want to introduce the reader to a poetic tradition that is as great as any, and very enjoyable to read.

Any visitor to Pompeii will know the thrill of feeling that ancient Romans trod these pavements, stopped at these bars, entered these houses, and gazed at these paintings while they ate. They also read the writing on these walls, for Pompeii is full of writing, from the illiterate scrawl of graffiti on the plaster of the walls to the carefully spaced, chiselled letters of formal inscriptions, via the colourful writing of the professionally painted advertisements. This writing reminds us that the people into whose lives we feel we have stepped spoke a different language. What did this place *sound* like? Language is much more than sound, of course, and a more important question to ask is how these people expressed themselves. Some of that is lost forever, because any conversation that has survived has been distorted by the written medium in which it has been reported. And so our knowledge of how Latin was actually used comes in a particular form. It is, for the most part, that special kind of language we call literature. This book concerns the most heightened form of speech of which a language is capable, namely poetry. By 'heightened' I don't mean 'elevated or 'removed from everyday speech'. Some of the poetry we will encounter is neither of these. Poetry is heightened language because it is memorable, powerful, and sensitive to complex nuances of feeling and meaning. It may signal its heightened nature by using metre and rhyme (we will come to that later), but most of us can tell that we are reading poetry simply by the way the language is used. When we read Latin poetry, we are coming as close to the texture of Roman experience as we are when we walk down the streets of Pompeii, because poetry displays the pleasure the Romans took in their language, and the experiences it made possible for them.

Poetry is the place where language performs, and so poetry shows us most clearly what a language can do, and what it likes to do; at the same time, in every different language poetry discovers new possibilities, and redefines itself. To read Latin poetry is to expand your sense of human expressiveness and thought, as well as of the nature of poetry itself. But to learn another language and to read its poetry is also to learn something about your own. Until you have had some experience of how people express themselves in a foreign language, you have little sense of what is characteristic of your own language. 'The person who does not know foreign languages does not know anything of his own,'

Goethe said, admittedly with some exaggeration. But can we call Latin a foreign language? True, it is not the language we speak, but neither is it an alternative language, one that another nation speaks. In the twenty-first century, Latin survives partly as the language of the great Latin writers and partly as a component of the English language itself, an element of the language we speak every day. Though English is not one of the 'Romance' languages directly derived from Latin (Italian, Spanish, and French), English is full of Latin derivates because of the influence of French on English, a fall-out of the Norman invasion. Until about the end of the seventeenth century, Latin was also a language in which new scientific, philosophical, and political ideas were discussed and spread across the boundaries of nations. So Latin haunts the modern West as the horizon of a common culture and a common language, shared with some ancient writers who lie at the heart of the Western tradition. It has exerted a powerful influence on Western poetry because, until recently, most poets encountered Latin poetry at the same time as (if not before) they did that of their own native tradition; many of them actually wrote Latin poetry before they wrote poetry in the vernacular. We can, for instance, read the prize-winning Latin verse composition of the teenage Rimbaud, written a few years before he went on to produce, in his native French, some of the most experimental poetry ever written.

Tradition is one way of describing our relation to the classical past. It is a concept that stresses continuity, identity, and inheritance. Tradition is an important part of what links us to the classical world, but tradition can be a burden, a source of stagnation as much as an inspiration. Ronald Knox, a brilliant classicist himself, put the case of many a modern Latin-sceptic in a passage from his book *Let Dons Delight*, in which one of his characters says:

God knows why it should be so, but as a matter of observation it seems to me quite certain that the whole legend of the 'English Gentleman' has been built upon Latin and Greek. A meets B on the steps of his club and says, 'Well, old man, *eheu fugaces* [alas, the fleeing years]. What?' and B says *'Dulce et decorum est pro patria mori'* [it is sweet and glorious to die for one's country], and the crossing-sweeper falls on his knees in adoration of the two men who can talk as learnedly as that.[1]

The second of the two Latin tags from Horace that Knox quotes is famously used by Wilfred Owen as the title for a poem on the horrors of modern warfare, which ends 'The old Lie: *dulce et decorum est pro patria mori.'* 'Old', here, is almost synonymous with 'lie'. Tradition, Owen reminds us, can mean what is taken for granted and unquestioned, preventing a fresh, unblinkered grasp of reality, and there is little doubt that Horace's words contributed to veiling the horrible realities of war from many a young recruit with a classical education. Sometimes a Latinate usage in English can produce startling results. When Thomas Gray speaks of 'the purple day' in his *Ode to Spring* we may think we have stumbled on an early case of surrealism, but in fact Gray is alluding to the Latin word *purpureus*, which, like many Latin colour words, emphasizes the aspect or sheen of an object more than its colour. *Purpureus* in Latin conveys a warm radiance, and not necessarily the colour purple. But Gray's 'purple' is poetic diction, signalled by its very remoteness from common experience; its Latin sense *denies* the English meaning of the word.

The elitist use of Latin, as a sort of secret handshake, should not distract us from the appreciation of Latin poetry, which can be as fresh and challenging as any in the modern vernaculars. My aim is to give the reader a glimpse of the brilliant colours beneath the brown, faded

---

[1] Ronald Knox, *Let Dons Delight* (London, 1939), 264–5.

patina that has accumulated over the words 'Latin poetry' in the minds of many. In the early twenty-first century, the world of elite privilege shored up by Latin, to which Knox alludes, seems far away. And that's a good thing, for it has allowed Latin poetry to become strange to us. We no longer assume that we understand Horace because he speaks like 'one of us', which was hardly surprising in the first place, given that schoolchildren had toiled for centuries to speak like him, or Cicero, or Ovid. Now Latin can be reborn as something other than the language of privilege, of secret knowledge and restricted access. Latin poetry can be recovered in all its difference as part of the record of what can no longer be said, but still has meaning for us.

Tradition is not the only way in which to think of our relation to the classical world. As Salvatore Settis has recently argued,[2] the classical world lives for us in a succession of rediscoveries and rebirths, of which the most significant would be the Renaissance itself. It is in the spirit of rediscovery that I want to read Latin poetry as a poetry worth experiencing afresh, now, in the twenty-first century. This is so not only because it has been such a presence in Western literature for so much of our history, and has infiltrated our modes of thought and feeling, whether we know it or not, but because we can, so to speak, dig it up out of an alien past and find that it 'speaks to us'. That's an easy phrase, much bandied about, but what does it mean? Latin poetry does not speak in our language or in our terms; it addresses its own very different world, so how can it speak to us? We used to go to the writers and thinkers of the past for wisdom about what is universally human, either because we thought that the ancients were wiser and less corrupted than us, nearer to an ideal state of being, or because

---

[2] Salvatore Settis, *The Future of the Classical* (Cambridge, 2006).

what has been filtered through different times and contexts, and has been consistently admired, must be what is essential. Now we are more likely to go to the past for an experience of difference, for surprises about the human spirit, for news. The world of ancient Rome is quite distinct from ours in its values, mores, politics, and aesthetics. It is this distance that makes it news. To some it will come as a surprise that Latin poetry is not only full of obscenity, but can make poetry of it. To others it may be news that poetry doesn't necessarily depend on striking phrases and the cultivation of the *mot juste*. This book will look at a number of ways in which Latin poetry is news—about poetry, about language, and about human expression. That, if you want, is what the strangeness of the past can offer us.

But the strangeness of Latin poetry is balanced by familiarity, for the history and literature of Rome has been constantly in view as a point of reference for modern writers. Antiquity has the curiously double status of being both the exotic place to which we travel to experience different ways of being human and the point to which we trace back the roots of modern attitudes. Much of the poetry I will be discussing formulates ideas, and uses means of expression, that have helped to shape the way we think and talk today. It is also the case that poetry is where we expect to find intimations of what can't be directly articulated by a culture—language that has been forced, or encouraged, to say what can't easily be expressed more directly. So, just as there are some things about these texts that we cannot understand as the Romans did, so there may be others that we can understand as they could not. Latin poetry may respond in interesting ways to the light shed by the concerns and experience of the modern reader.

Because Latin poetry has been speaking to us for hundreds of years, the Latin poets between them have come to mark out a map of emotions, styles, attitudes, and outlooks that has profoundly influenced our own ways of feeling and expression, via centuries of reading, translating, and imitation. Latin poetry is, among other things, a very varied collection of ways of speaking, of attitudes, of tones of voice. English translations and imitations of Latin poetry over the centuries are a series of attempts to match this tone in the vernacular, to bring a particular voice to life again, even to claim some of its authority. So the Latin poets have to some extent been domesticated, or 'Englished', so that they seem to speak like us. Translations feel natural, or that is usually their aim. Translators ask themselves 'How would this poet have written if he were writing English today (and what kind of a question is that?)?' Or 'What is the native equivalent of this particular foreign word/rhythm/tone of voice?' Or 'Is this good English, just as the poem being translated is good Latin?' Personally, I prefer a translation not to sound like an English poem, even if as a result it doesn't sound like good English. The Latin poets can be made readable at the expense of what makes them distinctive. Some of the greatest English poets have turned their hand to translating Latin poetry, and translations of the Latin poets continue to be produced today, many of them very good. Ovid's *Metamorphoses* and the poetry of Catullus, particularly, have proved an exciting read in English. But Vergil is a tougher proposition, and Horace even more so; in fact, anyone who reads Horace in translation can be forgiven for wondering what all the fuss is about. So I will be talking as much as possible about how the poems work in Latin.

My approach inevitably has its limitations. It is one thing to be taken through the workings of a poem in a language that behaves quite differently from your own, and another to feel these workings from the inside, so to speak. I hope some readers of this book may feel their curiosity piqued enough to learn Latin for themselves; others may be already embarked, or even advanced, on that path. But for those who are not, I want to offer an experience different from reading a translation. Of course, one can't help using translation in speaking of Latin poetry, and the mere fact that I am writing in English to readers of the twenty-first century means that I am translating. There is no explanation without translation, because what needs explaining depends on the native language of your reader. To a German, the fact that the Latin verb tends to come at the end of its sentence is hardly news, and the inflected nouns and adjectives will be more familiar. The vocabulary, on the other hand, will not be as familiar as it is to an English speaker, let alone a speaker of French or Spanish. The very difference of Latin is a difference *from* a particular language, in our case English. This book will stick as closely as possible to the *Latin* of Latin poetry. It is not a history of Latin poetry, nor do I attempt to 'cover' the subject in any systematic way. Rather, I want to provide a sample of the distinctive qualities of this great tradition in all its richness, variety, and power, and I have tried to do justice to the different styles and visions that it contains.

My chapters organize the variety of this poetry in different ways, whether by author, genre, subject, or style. At the heart of the book there are chapters on each of Rome's two greatest poets, Horace and Vergil, who were contemporaries writing during, and often about, the political revolution that made Augustus the first emperor. Before that we have a chapter each on the poetry of love and the poetry of hate, disgust, and blame, and after the two central chapters there is a chapter on two sensationalist poets of apocalypse from the Neronian period (Lucan and Seneca), followed by a chapter on two poets who present unique and fantastic visions of the way the world is

(Lucretius and the Ovid of the *Metamorphoses*). But now it is time to turn to Latin.

Perhaps the best point from which to approach Latin poetry in Latin is through English that is imitating Latin. Through translation and imitation English poets have tried to find ways of bridging the gap; of testing how Latin poetry might speak like us, or how we might speak like it. But, as I have indicated, there is not a complete separation between the two languages. In the past, one of the ways that English poetry might mark itself as a special kind of speech was by echoing Latin. For an English poet, both poetry and Latin were heightened forms of speech; poetry was a special realm of communication or utterance, and Latinate diction and syntax might be one of the ways to make it special, sometimes in the more dubious senses of 'elite', 'remote', 'inaccessible', or 'mystified'. But sometimes, intentionally or not, the result could be comic. There is a thin line between an elevated Latinate English and the uniquely dotty gibberish that is parodied by Rudyard Kipling in his 'translation' of Horace *Odes* 5. 3 (in fact, Horace only wrote four books of odes).

> There are those whose study is of smells,
> And to attentive schools rehearse
> How something mixed with something else
> Makes something worse.
>
> Some cultivate in broths impure
> The clients of our body—these,
> Increasing without Venus, cure,
> Or cause, disease.
>
> Others the heated wheel extol,
> And all its offspring, whose concern
> Is how to make it farthest roll
> And fastest turn.
>
> Me, much incurious if the hour
> Present, or to be paid for, brings

Me to Brundusium by the power
    Of wheels or wings;
Me, in whose breast no flame hath burned
    Life-long, save that by Pindar lit,
Such lore leaves cold. I am not turned
    Aside to it
More than when, sunk in thought profound
    Of what the unfaltering Gods require,
My steward (friend but slave) brings round
    Logs for my fire.

This is a brilliant parody, but of what? When I was an undergraduate, one of the exercises in Greek composition set in a classics prize exam was 'Describe a tennis match in the style of Herodotus'. Kipling is translating such a composition back into English. Kipling's Horace has to find ways of expressing concepts such as chemistry, germs, and cars that have no ancient equivalent. The resulting periphrases ('The clients of our body' for germs) are characteristically Horatian, and very funny. Finding ways of expressing modern ideas in Latin was the sort of exercise Victorian students might have been set for Latin verse composition. But Kipling is also parodying the translationese that flourished in cribs written to help fledgling Latinists and in schoolrooms where Latin was translated aloud. It is a language whose mustiness one can almost smell. Kipling is also parodying Horace himself. A typically Latinate separation between 'Me', at the beginning of the fourth stanza, and the verb that governs it ('leaves cold') is made faintly ridiculous by the emphatic repetitions of the accusative form of the pronoun I. English does not play with syntactic suspension in this way. The phrase 'much incurious', an oxymoron worthy of Horace, is also a parody of translations that use English derivatives of Latin words. *Cura* in Latin means 'care', so Kipling has given 'curious' a Latin sense and then coined the negative 'incurious' to mean 'indifferent' (there is in fact a Latin word *incuriosus*). Kipling's model for this poem is Horace's first ode of Book 1, which is cast in a common ancient rhetorical structure, to which we have given the name priamel (= preamble). It is a focusing device that lists alternatives in order to zero in on the subject ('some...others...but I...'), and it is common in lyric poetry. In his first ode Horace contrasts what other people value and pursue with his own preferences ('There are some who...but I...'). The mock-pedantic periphrasis 'the clients of our body' (i.e. germs) is typically Horatian, and Kipling wittily uses an English derivate in its Latin sense (Latin 'clients' were social dependants, on which more later). Kipling also pays ample homage to Latin poetry's obsession with saying things twice ('farthest roll and fastest turn', 'present, or to be paid for'; 'by the power of wheels or wings'). He also acknowledges Horace's attention to closural effects, and in particular his artful use of weak endings. The final stanza is worthy of Horace himself; its last line, 'Logs for my fire', is an ending in the authentic Horatian manner, inconsequential and yet satisfying. We are also reminded of the tendency of translations to gloss over the harsher realities of Roman life with words such as 'steward', where 'slave' is what is meant. The parenthetic 'friend but slave' is a wicked parody of 'enlightened' Roman attitudes to slaves.

Another weak Horatian ending, this one with more of a parodic edge, is the last line of the fifth stanza ('aside to it'), which ridicules the habit of using rhyme to translate Horace, and indeed all ancient poets. Classical Latin (and Greek) poetry does not rhyme, whereas in English poetry rhyme has played such an important role that unrhymed poetry has been called 'blank verse'. Appropriately, blank verse first appeared in English in a translation of Vergil's *Aeneid* (by Henry

Howard, Earl of Surrey, about 1554). Shakespeare brought it to perfection as a dramatic form, but it was Milton who made it a respectable medium for non-dramatic poetry. In a note prefacing *Paradise Lost* Milton claims to have rescued heroic poetry from the 'troublesome and modern bondage of rhyming', referring to rhyme as 'the invention of a barbarous age' and preferring the musical effect of ancient poetry, with 'the sense variously drawn out from one verse into another', to 'the jingling effect of like endings'. Here is the opening of Milton's *Paradise Lost*:

> Of Man's first disobedience, and the fruit
> Of that forbidden tree, whose mortal taste
> Brought death into the world, and all our woe,
> With loss of Eden, till one greater man
> Restore us, and regain the blissful seat,
> Sing heavenly Muse.

This is a typical Latinate sentence of the kind we call 'periodic', with many subordinate clauses and the main verb postponed until the end, at which point the syntax of the opening preposition ('*Of* Man's first disobedience') is finally resolved ('Sing'). Since the Latin verb usually goes at the end of its sentence, Latinate sentences tend to invert the normal English order (which would be 'sing of Man's first disobedience'). In Milton's sentence, the unpredictable way that the unit of sense expands, the changes of direction, and the temporary resting places ('and all our woe') are all typical of Latin poetry. Milton uses this Latinate sentence to outline the great Christian story, as though the Latin periodic sentence had been invented expressly for that purpose. The English poet claims pagan literature for his own uses, just as Vergil was to claim Greek literature to tell the Roman story (see Ch. 4).

A less obvious place to find the influence of Latin poetry on English is the poetry of the First World War poets. And yet we come across this from Wilfred Owen's poem *Insensibility*:

> Happy are men who yet before they are killed
> Can let their veins run cold.

Owen's word order is a poetic, Latinate inversion of 'Men who can let their blood run cold before they are killed are happy.' The paradox is given extra force by the inversion, which produces a first line containing the words 'Happy are men who... are killed'. It is an effect that he would have learned from his Latin studies, where he would also have come across the commonplace expression *felix qui potuit* (happy the man who could...). This expression usually precedes an appreciation of the simple, contented life, another very Roman sentiment. So Owen's use of this commonplace to make a point about the horror of modern war is savagely ironic. When I call Owen's 'Happy are men...' a commonplace I am translating the Latin *locus communis* (*locus* = place, cf. local). Commonplaces were standard ideas, themes, metaphors, or expressions that could be applied in many different contexts (i.e. common). Latin poetry draws on a large repertoire of commonplaces, which by modern standards doesn't sound like a very creative way of proceeding. But generating material from commonplaces fell, in Roman rhetorical theory, under the category of 'invention' (*inventio*). We, rather naively, think that writers *create* their material, but 'invention' comes from the Latin word for 'find', and a *locus communis* (common place) was a place where you could *find* material. English poetry takes many of its commonplaces from Latin poetry (*carpe diem*, for instance), and we shouldn't be put off by the existence of commonplaces. As I hope this book will show, the fact that Latin poetry is to some extent conventional in style and forms of expression does not prevent it from being original or surprising.

I have suggested that different languages stress different poetic values, depending on the character of the language, but there is little agreement over what makes a language suitable for poetry. For instance, the huge vocabulary and concreteness of English lead some to consider it a superior poetic language to French; but, for the French, English poetry is inferior to French in just this respect—its language hands sensations over bodily, a crude procedure by comparison with French, in which words act as promissory notes, on which the individual poet must make good. Another controversial characteristic of English is that it is particularly rich in monosyllables, which make up some of Shakespeare's most memorable phrases ('To be or not to be ...'). But Alexander Pope was not enthusiastic about this aspect of English, and he parodied one type of bad poetry with a line of ten monosyllables: 'and ten low words oft creep in one dull line' (*An Essay on Criticism*, 347). Pope is alluding to the fact that, more often than not, English monosyllables are Anglo-Saxon, hence 'low'. When English poets reach for something higher they often call on Latinate polysyllables, as does Shakespeare's Macbeth when he fears that the blood on his hands will 'the multitudinous seas incarnadine', which he then translates into good monosyllabic English, 'making the green one red' (II. ii. 59–60). Which version is more effective?

When it comes to comparing English and Latin as languages there is also room for disagreement. L. P. Wilkinson celebrated Horace's Latin for being 'So clean cut, so free from the fussy little words that blur our uninflected English.'[3] But Brigid Brophy saw it as one of the weaknesses

---

[3] L. P. Wilkinson, *Horace and His Lyric Poetry* (Cambridge 2nd edn., 1951), 145.

of Latin that, lacking the definite article, its juxtapositions tend to be crude (and its vocabulary tends 'to blare like a brass band').[4] Since Latin dispenses with the definite and indefinite article, words acquire a concrete solidity that has its visual equivalent in Latin inscriptions. Another comparison would be with the pidgin English foisted on Hollywood Indians ('white man speak with forked tongue'). But Latin dispenses also with words like 'with' in the phrase 'with forked tongue'. Being an inflected language, in which the grammatical case of a noun is expressed by modifications of the noun's ending, Latin has less use for prepositions (with, of, in, etc.). English inflects for the genitive, or possessive, case ('the king's English'), and for the plural ('the kings of England'), but otherwise very little. Without the 'fussy' articles and prepositions the juxtaposition of words becomes more stark.

English does not rely on prepositions alone to convey the cases of nouns. Word order is important too. It makes a big difference whether you say 'the dog bit the man' or 'the man bit the dog'. Word order allows us distinguish the subject from the object, the nominative from the accusative, which must come respectively before and after the verb. But in Latin the subject and the object might come next to each other and before the verb, as in the sentence *manus manum lavat*, 'hand hand washes', or 'one hand washes the other', which is the Latin equivalent of 'I'll scratch your back if you scratch mine'. The different inflections of the noun *manus* tell you that the first is the subject and the second, with the characteristic -*m* ending of the accusative, the object. The sentence tells you something else, as well: that you already know quite a lot of Latin, even if you've never learned it. 'Manual' and 'lavatory' are both derived from Latin.

[4] Brigid Brophy, response to *Arion* questionnaire on Horace, *Arion* 99. 2–3 (1970), 128.

Try this line of Horace, a bit more difficult:

Mors et fugacem persequitur virum.

Fugacem (compare our fugue, centrifugal) = fleeing; *mors* (mortal etc.) = death; *persequitur* (persecution) = pursues; *virum* (virile) = man. The accusative case, indicating the object of a verb, is usually marked by -*m* endings in nouns and adjectives. So 'death follows even the fleeing man (man who flees)'. The adjective *fugacem* modifies the noun *virum*, and we know this because the noun and adjective 'agree', that is, their inflections indicate that they are both in the accusative. Each noun in Latin also has a gender (masculine, feminine, or neuter) and the inflection of adjectives indicates gender as well as case, so that in many instances we can tell from a given form of the adjective whether it modifies a masculine, feminine, or neuter noun. This allows noun and adjective to be separated, as they are here by the verb *persequitur*. *Et* (even) is closely tied to the word *fugacem* (fleeing), emphasizing the paradox that is being expressed, and the verb *persequitur* (pursues), which does not have to follow its subject as slavishly as it does in English, has been juxtaposed to *fugacem* to produce a nice antithesis (fleeing pursues). Strictly speaking, the sentence is now complete, since the adjective without a noun is assumed to imply the noun 'man'.

The flexible word order of a language that does not rely on the position of a word to convey its syntax encourages elaborate patterning. Horace's poetry, which takes this capacity to the limit, has been compared to a mosaic. But, as we will see, Latin poetry (and prose) tends to like certain patterns, and the reader learns to makes sense of sentences with complicated word order by identifying those characteristic patterns.

Let us take a look at a short example of how sense, in Latin poetry, is 'variously drawn out', to quote Milton's suggestive phrase. Here is a line and a half from Lucan's epic poem on the civil war between Pompey and Caesar, written in the first century AD.

> merito Pompeium vincere lente
> gentibus indignum est a transcurrente subactis   (7. 73–4)
> (Justly do the nations who were subdued
> by Pompey as he passed resent that he is slow to conquer.)

The final showdown of the civil war between Pompey and Caesar is at hand. Pompey's soldiers are crazed for battle, but Pompey himself hesitates. Cicero, the great orator, is sent to make the case for immediate engagement. Why does Pompey delay this glorious victory? he asks. In his army are people from lands that he conquered in the name of Rome, and others are watching the outcome. They are understandably angry that, after he conquered them, as it were, *en passant*, he is now hesitating to defeat Caesar. We will take a closer look at Lucan's harrowing poem in Ch. 5. But let us see how Lucan makes this typically clever point, and how the sentence unfolds.

The first word, *merito*, means 'deservedly', so something is being approved, but what? The next three words introduce an indirect statement ('that Pompey conquers slowly'), expressed in Latin by an accusative (Pompei*um*) and infinitive (to conquer: vinc*ere*). So we are expecting a verb of speaking or thinking to govern this indirect statement (e.g. 'I think that Pompey conquers slowly'). Meanwhile, we wonder whether the adverb *merito* modifies the infinitive (i.e. 'that Pompey deservedly conquers slowly') or the main verb governing the indirect statement (for instance 'deservedly [i.e. understandably] I think that Pompey...'). In the next line we get our verb of thinking, but it is not directly expressed, rather it is implied in the phrase *indig-num est* ('it is shocking [lit. unworthy] that...'). *Gentibus* in the dative plural tells us who is shocked that Pompey conquers slowly: it is shocking 'to the peoples'. We must wait until the last word of the line to learn *which* peoples are shocked. Here Lucan uses the dative case of the very common past participle passive form (*subactis*—to the hav-ing been subdued [peoples]), where we might use a relative clause, such as 'to the peoples who have been subdued'. Latin does in one word (*subactis*) what takes five words to convey in English (to the [peoples] who have been subdued). Before *subactis* comes the phrase *a trans-currente*, which means 'by [Pompey] running past'. The characteristic -*nt*- of the Latin present participle appears in English words like 'present' (being there), 'current' (running), and 'errant' (straying). So the information unfolds as follows: 'understandably that Pompey conquers slowly to the peoples is shocking by-him-running-past con-quered'. The *merito* strikes an attitude: 'deservedly'. *Indignum est* deep-ens the mystery with a paradox: literally, 'deservedly... it is unworthy'. *Gentibus* tells us from whose point of view it appears *indignum*, and *a transcurrente subactis* explains why they might have this attitude. But it adds another paradox, neatly conveyed by the juxtaposition of verbs, compounded respectively with the prepositions *trans*- (across, through) and *sub*- (under, beneath): how could anyone moving *across* drive someone *under*? That is the point of the hyperbole.

A difference between Latin and English that we must confront immediately is that, though Latin is written with the same alphabet as English, the same letters and their combinations are pronounced dif-ferently. Over the centuries Latin has been pronounced in many dif-ferent ways, but a broad consensus has now emerged on how Latin must have sounded. A scene in the film of Terence Rattigan's play *Sep-*

arate Tables (1958) provides an amusing perspective on changes of Latin pronunciation. The David Niven character, who lays claim to a public school education that he has not had, tosses a Horatian tag into his conversation as corroborating evidence. *'Eheu fugaces'*, he says, quoting the first two words of Horace's Postumus ode (mentioned by Knox above), a characteristic lament on the passage of time (*'Alas, the fleeing* years, Postumus, slip by'). But he pronounces the second syllable of the word *fugaces* with a short a (as in 'man'). He is unmasked when another character points out that no public schoolboy would perpetrate a false quantity of this kind—it's 'few*gay*sees' says the schoolmaster. The a of *fugaces* is indeed long, but the pronunciation 'fewgaysees' is laughable by today's standards; we would say something thing like 'fugahkays'. The Latin c is always hard; the plural ending *-ces* is more or less like English 'case', and the u pronounced as in English 'butcher'. Though modern research has resulted in a large measure of agreement over how Latin was pronounced, older traditions and national differences still remain. Every nation used to think that the others pronounced Latin as though it were English, French, German, etc., rather than as it should be (which, to an outsider, sounded like English, French, German, etc.). What is curious, though, is that, in spite of the fact that Latin has sounded different in different countries, there has still been general agreement on which Latin passages or poets sound good, mellifluous, or harsh.

Why is it so significant that the David Niven character in *Separate Tables* doesn't know that the a of *fugaces* is long? The main marker of poetry in Latin is metre, and Latin metre is quantitative rather than accentual (unlike English). Every Latin syllable has a quantity; in other words, it is either long or short. A long syllable, in theory, takes twice as long to pronounce as a short syllable. The various metres of

Latin poetry are made up of different patterns of long and short syl-
lables. English metre depends on where the stress falls in the word,
not on the length of the syllable. Whether or not quantitative verse
can be written in English has been, and remains, a hotly contested
matter (I will give some examples later, which will help to give the
feel of some Latin metres). There are some rules for determining
quantity: diphthongs, for example, are long, and a syllable with a
vowel followed by two consonants is long. But the quantity of many
syllables simply has to be learned: a source of pain and suffering to
generations of schoolchildren, who were expected to compose
poetry in Latin metres until fairly recently. I cannot aspire to teach
the readers of this book the principles of Latin metre, but I will be
discussing the metre of some passages to give readers something of
the flavour of Latin verse.[5]

The sound of Latin is obviously an important dimension of the
poetry, and the reader should have a close look at the guide to pronun-
ciation at the end of this chapter before proceeding to the next. Poetry
was more of an oral, or aural, experience for the Romans than it is for
us, who usually read our poetry silently. But Latin poetry *was* written
poetry, and ancient readers didn't always read aloud, so there is a vis-
ual as well as an aural dimension to it. Besides, the difference between
reading aloud and reading silently has been exaggerated. Even when
we read poetry silently we create internal sound for the inner ear, so
that aural poetry is not necessarily oral.

[5] To supplement these discussions the reader is encouraged to visit one of the websites
with podcasts of scholars reading Latin poetry aloud. For more detail, I recommend Clive
Brooks, *Reading Latin Poetry Aloud: A Guide to Two Thousand Years of Verse* (Brooks
includes neo-Latin composition into the modern age), which comes with two very helpful
CDs. These are also a useful guide to the pronunciation of Latin.

This book is not a history of Latin literature, so a brief account of the historical trajectory of Latin poetry follows, to situate the poets who will appear in the following chapters. For more detail I recommend *Literature in the Roman World* (edited by Oliver Taplin), a stimulating and lively history of Latin literature in its cultural and historical context. Other suggestions appear in the Guide to Further Reading.

The core repertoire of classical Latin poetry, from Catullus to Juvenal, covers a relatively short period of about 170 years (*c.*60 BC to AD *c.*130), a period that saw enormous change in the Roman world. Rapid expansion of the empire, civil conflict, a change in political system from republican to monarchical government, and continual challenge to tradition are the marks of this period's history. The 'classical moment' at Rome was a time of considerable turbulence. It was during this period that Rome reached the apogee of its imperial confidence. Much Latin poetry celebrates Roman power, but not all of it does so uncritically; as we shall see, Latin poetry asks fundamental questions not only about power and empire but also about the role of art.

Latin literature is part of classical culture, the term we give to the amalgam of Greek and Roman civilization that became a common reference point for the West because of the success of the Roman empire. The Romans thought of Greek civilization not as one among many but as civilization itself. They, the Romans, were both the (victorious) successors to Greek empire and also the transmitters of what they called *humanitas*, civilization. There had been Greek colonies in southern Italy since the eighth century BC and, to the north, the Etruscans had been heavily Hellenized by the time of their ascendancy over Rome (late seventh century). So Rome grew and flourished in an Italy that was partially Greek. By the early third century BC Rome was in control of the Italian peninsula and was ready to take on the great powers of the Mediterranean, the Carthaginians and the Greeks. Roman literature was born at the time that Rome became a Mediterranean power, and it naturally adopted Greek forms and models. The earliest extant Roman literature dates from the period of the second Punic war (218–201 BC) and the conquest of the Greek kingdom of Macedon (175 BC), two of the most important wars in Rome's rise to dominance of the Mediterranean world. During that period, Plautus and Terence wrote the comedies that were to define the comic genre for the European tradition. They adapted, translated, conflated, and rewrote Greek comedies of Menander and others to produce something new and distinctive. Meanwhile Ennius (239–163 BC) wrote what was to be the national epic, until Vergil displaced it, tracing the history of Rome from the voyage of Aeneas down to Ennius' own day. Ennius wrote the *Annals* in the same hexameter metre that had been used by Homer, and all later Latin epic poets used the same metre. This is just one of the ways in which Ennius presents himself as Homer reborn, as he strives to produce for Latin culture what the poems of Homer had been for Greek. Ennius' *Annals* was still an important school text during the late Republic, but once Vergil arrived on the scene its importance diminished, and only fragments have survived into modern times. Throughout its history, Latin literature was in constant dialogue with Greek, from the micro-level of allusion to the macro-level of the adoption of Greek genres and poetic theories and the struggle to produce a rival canon.

Rome's growth, conquest of Italy, and imperial spread were inextricable from the development of its republican political system, which was conventionally supposed to have been born with the expulsion of the monarchy in 509 BC. But the enormous influx of wealth, and the opportunities for military glory and power that empire brought with it, sowed the seeds of decay for the Republic. This system had been geared to the diffusion of political power among the elite, and to the prevention of any one person acquiring overwhelming political influence; the fear of kings made Rome resistant to the change needed for the government and administration of a large and growing empire. However, successful generals such as Sulla, Caesar, Pompey, and Mark Antony were able to hang on to office beyond the legal limit of a year by virtue of their control of an army, often at the cost of waging war against their own countrymen. The fall of the republican system of government was preceded by fifty years of sporadic civil war, so that Romulus' killing of his brother at the foundation of Rome came to seem like a premonition of things to come. When the republic collapsed, in the second half of the first century, after more than four hundred years, its passing left a deep trauma on the Roman mind. Freedom (*libertas*) seemed to have been lost with the return of Rome to a monarchy (though under a different name), and four centuries of proud history to have been reversed. It was during the final, violent years of the Republic that some of Rome's finest literature was written. Cicero (106–43 BC), Catullus (*c*.85–*c*.54 BC), and Lucretius (*c*.95–*c*.55 BC) all flourished in the first half of the first century BC. Caesar, one of the men responsible for the death of the Republic, wrote accounts of his campaigns in a spare Latin that for many generations of schoolchildren was the gateway to Latin literature. Catullus' love poetry and Lucretius' philosophical epic, expounding the Epicurean philosophy, reflect their times more obliquely. The breakdown of trust and reciprocity in Catullus' relations with his beloved Lesbia, as well as Lucretius' attempt to give us the understanding to live a life of inner calm, both respond to the violence and divisions of the civil wars. In Catullus' poetry we also feel the tension as new forms of sophisticated behaviour begin to challenge the values and norms of a culture that was conscious and proud of its agrarian origins.

The civil wars saw great figures come and go, but finally Caesar's heir, Octavian (63 BC–AD 14), managed to stabilize his position and to turn the rule of one man into an institution in the years following his defeat of Mark Antony at the battle of Actium (31 BC). Octavian, who eventually took the name Augustus, associated his rule with a restoration of Roman tradition. This was a revolution that put Roman history and tradition centre stage, and it placed great importance on symbols, ideas, and representations. Small wonder, then, that this was a great age of Latin literature. Vergil (70–19 BC) wrote the national epic to rival Homer; Horace (65–8 BC) wrote lyric in the manner of the archaic Greek poets, but addressing the Augustan revolution (along with less momentous and more private concerns); and Livy (59 BC–AD 17) wrote the canonical history of Rome. Latin love elegy, a short-lived form, almost all of which was written in the twenties BC, was a phenomenon of the Augustan age, and its charting of a life devoted to love allowed the elegists (Propertius, Tibullus, and Ovid) to take an often subversive stance in relation to Augustus' project of moral regeneration.

The last of the Roman love elegists, Ovid (43 BC–AD 17), inaugurated a new wave of writers for whom the Republic was no longer a living memory, and monarchy a reality with which they had grown up. He was also the first poet to fall foul of the emperor, and was banished to the Black Sea for his subversive poem *The Art of Love*. Ovid never returned to the city he had celebrated for its pleasures and sophistication (emphatically not the qualities that Augustus was promoting), and his fate anticipates the tense relations that would often exist between paranoiac emperors and irreverent poets. But it is striking that the two other emperors whose reigns were most notable for the flourishing of literature were Nero (AD 54–68) and Domitian (81–96), two of Rome's 'bad' emperors. Both of them were the last emperors of their dynasty, the Julio-Claudian (founded by Augustus) and Flavian respectively. Of the authors who wrote under Nero, both the epic poet Lucan and his uncle, the tragedian and Stoic philosopher Seneca, were forced to commit suicide by the emperor, as was the novelist Petronius; only the satirist Persius, of the major Neronian authors, did not die violently. The two most important poets of Domitian's reign were luckier: the epigrammatist Martial (AD *c*.38–*c*.98) and Statius (AD *c*.54–*c*.95), who wrote epic (*Thebaid*) and occasional verse (*Silvae*), both flourished, and both wrote a good deal of verse flattering the emperor, which has not done their reputations any good.

There followed a long period of stability, attributable in no small measure to the fact that the emperors had no surviving sons, and so adopted their heirs. It stretched from the accession of Nerva (96), through the reigns of Trajan (98–117), Hadrian (117–38), Antoninus Pius (138–61) and Marcus Aurelius (161–81). This period includes all the remaining authors in the usual canon of Latin literature: the letter-writer Pliny (AD *c*.61–*c*.112), the historian Tacitus (AD *c*.56–*c*.118), the third (after Horace and Persius) of Rome's great verse satirists, Juvenal (fl. AD 120–30), and finally Apuleius (AD *c*.125–?170), who wrote one of the two surviving Latin 'novels' (*The Golden Ass*). In 312, under the emperor Constantine, Christianity was declared the official religion of the Roman empire, and this had a decisive effect on the literature that was to be written. The most important and exciting literature from the late second to the late fourth centuries was Christian, and some of that was poetry. But this book will not pursue the story of poetry in Latin further than the poetry of Martial, though this by no means ends the story of Latin poetry. There was a flourishing of Latin poetry in the classical style during the Renaissance, when writers such as Petrarch, Politian, Sannazaro, and Vida wrote significant Latin poetry, as did Milton in seventeenth-century England. Perhaps the last great poet whose Latin poetry is regularly published as part of his œuvre is the French poet Baudelaire (1821–1867), though his Latin poetry is not classical in style.

While we can place the Roman poets within the broader context of their times and culture, it is difficult for us to situate their works with any confidence within a biography. When it comes to modern poets, we have enough information about their lives to put together sizeable biographies, and we bring our knowledge of their lives to bear on our understanding of their poetry. In the case of ancient poets we have very little reliable information on their lives. Not only do we lack the usual records, especially letters, that allow us to construct the lives of modern poets, but what biographies we have of ancient poets are often little more than fantasies constructed from their poems; these ancient biographies are highly conventional, and similar motifs crop up in the lives of different poets, which is not encouraging. But what poets tell us about themselves is not reliable either. When ancient poets speak in the first person they are not necessarily talking about themselves. For instance, it is conventional for poets, especially love poets, to represent themselves as poor (all they have to offer is their poetry). Poverty was part of the persona of the love poet. The Augustan love elegist Tibullus was no exception to this, but in a verse letter addressed to Tibullus, his friend Horace says 'the gods have given you wealth' (Horace, *Epistles* 1. 4. 7). Tibullus is not trying to deceive anyone when he speaks of himself as poor; he is just adopting the persona appropriate to his genre.

The poet Martial represents himself as both married and unmarried in different poems, and some of the poems he writes to his 'wife' are so insulting that it is hard to believe that there was a real person involved. We should attribute no more reality to these poems than we would to a comedian doing a 'take my wife' routine, or, to take a more contemporary example, a columnist who writes weekly humorous columns about her boyfriend or spouse. It is unlikely that ancient poetry is confessional even when, as in the case of Catullus, it looks that way. So the lack of reliable biographical information about the poets need not impair our understanding of their poetry.

Genre was important in Latin poetry, and to write as a love poet or a satirist, for instance, meant adopting a persona, a mask that projected a particular type of character. The satirist is angry, the lover complains, the didactic poet takes pity on an ignorant humanity. More broadly, genre was hierarchical. At the top of the ladder came epic and tragedy, or, in prose, history. Other genres ranged themselves below the prestigious ones and found various ways of making a virtue out of their lowness, usually by taking pot-shots at epic. 'Why bother with all that irrelevant mythology?', says the satirist, 'My subject is what it's all about: human vice and folly.' 'Wasn't the Trojan war really just an appendage to a love story?' asks the love poet. 'I don't use high-falutin' language', says the epigrammatist of his obscenity, 'I call a spade a spade and speak plain Latin.' The first of my chapters will focus on one of these genres, elegiac love poetry, but before that we will have a look at two introductory poems addressed to the reader.

A GUIDE TO THE
PRONUNCIATION OF LATIN
(*English equivalents are approximate*)

CONSONANTS:

b   as in English.

c   is hard.

g   is hard.

gn (e.g. *magnus*) like -ngn in English *hangnail*.

h   is always sounded.

i   can be used as a consonant as well as a vowel, as, for instance, in *iam* (already), pronounced yam.

q   is only used before u and has the effect of making the u consonantal (as in *quick*).

r   is rolled.

s   is always as in *sea*, never as in *ease*.

v   is pronounced as English w.

VOWELS:

All vowels are sounded, except in the diphthongs, which in Latin are *ae, au, oe, ei, ui,* and *eu*. So, *cogite* is a three-syllable word.

Vowels can be long or short:

a   when short (e.g. *amo*), is pronounced as in *man*; when long (*basium*), as in *father*.

e   short (*ille*), as in *net*; long (*veni*), as in *feint*

29

i short (*igitur*), as in *fit*;
     long (*ite*), as in *feet*.

o short (*amor*), as in *pot*;
     long (*amo*), as in *hope*.

u short (*ubi*), as in *put*;
     long (*utor*) as in *boot*.

DIPHTHONGS:

ae as in English *high*.
au as in English *now*.
ei as in English *rein*.
eu both letters are pronounced, but run together very quickly (e-oo).
oe as in English *boy*.
ui as in French *oui*.

PRELUDE

To the reader

We begin with two short poems that say very little, one by Martial and one by Catullus. Each is the introductory poem heading a collection written and circulated as a single book, and it was customary for the poem in this position to be a dedication. But these two poems are not exactly what would have been expected. The first is by the father of epigram, Martial, a poet who wrote under the infamous emperor Domitian. His reputation has been harmed by the fact that he wrote some very obsequious epigrams flattering the emperor, balanced by a lot of poems that are scatological, obscene, or both. But we will start with something dignified.

> Hic est quem legis ille, quem requiris,
> toto notus in orbe Martialis
> argutis epigrammaton libellis;
> cui, lector studiose, quod dedisti
> viventi decus atque sentienti,
> rari post cineres habent poetae.   (*Epigrams* 1.1)

> (This is the one you read and ask for,
> known throughout the whole world—Martial.
> Famous for his witty little books of epigrams;
> the glory that you've given him, gracious reader,
> while still alive and feeling
> is such as few poets acquire once they're ashes.)

A simple statement, devoid of poetic imagery, striking choice of words or rhetorical devices is made into poetry by Martial's use of the possibilities of Latin word order and grammar. The flexibility of Latin word order allows Martial's simple statement to unfold in a strategic way, both anticipating and suspending information as it proceeds to build up a complex state of affairs. As we read these lines, we might think of Milton's apt description of blank verse, in which the sense is 'variously drawn out from one verse into another'.

This is not a profound poem, at least if one judges by its content: 'I'm an international sensation, with devoted readers all over the world, and famous before my death.' It's not a modest poem, either, but modesty was not a virtue in the ancient world, and in some cases it may even have been a vice. What is less immediately apparent is that this is in one respect a revolutionary poem. Martial was the first poet in the European tradition to speak to and of his readership with any regularity. Most Roman poets addressed themselves to a small coterie of like-minded souls known personally to each other. The poetry of Catullus, author of the poem to which I will turn next, gives a lively impression of a group of friends with its own in-jokes, slang, and aesthetic credo. Latin poems are nearly always addressed to someone, usually named, and the first poem of a book can be expected to be addressed to a dedicatee, often an important patron. But here Martial addresses the anonymous reader, already a fan, in this, the first of his twelve books of epigrams. Martial's special relationship with his unknown reader is the beginning of a virtual relationship between readers and writers that will have a long history.

Martial's poem divides into two parts, of which the first emphasizes space (famous the world over) and the second time (famous before his death). But, grammatically, it unfolds as a single sentence, the two halves welded together seamlessly by the relative pronoun *cui* (to whom). The relative pronouns are the key to this poem. In theory, a Latin sentence could continue to tack on relatives ad infinitum, constantly extending the sense unit in unpredictable directions. Each of this poem's two parts begins with a line that contains two relative pronouns. Martial is the poet *whom* we read and *whom* we ask for, the creation of his readership. He is the person *to whom* we have given glory, and the glory *which* we have given him while still alive is such as few poets achieve after death. The prominent relatives make Martial the still centre of his world, the point at which adulation and demand are directed. 'Here I am', says Martial, which is what we might expect in the first epigram of his twelve books. But this gesture is diverted into something rather different: 'Here is the me that *you* have made (devoted reader).'

The relative pronouns are given heavy emphasis by the word order, which cannot be imitated in English. In the first line, the main clause *Hic est…ille* (here is that [famous] man) has been infiltrated by the relative clause *quem legis* (whom you read), so that when the demonstrative pronoun *ille* arrives Martial has been identified, almost created, by our enthusiasm, an enthusiasm that is made vividly present by the repetition of the relative pronouns: **quem** *legis* (cf. legible)…**quem** *requiris* (cf. require). We can't get enough of him. The introduction of the author is only completed when the name of Martial appears at the end of the second line. One could represent the unfolding of the sense as follows: 'Here, the one whom you read, is he, the one whom you ask for, known the whole world over, Martial, known for his witty books of epigrams.' New energy is constantly supplied to Martial's utterance as the sense extends itself in unpredictable ways. The first three lines of this poem, then, say to the reader 'Here you are;

here's what you want (Martial).' The second three lines turn to what the reader has given Martial (to whom you've given fame before his death), and the relative *cui* (to whom) puts Martial in a different position in relation to the reader from the previous line's accusative *quem* (*whom* you read). But the second relative clause is infiltrated by another relative: 'to *whom*, keen reader, *what* (*quod*) you gave is *such* glory as most poets only get after they are dead'. And embedded in this statement is the phrase *viventi…atque sentienti* (to him alive and feeling; present participles in the dative): **quod dedisti *viventi* decus *atque sentienti*.** With the embedded present participles the emphasis shifts from what you gave Martial to when you gave it. This sentence draws our attention to an important feature of Latin, which, along with the absence of definite and indefinite articles, contributes to its powers of compression. The present participles *viventi* and *sentienti* are equivalent to a whole phrase in English (to him while he is alive) by virtue of the fact that the participle can be inflected just like an adjective. Latin makes frequent use of such participles. In English we would have to say 'few poets achieve after death the fame that you have given me while still living'. In Latin we have 'to whom, dedicated reader, what you have given, (while he was) living, (in the way of) fame, and (while he was) conscious, few after (they have become) ashes have achieved it, poets (that is)'. Of course, it sounds ridiculous in English, partly because I have had to add lots of those little words ('in the way of', 'that is') in parentheses to make the stark juxtapositions of the Latin comprehensible in English, though the Latin inflections leave no room for ambiguity here. But my lumbering 'translation' is meant to convey the way in which the sense unfolds, the temporal experience of accumulating meaning. Words are picked out, almost isolated, like colours in a primitive Flemish painting that refuse to resolve into a harmony. The Romans had a word for this effect, which they compared to the flowers in a meadow, whose different colours stand out from each other: such a visual field was *varius*. Milton's 'sense variously drawn out' alludes to this Latin meaning.

It is quite common for an ancient poet to imagine or predict his survival into posterity; sometimes this comes in the form of an epitaph. 'Don't weep for me,' says the epic poet Ennius in his epitaph, 'I fly, live, through the mouths of men.' Martial is saying something similar, but he is not speaking from a grave. An epitaph would commonly begin *Hic iacet*, 'here lies'. Martial alludes to this convention, but only to emphasize that his poem is *not* an epitaph. The proud boast that he makes in the second half of this epigram is that he has not had to die to achieve fame. Martial is basking in his reader's appetite for his poetry and the celebrity that this has brought him, but he is also making the reader part of something remarkable that is happening right now. It is not only Martial who benefits from the virtual relationship that is created by an anonymous readership, but also the individual reader to whom the poem is addressed. The addressee ('keen reader') is both singular and plural, for the individual reader is in touch, through Martial and his books, with many others who share a similar taste for their poet, so that they are all participants in an event. If we try to specify the speech act of this poem, we find ourselves in difficulties: it is not quite a boast, nor yet quite an act of gratitude; it puts something unprecedented on record, and in the process struggles against the impulse to shout it from the rooftops in order to register a more complex statement. We moderns recognize here the heady love-affair between public and celebrity that is so central to our world, but we recognize it in an alien form: instead of the flash of cameras, we have the measured exactness of an inscription, the almost solemn pronouncement of a relationship in a formal structure that is bursting at the seams. We could think of those relative pronouns in their different cases (*quem, quem, cui, quod*) as camera flashes going off from different positions around a focal point (the star), and we would have something of the effect of this poem. But what we would miss is the poem's unfolding of a complex statement, the diversion of space (the whole world over) into time (after death), and the way that the climactic statement which completes the sentence withdraws slightly from the initial boast (known the *whole* [*toto*] world over) to the more restrained '*few* poets' (*rari*). Martial's poem achieves its effects not through striking vocabulary or original metaphors, but through the way that it unfolds, exploiting the distinctive capacities of Latin grammar, syntax, and word order.

As I said earlier, this is an unusual opening poem, in that it is addressed not to a named individual, a patron, but to an unnamed reader. What difference does that make? Let us look at a more typical opening poem, written over a hundred years earlier, in the same metre as Martial's, by the poet he most often names as his model, Catullus:

> Cui dono lepidum novum libellum
> arida modo pumice expolitum?
> Corneli, tibi, namque tu solebas
> meas esse aliquid putare nugas,
> iam tum cum ausus es unus Italorum
> omne aevum tribus explicare cartis,
> doctis, Iupiter, et laboriosis.
> quare habe tibi quidquid hoc libelli
> qualecumque; quod, o patrona virgo,
> plus uno maneat perenne saeclo.   (*Poem* 1)

> (To whom do I give this chic new little book
> freshly smoothed by the dry pumice?
> Cornelius, to you; for it was you

who used to think my trifles *were* something,
when you yourself had dared, alone
of the Italians, to expound all history
in three most learned and laborious volumes.
So have this little book, for what
it's worth, and, O my virgin patron,
may it remain fresh for more than one generation.)

Once again, a complex situation unfolds in a single syntactical sweep, which can be represented as follows: 'To whom do I give this book? To you, Cornelius, *for* you used to encourage my dabblings *when* you yourself were working on something much grander, *so* have this book, *which*, patron Muse, I ask you to keep fresh for more than one generation.' The simple gesture of giving the book to its dedicatee ('Cornelius, to you') becomes more and more complicated as the poem unfolds.

Catullus' poem has all the usual ingredients of the opening of a Latin literary work: a named dedicatee, who is honoured by this gift; a statement that the author has been encouraged and urged to publish by this 'patron'; and praise of the patron's own achievements. In these respects, Catullus' opening poem differs radically from Martial's. We run-of-the-mill readers look over the shoulders of the more privileged addressee, modelling our relation to the poet by analogy and by difference. We may imagine ourselves as friends, but we cannot fail to reflect that, in fact, that is not the case. By contrast, Martial celebrates a virtual relationship with all his readers, whether he knows them or not.

Catullus' tone is conversational, and his language is permeated by the jargon of a clique. He calls his book (*liber*) a *libellum* (booklet), a diminutive form that signals his poetic principles (a little book, highly polished) while giving off a provocative air of preciosity. The phrase *habe tibi* (literally, have it for yourself) is colloquial and throwaway, as is *quidquid hoc libelli* (this whatever-it-is of book). By contrast to Martial's bursting pride, Catullus' arch modesty is disarming. But it is not consistent. Catullus swerves away from Cornelius in the last two lines to introduce another patron, the Muse, and with this comes a more ambitious attitude to his work. The last word of the poem, *saeclo*, from which we derive 'secular' (having to do with time, not eternity), links Catullus' book with 'the whole of time' (*omne aevum*, cf. medi-*eval*) that was the subject matter of Catullus' addressee, the historian Cornelius Nepos, to give him his full name. How are we to assess Cornelius' own work by the standards of Catullus' 'little book'? Three volumes for the whole of history is not a lot (at about 1,000 lines a book), but the undertaking itself sounds presumptuous. 'Learned' (*doctis*) is very much a positive quality for Catullus and his friends, but what are we to make of *laboriosis*, which could mean 'the product of much labour' or 'laborious' (hard work *for the reader*)? In Catullus, tone is important, but since this is a written poem we cannot always gauge it. Though the written medium here conjures up the sound of speech, we feel that we are missing something, deprived of the usual accompaniments of voice, expression, and context. What kind of exclamation is this, admiring or ironic? Catullus teases his reader with the possibilities.

But he teases Cornelius too. For we might ask whether the physical book that he gives Cornelius, all polished at the edges, can be the same as the book that Catullus consigns to the Muses, which is a 'work'. In the beginning of the poem Catullus is describing a book-roll (*volumen*), which was the standard form of the book throughout most of antiquity. It was a scroll of papyrus, with handles at each end that enabled the reader to unroll the text still to be read with the right hand, as he or she rolled up what had been read with the left. When Catullus says that Cornelius has 'unrolled' (*explicare*) all of history in three volumes he is being both literal and metaphorical at the same time. The edges of the papyrus scroll were smoothed by pumice, but pumice was also used as an eraser, so Catullus' *pumice expolitum* (smoothed by pumice) refers both to the stylistic perfection of the revised work and to the elegant look of the physical book itself. A hundred years later, Martial refers to his book as *membranum* (parchment), which is a different kind of object altogether. The reason that Martial can identify himself as an international star already, at the beginning of the work that has secured his reputation for posterity, is that this book is a second edition, and it is not in the usual format of the book-roll. As the word *membranum* indicates, his book is a codex, the ancestor of our modern book, with its pages bound between covers. Even in Martial's time book-rolls were more common than codices, and it is thought that the codex first came to be standard with Christian writers, who needed to be able to find individual passages in their sacred texts swiftly and conveniently, which would have been difficult with a book-roll.

Catullus and Martial are the earliest and latest of the poets we will read in this book. They are very different, not only as to the kind of physical book they assume, but also in tone, style, and persona. Both of them, like so many Roman poets, were provincials, Martial from Spain (the home also of Lucan and Seneca) and Catullus from Verona. Both spent most of their adult lives in Rome. But Catullus writes as a member of a tight social elite, whose other members he can address on equal terms, whereas Martial casts himself as a dependant of rich patrons, whom he flatters and sometimes berates for their stinginess. In fact, Martial probably came from a well-off family, and his pose of poverty is dictated by the 'low' genre in which he writes. Catullus, who we know was well connected and rich, also claims in some of his poems that he is short of cash. In spite of their different personas, Catullus was an important influence on Martial, who specifically claimed Catullus as his model. This doesn't preclude a competitive aggression in some of his allusions to the earlier poet. For instance, Catullus had invited his friend Fabullus to dinner in a teasing poem (13) in which, pleading poverty, he asked the guest himself to bring food, drink, and a nice girl. In return, Catullus promised to provide an exquisite perfume, and once he smells it, Fabullus will wish he were 'all nose' (anointing oneself with perfume was one of the luxuries of Roman dinner entertainment). Martial's reply to this poem is addressed to a host, called Fabullus, who has provided his guests with perfume, but has been stingy with the meat. Martial turns Catullus' elegant and confident tease into a devastating quip at the expense of the host. (In order to understand the joke of this poem you need to know that corpses in Rome were anointed with perfume.)

> Unguentum, fateor, bonum dedisti
> convivis here, sed nihil scidisti.
> res salsa est bene olere et esurire.
> qui non cenat et unguitur, Fabulle,
> hic vere mihi mortuus videtur. (*Epigrams* 3. 12)

> I admit you gave your guests a good perfume
> yesterday, but you carved them nothing.
> It's amusing to smell nice and go hungry.
> He who doesn't dine but is anointed, Fabullus,
> really seems to me a dead man.

What better way for Martial to say 'Catullus is dead, long live Martial'? It is quite common for Latin poets to allude to each other, and to engage in friendly, or not so friendly, rivalry. That is one of the ways in which the poets of ancient Rome self-consciously situate themselves within a tradition. One of the most important bearers of tradition was genre, and the chapter that follows takes a look at Roman love from the perspective of a poetic genre.

1

....

LOVE, AND A GENRE

Awkward sincerities: Sulpicia

Tandem venit amor, qualem texisse pudori
(At last it has come—love, and such a love as for me to
    hide would be more shameful)
    quam nudasse alicui sit mihi fama magis.
    (than to bare it to someone, once word gets out.)
exorata meis illum Cytherea Camenis
(Won over by my imploring Muses, the Cytherean (Venus))
    attulit in nostrum deposuitque sinum.
    (has brought him to my lap and set him down.)
exsolvit promissa Venus: mea gaudia narret,
(Venus has made good on her promise: my joys can be told)
    dicetur si quis non habuisse sua.
    (by anyone who is known not to have her own.)
non ego signatis quicquam mandare tabellis,
(I would not consign anything to sealed tablets)
    me legat ut nemo quam meus ante, velim.
    (just so that no one could read me before my own one does, far
      from it.)
sed peccasse iuvat, vultus componere famae
(But I'm pleased to have sinned, tired of composing a face for
    reputation.)
    taedet: cum digno digna fuisse ferar.   (Sulpicia, 1)
    (I want to be spoken of as worthy of his love and he of mine.)

We start this chapter with a very unusual poem. Unusual because the speaker is a woman, Sulpicia, though the poem belongs to a genre that is very emphatically male. It is not until the last line that we can be sure that the speaker is female: the adjective *digna* (worthy) has a feminine ending. By the time we get to the end of this poem we have probably gathered that it is an unusual love poem, as concerned with the act of telling as it is with the love itself. It begins, straightforwardly enough, with a sigh of relief, or perhaps a jubilant exclamation, or even a defiant claim. *Tandem* (at last) *venit* (it has come) *amor* (love). This is echoed in the final couplet by the three words *sed peccasse iuvat* (but I'm pleased to have sinned). The Roman reader would notice that these three words in the final couplet have exactly the same rhythm as the first three words, echoing their boldness, and also that this last couplet brings back the crucial word *fama* (reputation, fame) from the second line, to make an even stronger statement. The speaker will no longer compose a face for reputation, she will compose (*componere*) poems, nor does she care if she is the object of gossip. She is worthy of a worthy man (*cum digno digna*). But the confident clarity of the first three words is not the tenor of the whole poem. The syntax can be awkward, complex, and baffling, particularly in what follows the opening statement to complete the first couplet. Sulpicia's difficult syntax used to be called feminine, which meant little more than uneducated, or incompetent, but over the last twenty years its expressive qualities have been recognized, and a very distinctive poet has come into view.

Let us pick up the poem after the opening announcement, *Tandem venit amor*. *Qualem* (such as) prepares us for some qualification of the love that has been given such a welcome. The shape of the first sentence changes before our eyes, as the bold statement becomes a convoluted comparison. And the meaning of this sentence is not what we would expect. The womanly thing would be for Sulpicia to cover (*tex-isse*) her love *out of* shame or decency (*pudore*), but that is not what we hear, because she writes *pudori* instead of *pudore*, putting *pudor* in the dative, instead of the ablative, case. Why? Only as we read on does it become clear that this is the dative of cause: to hide her love would be a *cause* for shame, not a result of it. Sulpicia's word order allows the picture to come slowly into focus (to have covered...rather than to have revealed it to someone...**that** reputation would be a greater cause **for** shame). Throughout this short poem, Sulpicia's speech veers between clarity and obscurity as she expresses the difficulty and the satisfaction of speaking out as a woman. She does not avoid confronting the disreputable implications for a Roman woman of exposing her love life. In fact, she contrasts covering or hiding (*texisse*) her love not with revealing it but with laying it bare (*nudasse*). Sulpicia takes on defiantly, perhaps provocatively, the self-exposure that comes with committing herself to writing.

Latin love elegy is composed in a series of couplets, usually self-contained in meaning, and Sulpicia makes no attempt to break out of this structure. This courts monotony, but it also invites the writer to display variety in the structure, sound, and syntax of the couplets. The opportunity for symmetry and balance is increased by the metrical division of each line into two halves. Sulpicia allows these metrical divisions of the line to coincide with the sense division in lines 1 (*Tandem venit amor*), 5 (*exsolvit promissa Venus*), and 9 (*sed peccasse iuvat*), but otherwise she plays against it. Though all the couplets are self-contained in sense, Sulpicia finds different ways of distributing the sense of the couplet across its two lines. In two cases the sense simply runs on over the line-break in one sweep, but in others the couplet is divided into two or even three sections. The first two couplets are starkly contrasted in structure. Unlike the first couplet, with its complex syntax and asymmetries, the second features structures that are common in Latin elegy, and its architecture is clear and marked. Its first line can be represented as follows, marking the words that go together with the same font: **exorata** (implored) *meis* (by my) illum (him, object) **Cytherea** (Venus, subject) *Camenis* (by the Muses). The line has no main verb, and we must wait for the next line to discover what is being done to 'him'. Around this suspended object (*illum*), the two phrases *exorata Cytherea* (Cytherea, implored) and *meis…Camenis* (by my Muses) are arranged in an interlocking pattern with the two adjectives next to each other, and similarly the two nouns (*aAbB*). The effect is as much visual as auditory, and the juxtaposition of words that do not combine in sense has the effect of isolating each word as we hold it suspended in our mind, reading on until the pattern is completed. The second line of this couplet is equally, but quite differently, patterned. Instead of a central pivot with symmetrical flanks, this one emphasizes the division of the line into two by having each element of the noun–adjective pair *nostrum…sinum* (our [i.e. my] lap) mark the end of half a line. Two verbs are disposed to interlock this pair (i.e. 'brought into my…and set down…lap'). The verbs Sulpicia has chosen both have a prepositional prefix, **attulit** (brought *to*) and **deposuit** (set *down*). So each half of the line begins with a prepositional prefix, and this effect is continued at the beginning of the next line with *ex*solvit (carried *out* her promise).

Sulpicia has begun her poem with two couplets that present a complete contrast: the first begins with a bold statement, and then hedges it in a dense thicket of taboos and expectations, against which her resolution struggles. The second is triumphant and straightforward, and handles conventional structures with complete confidence and ease. This contrast is the stylistic equivalent of Sulpicia's struggle with the norms of behaviour expected of an elite Roman woman. She is confidently speaking from the position usually taken by a man in this genre (more of that later) and she is at the same time acknowledging the power of the restraints that she is flouting. In each of the remaining three couplets Sulpicia declares that she will make her love publicly available to all who read her. But the fourth couplet puts this in the negative: 'I would not write sealed love letters so that nobody reads me before my lover'. In other words, 'You the reader get me before he does'! It is an extraordinarily bold statement, but it is made in a very roundabout way. The awkwardness of the language stems from the fact that the sentence is really its own opposite negated. We would expect Sulpicia to say that she will consign her thoughts to sealed letters so that her lover will be the first to read her thoughts. But in fact she says just the opposite. In Sulpicia's sentence the expected statement shines through its negation quite clearly, and the conflict between them expresses not only her precarious position as a woman who speaks publicly about her love, but, more generally, the tension between being a poet and being a lover. Who is the primary, or first, audience of a love poem: reader or beloved? Beloved as reader, or reader as beloved? Sulpicia plays with the provocative idea that in speaking up she is exposing herself to us, naked and unsealed, but she also asks us to see her self-revelation as a mark of pride in a worthy lover, of whom she herself is worthy.

Sulpicia's first and last couplets stress the matter of pride: *this* is no love to be ashamed of. It is very common for the end of a Latin poem to recall the beginning, a technique that is known as 'ring composition'. But more elaborate forms of patterning occur too. In this poem there are five couplets, and not only do the first and last correspond, but the middle one makes a nice pivot by suggesting that a woman might have an undesirable reputation for *not* having a lover. Sulpicia kindly offers to let the loveless woman relate as her own the joys described in this poetry. She is in a sense doing for these women what Venus does for her: putting love in their lap. *Sinus*, the word translated as 'lap', means 'the fold in a garment'. Our words 'sinuous' and 'insinuate' are derived from it. *Sinus* can, by extension, also mean a breast, an embrace, or a pocket. So, Venus sets down her lover in Sulpicia's embrace, or puts him in her pocket (*deposuit* can have the same financial connotations as the English word 'deposit', which is derived from it). But what Venus consigns to Sulpicia for safe keeping Sulpicia broadcasts to the world, for in the fourth couplet Sulpicia tells us that she would not want to consign anything (*mandare*, compare 'remand') to sealed tablets. These tablets would be made of two wooden leaves coated with wax and threaded together (like our books), and they were the usual form in which more ephemeral letters were sent; important writings would be written on a papyrus scroll. The message, inscribed in the soft wax, could be smoothed away by the recipient, who would then write a response on the same tablets. Sulpicia's love-story, she tells us, will be written on the more public papyrus scroll, rather than the wax tablets exchanged by lovers. She ends the poem by imagining the reputation that her poetry will bring, and by playing off one form of good reputation, the sort that requires her to compose her expression and dissimulate (*vultus componere*, to compose a face) against another, the sort that would come from composing poetry (*versus componere*, to compose poetry).

Let us now put this poem of Sulpicia in a little context. Sulpicia is one of the very few female poets whose work survives from the ancient world. The most famous is the Greek poet Sappho, also a love poet. Sulpicia is writing in the short-lived but highly stylized genre that we know as Latin love elegy ('elegy' refers to the metre of this poetry, on which more later). It survives in the work of Propertius, Tibullus, and Ovid, all of whom published their books of love poetry within a short span of about thirty years, after which the genre died out. This period covers the rise to power and the rule of the first emperor Augustus, and many have seen the elegists' irreverence and indifference to traditional moral attitudes as a slap in the face to Augustus' programme of moral regeneration. Ovid tells us that he was banished by the emperor at least partly because of his love poetry.

We can speak of Latin love elegy as a distinctive genre mainly because the three poets who exemplify it all present a similar persona. The Latin word *persona* means mask (so the *dramatis personae* is the list of masks that will be employed in a play), and masks, literal or metaphorical, were important to the Romans. Death masks of ancestors were proudly kept in the entry halls (*atria*) of the great families, and probably inspired the great Roman traditon of sculptural portraiture. Roman portrait heads are often called realistic, but the hardbitten, warts-and-all features that look out at us from republican portrait heads are, in fact, presenting us with an ideal image of the austere, severe, and restrained Roman *paterfamilias*. Latin literature, too, is very much concerned with *ethos*, the presentation of character, and it is typical of Latin poets to construct a persona for the speaker in their poems. But in the case of love poetry this character is by no means an ideal, since, in the ancient world, passionate love was not regarded as an ennobling experience; it was more like a madness or disease. In tragedy, love causes disaster, and in the comedies of Plautus and Terence it tends to make a laughing-stock of the lover. The lover of Latin love elegy is everything a good Roman male shouldn't be, and defiantly so. He is, first of all, a poet. This means that, by convention, he is poor (whatever the poet's real circumstances, usually very comfortable).

He has rejected more lucrative and, above all, honourable callings to devote himself to the twin lives of love and poetry, and he embraces defiantly the insults that come his way as a result. Yes, he is soft (*mollis*), unfit for war (*imbellis*), lazy (*desidiosus*), and, yes, he is a traitor to his sex in being the slave of a hard (*dura*) mistress. But, he asks us, what good has the macho ethic of the warrior done for Rome, which was emerging, as these poets wrote, out of a long and murderous series of civil wars? If there had been more lovers there would have been less civil war. Or so the poets imply.

It is consistent with the importance of persona that the main unit of Latin poetry is not the poem but the book, and Sulpicia's poem is the first and introductory poem in a sequence of six poems that make up the shortest book in extant Latin poetry. The three canonical male love poets each wrote several books of love poetry revolving around a particular relationship with a beloved, who is given a Greek pseudonym. The books run to twenty or so poems, varying in length, but averaging about forty lines. Each book is carefully composed as a self-contained unit, but it does not tell a story, though it may allude to episodes in a love affair. Poems addressed to the beloved are mixed with poems addressed to other men, whether patrons, rivals, or fellow poets. The love elegists' subject is not simply the love for a particular woman, but rather the life of love more broadly, with all the choices, attitudes, and perspectives that entails.

How, then, can love elegy be written from the perspective of a woman? Quite different expectations govern her reputation, which should be safeguarded by the exercise of *pudor* (modesty, shame) and would have been jeopardized by any attempt to make a spectacle of herself. On the other hand, for a woman to take the position of the slave of love, to be subservient to her lover and to reject military life, would be to act *in accordance* with her role as a woman, and that would conflict with the counter-cultural spirit of elegy. In her opening poem, Sulpicia finds her own equivalent of the counter-cultural pose of the male elegists by rejecting the decorum that is foisted on her as a woman. She then allows aspects of the ready-made male persona to take on new meanings in the mouth of a woman. For instance, if writing poetry is the one way that a male love poet does exhibit the ambition proper to his gender, Sulpicia makes of it a not exactly respectable form of self-revelation, almost a striptease. For a woman, the mere act of writing love poetry would be compromising.

So, who is this Sulpicia who so recklessly risks her reputation? In one of her poems she identifies herself proudly as 'Sulpicia, the daughter of Servius'; her father is probably Servius Sulpicius Rufus, who was married to Valeria, the sister of Messalla Corvinus, one of Augustus' generals and the patron of the most distinguished literary salon at Rome. She is, then, a member of the aristocracy, and she speaks from a position that is socially more eminent than that of any of the contemporary male poets; what's more, she is not afraid to pull rank, something the male elegists (or their personas) are never in a position to do. It is Sulpicia's connection with Messalla that accounts for the survival of her poetry, which is contained in a manuscript that comes down to us under the name of Tibullus, her uncle's most famous protégé. The third book of Tibullus' corpus is a collection of writings by various hands, all of whom seem to have been connected with Messalla; Sulpicia's poetry shares the manuscript with a 200-line poem in praise of Messalla and a collection of quite conventional love elegies by a certain Lygdamus, otherwise unknown.

But let us return to Sulpicia's 'book'. A quick survey of the six poems will show how she adapts the conventions of the male elegists to her own purposes. In the opening poem, for instance, she adopts the pose of the 'teacher of love' to which the male elegists lay claim. The male elegists admit that they are lazy, servile, and unambitious, but as old hands in the painful business of love they can at least warn and advise others. Sulpicia, for her part, offers her story to be told by those who have not themselves experienced love. The second poem brings in a character that we expect to appear early in any collection of Latin poetry, the patron. In this case, the role is played by her uncle Messalla, the patron of Tibullus, but standing in a quite different relation to his niece Sulpicia. Sulpicia's birthday is looming, and Messalla wants her to spend it in the country, without her beloved, Cerinthus. She complains that Messalla is too protective of his niece and won't allow her to be her own mistress. Here she plays a clever variant on the first poem of Tibullus' first book of love elegies, where he declines to accompany his patron Messalla on a military expedition, claiming that he is chained (like a slave) to his mistress's door. Tibullus longs for the country, the traditional place for a contented and simple life, but Sulpicia strikes a different, though equally conventional, pose when she complains that the country is a drag (*molestus*, from *moles*, a lump) and that nothing is sweeter than the city, which is in any case more suitable for a girl. In the third poem, Sulpicia announces joyfully that Messalla has changed his mind and she can celebrate with Cerinthus. But, as always in Latin love elegy, the course of love does not run smooth. The mistress of the male elegists is fickle or reluctant, and Sulpicia too complains of a rival, but in a quite different tone. The rivals of the male love elegists are rich, so that the poets, poor but talented, must use their full powers of poetic persuasion to prevail. By contrast, Sulpicia is confident of her social superiority, and in the fourth poem she lets Cerinthus know it. I quote the entire poem in the translation of Mary Maxwell:[1]

> I'm grateful that, now you've so blithely left me behind,
>   I am saved from taking a precipitous fall.
> You prefer the simple toga and a basket-burdened
>   Whore to Sulpicia, daughter of Servius:
> Others worry about me and the pain it would cause
>   Should I yield my high place to an inferior.

Sulpicia haughtily identifies herself by name as 'Sulpicia, daughter of Servius' (*Servi filia Sulpicia*), the s's of the names echoing the derisive *scortum* (whore) in the same line. The translation captures well the slightly awkward, pained sarcasm as Sulpicia struggles to maintain her dignity. The following poem finds Sulpicia ill, another conventional motif. She asks Cerinthus if he is anxious on her behalf, and protests that she would only want to recover if that is what he wants. But what is this illness? Since the conventional metaphors of love are of disease and burning, the description of Sulpicia's illness is ambiguous. Is it real or metaphorical? The burning of love returns in the next, final poem, and the content of this poem comes as a surprise. Far from closing down the affair, triumphantly or tragically, it seems to circle back to the beginning, or at least a beginning:

> Ne tibi sim, mea lux, aeque iam fervida cura
>   ac videor paucos ante fuisse dies,
> si quicquam tota commisi stulta iuventa
>   cuius me fatear paenituisse magis,
> hesterna quam te solum quod nocte reliqui,
>   ardorem cupiens dissimulare meum.   (Sulpicia, 6)

---

[1] In Diane Rayor and William Batstone, eds., *Latin Lyric and Elegiac Poetry* (New York and London, 1995), 84.

(May I never be, my darling, such a burning thought for you,
as I seem to have been a few days ago,
if I have ever in my foolish youth done anything
that I can say I have regretted more
than that last night I left you on your own,
yearning to hide this fiery passion.)

In this final poem, Sulpicia echoes the opening poem of her book, for here too she rejects dissimulation, but this time not in the eyes of the world. If the first poem seems to bypass Cerinthus in favour of the readers to whom Sulpicia bares her thoughts, here we feel we have intruded on something that is not for our eyes or ears. Sulpicia addresses herself to Cerinthus, and her regret is as intimate as her defiance was public in the opening poem. The poem unrolls as a single sentence, which gathers power and complexity in its deliberate progress, as though Sulpicia were trying to express a regret as absolute as the irrevocability of the moment that has been lost. Each couplet divides its statement into two parts, corresponding to the division between hexameter and pentameter (the two lines of the elegiac couplet), and this produces a methodical effect that only increases the emotional power. Each couplet also introduces a different scale of time, beginning with 'a few days ago', the poem broadens out to 'ever in my youth' and then comes to a quivering rest on 'last night'.

One of the reasons that Sulpicia's poems are so much shorter than those of the other elegists is that they are totally devoid of the mythological comparisons and allusions that permeate the poetry of her male colleagues. Elaborate similes, too, are avoided as Sulpicia concentrates on the unadorned statement. In modern terms we might describe Sulpicia's utterance in this final poem as a confession, but in fact she is declaring an oath, which takes the conventional form 'May I never... If I have ever...' In an epic poem it might be 'May I never return safe from battle if I do not avenge my comrade's death.' The oath is a special kind of speech, claiming a magical effectiveness in its very utterance. Poetry too is a special kind of speech, and myths like those of Orpheus, Arion, Amphion, and others illustrate its magical effects. The Latin elegists emphasize this capacity of poetry with a favourite pun on the double meaning of the word *carmen*, literally 'a song', but also both a poem and a magical incantation (English 'charm' is a derivate). But there are no love charms or witches in Sulpicia's poetry, and this oath is intended to impress the addressee by the power with which it binds the speaker. So, though Sulpicia's final poem ends the sequence with regret for a moment of irrevocable loss, trailing away in a subordinate clause, it also stresses the power of her speech to have a persuasive effect on its addressee.

Sulpicia's poem is both powerful and original, but to modern tastes it may lack something. Modern poetry lays great stress on the precision and freshness of its vocabulary. Metaphors become hackneyed and can no longer be used; yesterday's daring usage becomes a cliché, and to repeat it is to be branded as lazy. Finding the *mot juste* has almost become synonymous with writing well. As we shall see, Latin poets did recognize the power of the unexpected word, strategically placed, but for the most part they worked with conventional vocabulary and the stock of conventional metaphors written into it. Sulpicia uses few metaphors in this poem, but those she does use are utterly conventional. *Fervida* in the first line and *ardorem* in the last, both of which have English derivates, cast love as burning. The word I have translated as 'darling' in the first line means 'light', a standard figure of speech for a precious being. It works well by association with *fervida*, and gathers further power from the contrasting *nocte* (night) in the penultimate line. Will Cerinthus continue to be her 'light' after what

53

she did last night? In isolation, none of the usages is striking, but Sulpicia puts them together in such a way as to increase their individual power by association with each other.

The poetry of the male elegists plays constantly, and often ingeniously, on a few oppositions: soft (*mollis*) and hard (*durus*), love (*amor*) and soldiering (*militia*), slavery (*servitium*) and domination (*dominatio*). These contrasts are, as it were, the soundtrack of the genre. There is none of this in Sulpicia, except perhaps the contrast between city and country in the second and third poems. The keynote of the genre is struck instead by certain characteristic words, and these can be very broad in meaning. *Cura*, in the first line, is a perfect example. The line runs, literally, 'may I not be to you, my light, equally now a burning care (*fervida cura*)'. English 'care' is derived from *cura*, and has something of the range of the Latin word, which can mean 'concern', 'worry', 'devotion', 'attention', or the object of any of these. Love, in the Latin elegists, is suffering, so the combination of meanings goes to the heart of the genre. Sulpicia has used the word in the previous two poems. In the first of these, Cerinthus' attraction to her rival was described as *cura togae* ('attention to a toga'; prostitutes were compelled to wear the toga—in the case of a woman a mark of disgrace). This rather decorous circumlocution is phrased to contrast with Cerinthus' attitude to Sulpicia, towards whom he is *securus* (confident, negligent, secure), a word compounded of a separative prefix *se-* (compare se-duce, meaning lead *astray*) and *cura*. In the following poem Sulpicia asks whether Cerinthus has a *pia cura* (dutiful concern) for her, now that she is ill. In the following, and final, poem the heat of illness has been transferred to the *cura* itself: Cerinthus has exhibited a burning care (*fervida cura*) for Sulpicia, but now it is she who has failed him, rather than vice versa. In each of these phrases *cura* is the opposite of the *mot juste*; it is rather a word that conjures up a melange of generic associations, the combination of concern, dedication, and pain that produces the emotional unease of the elegiac lover.

Sulpicia's collection, short though it is, has episodes and events and even a trajectory. It begins with an initiation into love and a (poetic) debut: Sulpicia the poet steps forward and Sulpicia the woman asserts herself. The sequence ends with a different kind of beginning, as a sexual encounter looms, or beckons, and language becomes a more private matter. Though Sulpicia begins defiantly with a reckless attitude to the *fama* that a woman is supposed to guard, at the end of the sequence she is more deferential. The flirtatious self-revelation of the first poem becomes a maidenly combination of fear and attraction to sex in the last. In between, the male patron/guardian is acknowledged and (politely) challenged, and the claims of Sulpicia's family are proudly maintained when she names herself as her father's daughter. It is an attractive conjecture that these poems celebrated the impending marriage of Sulpicia, cleverly adapting the conventions of love elegy to a society event. If so, is Sulpicia really the author? It is quite possible that one of the poets of Messalla's circle produced these poems in honour of the event, in which case we would lose the work of classical Rome's only extant female poet. Does 'Sulpicia''s distinctive syntax and original handling of a conventional genre guarantee that we are dealing with the true feelings of a real woman? Or has a male poet cleverly ventriloquized the female voice, containing potentially rebellious attitudes within a reassuring trajectory towards marriage? The final poem, after all, suggests that there has been no sexual activity *yet*. To makes matters more complicated, the same manuscript that contains these poems also includes a collection, known as 'The Garland of Sulpicia', in which poems speaking about Sulpicia's love for Cerinthus alternate with poems spoken in her own voice. The poems in 'The Garland' are longer, and much more conventional, treatments of some of the same incidents or themes that occur in the Sulpicia sequence, and the contrast makes the six Sulpicia poems look like a different order of poetry. It almost seems as though the author of 'The Garland' felt compelled to step in and clothe the naked self-expression of Sulpicia. But these two collections could equally be the contributions of two different male poets to the celebration of Sulpicia's impending marriage. The marriage theory is only that, a theory, and the question of whether the author of 'Sulpicia' is a woman or not cannot be answered with any confidence, though it does force us to consider what is at stake in the issue. Is there such a thing as female writing, and does it have to be written by a woman? What were the limits of an elite woman's licence to express herself in ancient Rome?

Love, the flip side: Ovid

Sulpicia begins her sequence with the words *Tandem venit amor*. The world of her poetry begins where love begins. Propertius, the first of the extant male love elegists, opens his first book similarly, with the statement 'Cynthia was the first to take me (wretched) with her eyes | I who till then had not been tainted by desire'. Ovid, the last of the three, starts not with the first experience of love, but with—metre! He was happily writing epic poetry (the really important stuff) in the appropriate hexameters, he explains, when Cupid came in on him and stole a foot from his metre. And look, he's writing love poetry!

Latin love elegy gets its name from its metre, the elegiac couplet. Metres in the ancient world tended to have associations with particular kinds of subject matter. The hexameter is the metre of epic, iambics are associated with invective and insult, and elegy is the metre of lament. In English, the word 'elegiac' conjures up a muted, possibly nostalgic sadness, and lament was the basic association of elegiac metre in the ancient world. Love elegy was the genre of the lover's lament and complaint. The regular appearance of the word *'miser'* (wretched, unhappy) reminds us that we are, indeed, reading love elegy. Ironically, the poet who made the most of the elegiac couplet, which almost becomes a character in his love poetry, is Ovid, the least 'miserable' of the canonical three. Ovid is the last of the love elegists, and it is often said that he kills off the genre by sending it up. He is certainly the funniest of the three, but that would not be a difficult achievement. Ovid is the wittiest, most irreverent of all the Latin poets, and one of the most enjoyable to read. His *Metamorphoses,* a sequence of mythological tales of epic propor-tions, has caught the contemporary imagination, with translations, imitations, and dramatizations appearing in their scores over the last twenty years (more on this in the final chapter). His love poetry is less well known.

Ovid's claim that Cupid stole a foot from his epic hexameters pro-vides a neat description of the elegiac couplet, which is made up of two lines, one of six metrical feet (the hexameter) and the other of five (the pentameter). Ovid reminds us, outrageously, that when you shorten every other line of the epic metre by a foot it becomes elegiac. The elegiac couplet shares the same basic metrical foot with the hex-ameter, namely the dactyl, which consists of a long syllable followed by two shorts (– ◡ ◡, or, phonically, 'dum da da'). So the simplest schema for an elegiac couplet looks like this:

$$– ◡ ◡ – ◡ ◡ – // ◡ ◡ – ◡ ◡ – ◡ ◡ – ◡$$
$$– ◡ ◡ – ◡ ◡ – // – ◡ ◡ – ◡ ◡ –$$

The slanting lines mark the point where there is usually a break (called a caesura) between one word and the next, dividing the line into two parts. In the pentameter, a more conclusive feel is given to the line by making the fifth foot a spondee (two longs) and dividing it between the end of the first half of the line and the end of the second half. Putting it phonically (with commas marking off the feet):

Hexameter:
Dum da-da, dum da-da, dum // da-da, dum da-da, dum da-da, dum da.
Pentameter:
Dum da-da, dum da-da, *dum*, // dum da-da, dum da-da, *dum*
(the italicized 'dums' between them produce the fifth foot).

Latin metre is quantitative, based on the length of syllables, whereas English metre is based on stress. Whether one can write quantitative verse effectively in English or not is debated; there have been many attempts to do so, more or less successful. But we can get a sense of the rhythm of an elegiac couplet from Coleridge's English version of it, which is also a description:

> In the hexameter rises the fountain's silvery column;
> In the pentameter aye falling in melody back.

In order for the first line to work as a Latin hexameter you need to put a stress on the first word, 'In', and on the second syllable of the word 'hexameter' (hex**am**eter). But not all of this line can be read as dactylic. The word 'fountains', for instance, consists of two long syllables, a foot called a spondee (– –). Since Latin metre is quantitative, marked by the time it takes to pronounce a syllable, a long syllable is regarded as equivalent to two shorts, and in the elegiac couplet spondees can be substituted for dactyls in all but the penultimate foot. This allows necessary variation in the lines, which would be monotonous if they were always made up entirely of dactyls.

The first line of the elegiac couplet, the hexameter, is the metre of epic. As Ovid puts it: you only have to steal a foot from every other line to turn epic hexameters into unwarlike elegiac couplets, in which the hexameter is followed by a five-foot dactylic pentameter. Coleridge compares this to the rise and fall of a fountain. Ovid's metaphor is less decorous. After Cupid steals a foot from his (alternate) hexameters, Ovid complains, in his opening elegy:

> Cum bene surrexit versu nova pagina primo,
>   attenuat nervos proximus ille meos;   (*Amores* 1. 1. 17–18)
> (When the new page successfully hoists itself up in the first line,
>   the one that comes next then slackens my sinews.)

Having just dramatized the choice of genre as a descent from the metre of epic to elegiac couplets, Ovid now suggests that the elegiac couplet is the right metre for love poetry, because it imitates the cycle of erection and detumescence, love's endlessly repeated narrative.

The right metre may be a crucial ingredient of love poetry but so, surely, is someone to love, and Ovid now complains to Cupid that he still needs 'either a boy or a girl with long, well-dressed hair'. Cupid bends his bow and replies, 'Here you are, then, poet, here's a work to sing'. The arrow finds its mark, and Ovid concludes his opening poem by confirming that metre is destiny:

> Sex mihi surgat opus numeris, in quinque residat:
>   ferrea cum vestris bella valete modis!   (*Amores* 1. 1. 27–8)
> (Let my work rise in six feet and fall back in five
>   iron wars farewell, and your metre to boot.)

Ovid's work, *opus*, takes two different forms: the book of love poetry that he has embarked on and the 'job' that is sex. The pun on *opus* (literary work, job) is one of his favourites, and Ovid finds plenty of opportunity for double entendres, given that Latin love elegy (quite unlike, for instance, the lyric of Catullus) is a decorous genre that avoids four-letter words and overt eroticism in favour of euphemism. Ovid sees that as an opportunity rather than a restriction.

In his introductory poem to the first book of *Amores* (loves, love poetry), Ovid flippantly takes metre as destiny. Since he is writing elegiacs now, he tells himself he must be in love. The particular object of this love is yet to be determined, and it is not until the fifth poem of the book that she is named as Corinna. But though Ovid makes the conventional protestations of devotion and fidelity to the woman he has named, or nicknamed (Corinna is a pseudonym), he reserves the right to contradict himself. Later on, in the second book of *Amores*, he confesses that he is a philanderer; he hates himself for it, or so he claims, but he just can't help it. Ovid goes on to describe how he is attracted to all women, fat or thin, tall or short, demure or forward, rustic or sophisticated. As he puts it in a summarizing pentameter:

> Conveniunt voto longa brevisque meo.   (*Amores* 2. 4. 36)
> (The tall and the short suit my desire.)

The line has a typically neat construction, in which the verb comes first, unusually and therefore emphatically (*conveniunt*, literally 'they come together', so 'suit'), while the noun–adjective phrase *voto…meo* (my desire, cf. vote) is split up and the two elements are placed at the end of each half of the line; in between, *longa brevisque* (the tall and the short) come together (the *que* tacked on to *brevis* is the equivalent of an 'and' before it). Not only do the long and the short both suit (*conveniunt*) Ovid's amatory desire but the long and the short, hexameter and pentameter, also come together (conveniently) to form the elegiac couplet in which Ovid writes. It is hard to disentangle Ovid's erotic life from the medium in which it is described, for the elegiac couplet itself is one of the most important characters in Ovid's love poetry.

In the lines that follow, which must surely be the inspiration for Leporello's Catalogue Aria in Mozart's *Don Giovanni*, Ovid plays dazzling variations on the couplet's aptitude for symmetry, opposition, and alternation as he lists the different types of women that take his fancy. One couplet describes the attractions of the modest girl ('her downcast eyes ambush me') and the next those of the forward ('I can expect her to be active in bed'). Or the hexameter tells of the attraction of the frump ('imagine what a make-over would do'), while the pentameter praises the elegant woman ('she puts her assets on display'). But there are other ways of using the couplet to structure the opposition. For instance, it can be unevenly divided between the lines:

> molliter incedit—motu capit; altera dura est—
> at poterit tacto mollior esse viro.   (*Amores* 2. 4. 23–4)
> (One walks languidly—she snares me with motion; the
> other is stiff—
> but she might become soft at the touch of a man.)

Or each line can express a parallel opposition:

> me nova sollicitat, me tangit serior aetas;
> haec melior, specie corporis illa placet.   (*Amores* 2. 4. 45–6)
> (The youthful excites me, the later age also touches me;
> one's better, the other pleases by its bodily form.)

My translation of this last couplet gives little sense of its elegance (or rhythm). The backbone of the hexameter is the balanced pair *me ... sollicitat ... me tangit* (excites me ... touches me). Though the order pronoun–verb is repeated in each half (*me sollicitat, me tangit*), the position of the other element changes. *Nova* (young) is wedged between *me* and *sollicitat* (cf. solicit, solicitude); it is an adjective that as yet has no noun. For that we must wait until the last word of the hexameter, *aetas* (age), the noun that is shared by *nova* and *serior* (literally, later). The fact that we have been kept waiting for *nova*'s noun gives the phrase *serior aetas* at the end of the line a climactic effect: the later age, after all, is better. Of the two adjectives, *nova* comes before the verb, whereas *serior* comes after it. This structure, in which a unit with two elements is repeated with the order of its elements reversed (*abba*: here adjective–verb/verb–adjective), is called chiasmus, and it is an extremely common way of achieving the variety that Latin writers so prized. Another way of achieving this variety is exhibited in the pentameter, where two different syntactic constructions, of unequal length, are used for the two halves of a simple opposition. 'This (age is) better (*haec melior*); by the attraction of the body that age pleases.' Ovid's list, in which each of the couplets is self-contained, is a virtuoso performance that exhibits constant variety of expression and structure within the potentially monotonous succession of lines and couplets, both of which divide into two halves. His desire is constant across the infinite variety of women who attract him, or, alternatively, his unwavering desire for women finds an infinite variety of forms in which to express itself.

All educated Romans learned to express themselves by mastering the art of rhetoric in a graded sequence of exercises that taught them how to generate and elaborate material on any topic that they might encounter. The purpose of this education was to ensure that a speaker would never dry up, never run out of things to say. *Copia* (copiousness, abundance) was a prized attribute, and the ability to say the same thing in a multitude of different ways was the main means of achieving this *copia*. We know that Ovid was a trained and celebrated rhetorician, and throughout his poetry he reminds us of this.

Later in the second book of *Amores* Ovid makes a quite different point about the couplet's suitability to his subject matter. Corinna, the main subject of his love poetry, is haughty and recalcitrant because she knows her own beauty. But, Ovid argues, she should not reject him as unworthy of her, since there are plenty of precedents for unequal pairings. Cue another list, this time of goddesses who deigned to love mortal, or otherwise unsuitable, men. Venus, for instance, was married to Vulcan, the god with the limping foot. The word 'foot' allows Ovid to jump to quite another category for his next example: 'the form of this poem itself is unequal, but it is apt that an epic metre (hexameter) be joined with a shorter one (pentameter)'. So, the elegiac couplet itself supports the ill-matched pair. Once again, metre is destiny. But Ovid now proceeds to shoot himself, quite deliberately, in the foot, with an argument that is contradicted by this very point. Corinna, he argues, should stay with him because he will be grateful, servile, and faithful. It is impossible that another woman could be celebrated in his poetry, as impossible as... different rivers flowing in the same bank:

> sed neque diversi ripa labuntur eadem
> frigidus Eurotas populiferque Padus,   (*Amores* 2. 17. 31–2)

> (but different rivers do not glide along in the same bank:
> the cold Eurotas and the poplar-bearing Po.)

This supposed impossibility, euphoniously realized in the pentameter, is the very principle of the couplet that Ovid has been emphasizing all along. The elegiac metre, in this case, is a charter for deceit.

Ovid's winking insincerity, his copious variety, and his sheer facility, are at the opposite extreme to Sulpicia's laconic, sometimes awkward, intensity, and between them Sulpicia and Ovid exemplify two expressive poles of Latin poetry. At one pole we have the solemn utterance: the declaration, the promise, the enunciation of intent, the expression of outrage or demand for redress, all of which call on the reader as witness. This is the poetry that derives strength from its allusion to the language of Roman legal formulas or contracts, or to those bargains with the gods that give Roman religious practice its legalistic hue. At the other pole we have the facetious or urbane conspiracy with the reader not to take anything the poet says too seriously. Here the poet draws us into the atmosphere of sophisticated dinner parties, of casual chit-chat and gossip, and of self-deprecating wit, all of which is summed up by the word *urbanitas* (cityness). This could be contrasted either with the rusticity of those who lacked urban refinement and education or with the *ineptia* (clumsiness, gaucheness) that the Romans liked to attribute to pompous, over-intellectual, and self-important Greeks.

Having it both ways: Catullus

But these two expressive poles or modes of utterance, the solemn and the urbane, may be found in the same poet, and the work of Catullus is a striking example of this. The poems of Catullus' small œuvre cover a remarkable variety of subject matter, tone, metre, and scale. Much of it is love poetry, and Latin love elegy, beginning in the generation after Catullus, owes a great deal to his example. The male love poets, however, did not imitate the epigrammatic quality of many of Catullus' love poems. It is left to Sulpicia to continue in the line of poems like this:

> Nulla potest mulier tantum se dicere amatam
>   vere, quantum a me Lesbia amata mea est.
> nulla fides ullo fuit umquam in foedere tanta,
>   quanta in amore tuo ex parte reperta mea est.   (Poem 87)

> (No woman can say she's been loved as much,
>   truly, as my Lesbia's been loved by me:
> there was never a guarantee so strong in any contract
>   as that found, on my part, in my love for you.)

Here, Catullus actually compares his love to a contract (*foedus*) and, like a legal document, his poem allows no loophole, straining to have the last, definitive word. Catullus takes himself very seriously here, and he calls on some very serious concepts, deeply engrained in Roman tradition, most notably the crucial *fides* (trustworthiness, cf. fidelity) from which the word *foedus* (contract, cf. federal) is derived. The language is completely straightforward and there are no figures of speech, or even descriptive adjectives, to distract from the statement. Each couplet divides into two parts signalled by the correlatives *tantum…quantum* (as much…as). Each couplet makes the same statement in slightly different form. But the exaggerated symmetry of this poem makes the asymmetries all the more striking and effective. The first couplet speaks of Lesbia in the third person, and so calls the reader to witness Catullus' claim, while the second turns to Lesbia herself. We hear the first couplet, perhaps, as a cry to anyone who is listening, or can be made to listen, and the second as spoken in a lower voice, with a mixture of tenderness, desperation, hope, and resentment. It is left to the reader to choose the appropriate registration for the contrast of addressees. Catullus helps us to make the distinction by adding the vowel o to the poem's predominant colouring of u and a in the second couplet, but it is the careful play of symmetry and asymmetry that requires us to realize the two halves of the poem in contrasting tones of voice. Perhaps the most subtle play with symmetry is achieved in the pentameters, where Catullus' language emphasizes the first person. In the first pentameter there is both *me* and *mea* (me, mine), but in the second pentameter Catullus opposes *tuo* to *mea*, 'yours' to 'mine'. Or so it seems. In fact the phrase *amore tuo* means 'your love' in the sense of '(*my*) love of you'. The balance between 'I' and 'you' is illusory. There is only one person concerned, and the 'contract' is one-sided, which is of course absurd.

This poem comes from a section of the Catullan collection in which all the poems are in elegiac couplets. The love poems in this section tend to be solemn and self-righteous, exploiting the couplet's capacity for symmetry, contrast, and balance. By contrast, the hendecasyllabics (11-syllable lines) of the poems earlier in the collection tend to be more conversational. We can judge the difference by looking at a poem in hendecasyllables which shares some of the characteristics of the elegiac poem I have just quoted, but to quite different effect. This poem will provide a transition from love to the more aggressive emotions that will concern us in the next chapter. Just how sincere is the protestation of friendship expressed in the following lines?

> Disertissime Romuli nepotum,
> quot sunt quoque fuere, Marce Tulli,
> quotque post aliis erunt in annis,
> gratias tibi maximas Catullus
> agit pessimus omnium poeta,

> tanto pessimus omnium poeta,
> quanto tu optimus omnium patronus.   (Poem 49)

> (Sweetest-spoken of Romulus' descendants,
> all that are, or have been, Marcus Tullius,
> and all who will yet be in other times—
> the greatest of thanks to you from Catullus,
> who's the worst poet of all the poets,
> by as much the worst of all the poets
> as you're the best of all the lawyers.)

Here we have the same attempt to measure (*tanto...quanto...*: as great...as...) and a similarly restricted and straightforward vocabulary, but the effect is jauntier, mainly because of the different metre, which is the same as that of the introductory poems of Catullus and Martial discussed above.

An English version of Catullan hendecasyllables is attempted quite successfully by Tennyson:

> O you chorus of indolent reviewers,
> Irresponsible, indolent reviewers,
> Look, I come to the test, a tiny poem
> All composed in a metre of Catullus,
> All in quantity, careful of my motion,
> Like the skater on ice that hardly bears him,
> Lest I fall unawares before the people,
> Waking laughter in indolent reviewers.

The hendecasyllable is composed of an introductory spondee ($-\,-$, i.e. dum dum; 'O you'; 'Look, I'; 'Lest I'), followed by a choriamb ($-\,\cup\,\cup\,-$, i.e. dum da da dum; 'come to the test'; 'skater on ice'; 'fall unawares') and finished with two iambs and a completing long ($\cup\,-\,\cup\,-\,-$, i.e. da dum da dum dum; '-dolent reviewers'; 'that hardly bears him'; 'before the people'). So the whole line goes dum dum, dum da-da dum, da dum da dum dum.

It's jaunty, swift-moving, and the perfect vehicle for Catullus' more urbane utterances.

Returning to Catullus' little thank-you to Cicero, we might ask what makes this a poem rather than a piece of versified politeness. First of all, can we be sure that it really is so polite? In Catullus' Latin, awkward jingles, bare symmetries, and a restricted and repetitive vocabulary all lend a dutiful sound to the string of superlatives (most eloquent, best, worst, greatest). It is as though Catullus wanted to give the impression that he was taking dictation. Even Cicero's name, Marcus Tullius (*Marce Tulli* in the vocative case) is made to form a jingle with Catullus' own name. Such is the baldness and exaggeration of the comparison in the last three lines that an awkward silence seems to descend as the poem ends. Even Cicero, who was not a modest man, must have suspected that there was more to this than meets the eye. Was Catullus parodying the orotund symmetries of his prose? There is a nice effect in the second and third lines, where each element of the tripartite division between past, present, and future is longer than the last. Cicero's speeches are full of this device, which is called a tricolon crescendo. But Cicero might also have suspected that Catullus was mocking his high opinion of himself. The great orator was notoriously self-important, and he was well aware of this reputation. Was Catullus trying to immortalize him as the sort of person who might swallow flattery this bald? Or were all these speculations paranoid imaginings, and Cicero should accept the compliment graciously? We readers are in much the same situation as Cicero, not sure whether we are in on the joke or not. Like Cicero, we do not want to be dupes, and so we return to the poem again and again, trying to catch a tone of voice. But the poem maintains its deadpan.

This is all quite a contrast to Sulpicia, or even to the parts of Catullus' own œuvre that seem to anticipate her strained intensities, but it is also a long way from Ovid's conspiratorial facetiousness, which lets us in on the joke. With Catullus' possibly ironic thank-you to Cicero we move out of the sphere of love towards the more aggressive attitudes struck by some of the Latin poets, which will be the subject of the next chapter. In that chapter we will meet a Catullus whose insults are not shy to declare themselves.

2
....

HATE, MOCKERY, AND THE PHYSICAL WORLD

From love we turn to hate, mockery, and abuse. Enemies were as inevitable a part of a Roman's world as were family or friends. It seems shocking to us that, for a Roman, the obligation to harm your enemies was the other side of the duty to help your friends. But turning the other cheek was not the Roman way. The most important weapon in this aggressive society was verbal abuse. Roman lawcourts, where most members of the elite would perform at some point in their career, dealt in insult and character assassination more than evidence or proof, and debate in the senate was neither gentlemanly nor decorous. Crime was not policed by the impartial institutions of public order on which we rely, and one way of claiming back stolen property was to gather together some friends and accost the thief in the marketplace, or to stand outside the house of the thief and loudly declaim his crime, shaming him, or her, into compliance. When all else failed, cursing was a common way to achieve justice, as the survival of so many buried curse tablets from the ancient world attests.

Abuse was not only a vital resource, it was also an art. A good insult was recorded, repeated, and passed around. It required the economy, power, and memorability that are the marks of good poetry, and so it is hardly surprising that a number of poetic genres specialized in the art of abuse. But we must remember that the spoken and written word

were regarded as a source of effective power, not just a means of com-
munication or persuasion. Curse tablets and magic incantations were
known in Latin as *carmina*, which was also a common term for poetry.
The figure who stands at the origin of iambic, the genre of invective
named after the usual metre of this kind of poetry, was the archaic
Greek poet Archilochos. According to a well-known story, Archilo-
chos was engaged to be married to Neoboule, but her father Lykambes
broke off the engagement. Archilochos subjected the family to such a
torrent of public (and poetic) abuse that both of Lykambes' daughters
committed suicide. In this chapter I will look at poetry, in a number of
genres, that deals out insult, criticism, or outrage. The poetry we will
be reading differs from love elegy not only in the character of the emo-
tions it expresses but also in its diction, which is one of the ways it
acknowledges the fact that we live in a physical world.

Polluted mouths

Latin love elegy is not much concerned with the physical aspects of
love, nor is the poetry of the elegists generally erotic or titillating. Its
language is decorous and euphemistic; double entendre is cultivated,
especially by Ovid, but obscenity is taboo. Yet Latin poetry can be
breathtakingly obscene and physically explicit. A surprisingly high
proportion of the Latin poetry that has come down to us 'does not
lend itself to comment in English', as the author of an important com-
mentary on Catullus put it, as late as 1961.[1] We should remember that
for those generations of schoolchildren that I have occasionally evoked,
Latin was not only the source of endless tasks of memorization and the

---

[1] C. J. Fordyce, *Catullus* (Oxford, 1961), p. iv.

fount of lofty sentiments but also, if you knew where to look, a treasure trove of obscenity. Significant gaps in school editions, translation into Italian rather than English in parallel texts, lapses into Latin in commentaries or dictionaries: all these were an invitation to hunt down an original text and puzzle it out for yourself. But most of this poetry is not what we would consider erotic. In Latin poetry, obscenity features generally not in the context of love but of hate. Horace's *Odes* can be erotic, but they are never obscene, whereas his *Epodes*, modelled on the invective of the Greek poet Archilochos, have passages that cross the line dividing the obscene from the revolting. There are many poems in Latin that are really no more than insults. Can we call them poetry? Try this poem of Catullus, which culminates in what must be the most disgusting line in Latin poetry:

> Non (ita me di ament) quicquam referre putavi
>   utrumne os an culum olfacerem Aemilio;
> nilo mundius hoc, niloque immundius illud,
>   verum etiam culus mundior et melior:
> nam sine dentibus hic: dentis os sesquipedalis,
>   gingivas vero ploxeni habet veteris,
> praeterea rictum qualem diffissus in aestu
>   meientis mulae cunnus habere solet.
> hic futuit multas et se facit esse venustum,
>   et non pistrino traditur atque asino?
> quem siqua attingit, non illam posse putemus
>   aegroti culum lingere carnificis?   (Poem 97)

> (So help me god, I thought it made no difference
>   whether I smell the mouth or arsehole of Aemilius.
> The one's no cleaner, the other no dirtier;
>   in fact, the arsehole's cleaner and better,
> for it has no teeth. The mouth has teeth half a yard long,
>   and gums like an old wagon-box.
> What's more, it gapes like the cunt of a pissing
>   mule split open in the heat.

This guy fucks a lot of women and thinks he's charming,
and he's not consigned to the mill and the ass?
If any woman touches him, wouldn't you think she could
lick the arsehole of a sickly executioner?)

The defiled mouth is one of the most common topics in the Latin
poetry of insult, as we shall see, and Catullus' whole poem is built
around the relation between mouth and arsehole. The final line brings
them closely together in a physical act which draws the poem to a sat-
isfyingly repulsive close. If it doesn't make any difference which end of
Aemilius you smell, then you may as well lick the one as kiss the other.
In the middle of the poem, Aemilius' laughing mouth dissolves into
an image one would rather had not intruded on one's consciousness.
Now that it has, can one ever see Aemilius laugh without turning away
in disgust?

But who is this Aemilius, and what is his sin? The ninth line tells us
that he fancies himself as a loverboy, putting it at first crudely (*hic
futuit multas*: this [guy] fucks many [women, since 'many' is in the
feminine]) and then more decorously 'and makes himself out to be
charming' (*se facit esse venustum*). *Venustus*, an adjective derived from
the name of the love goddess herself, is one of the untranslatable
watchwords of Catullus' circle. It comprises sexual attractiveness, but
is much broader and less definable. A good portion of Catullus' poetry
either confers the accolade of sophisticated charm that is the highest
value of his circle or witheringly withholds it from people who delude
themselves, and perhaps others, that they possess it. Originally, the
Latin word *venus* meant 'charm', but the connection of Venus with the
Greek Aphrodite added the more explicit sense of 'sex'. Aemilius'
claim that he is *venustus* on the basis that he fucks a lot of women is a
crude shrinking of the term's associations, and shows that he has

missed the point. For Catullus, *venustas* and sex overlap, but they are not equivalent.

Catullus provocatively pits one kind of diction against its opposite by using a bald obscenity (*futuit*, cf. French *foutu*) at the beginning of a line that ends with one of the undefinable watchwords of an in-group. In fact, the whole poem is paradoxical in tone, with its casual logic, which scarcely deigns to be angry, standing in sharp contrast to its four-letter words. The arc of the poem is marvellously controlled, as Catullus warms to his theme. Beginning with a pedantic indiffer-ence, Catullus then settles on Aemilius' mouth, and the poem reaches its climax when mouth and arsehole, which are alternatives in the first couplet, are brought revoltingly together in an image to which no one can be indifferent. On the way, we pause at the image of the pissing mule. It is only at this point that we are told something about the source of the poet's anger (line 9). But the thought of Aemilius fuck-ing lots of women is inevitably contaminated by the image of the piss-ing mule, which manages to combine both partners of the sexual act. The mule belongs to the wagon that is compared to Aemilius's gums, and in turn it suggests the miller's ass to which Aemilius should be consigned: for a Roman slave, the worst threat a master could make was to hand that slave over to work at the mill, and the final line of the poem picks up the theme of slave punishment with its last word *carnificis*, executioner (literally, flesh-maker).

Let us look more closely at Catullus' thoroughly unpleasant final couplet, which winds itself up in the hexameter in order to unwind in the pentameter's carefully measured delivery of physical disgust. Catullus consigns everything but the bare act to the hexameter: 'Whom (*quem*), if any woman (*siqua*) touches (*attingit*, compounded from *ad* and *tango*), (would) not she be able (*non illam posse*), we would think (*putemus*) to...' The verb we are anticipating does not come until the second half of the pentameter (*lingere*, to lick), preceded by an object that gives us a fairly conventional image of humiliation, in Latin as in English (*culum*, arsehole). But the image is enhanced by the phrase *aegroti carnificis* (of a sickly executioner), split up to enclose the line. Putting the adjective first keeps us waiting for the noun, so that the line becomes a crescendo of disgust. We can only imagine what the significance of the executioner's sickliness might be, but that is just what Catullus wants us to do! For an English reader, there is the added bonus (?) that our word 'linger' (no relation) comes to mind as the tongue goes about its work. That is not inappropriate, since the reader, putting together the line's four words, each of which elicits disgust, must linger over the assembly of the total picture. Catullus' poem humiliates Aemilius by making his body self-defiling, a place where pure and impure are indistinguishable. The girlfriend of Aemilius is performing a degrading act merely in kissing him. But what of the person who fills his own mouth with obscenities, who gets his tongue round 'the arsehole of a sickly executioner' or 'the cunt of a pissing mule'? And who is that person? Reader or writer? Catullus' poem does not raise the question directly, but it leaves us carefully articulating those four words on which the whole weight of the poem falls, at the same time as we turn away in disgust from the picture they (we? Catullus? the girlfriend?) have formed. The elegant language holds Aemilius at arm's length, but the physical images thrust themselves on our consciousness and, yes, our tongue. How much does it matter, Catullus seems to ask, that poetry comes from, and is articulated by, the mouth? This may seem an unlikely connection, but Roman authors were particularly sensitive to the relation between writer and reader, and they often expressed this relation in sexual terms. Sex, in fact, was a common figure for all relations of dominance and subordination, so important in a society in which respect was the most valuable of commodities; conversely, sexual relations themselves were often seen in terms of dominance and humiliation. Perhaps Horace is playing a similar game with the reader when, in one of his *Epodes*, he ends a poem addressed to a woman he doesn't fancy by telling her that, if she wants him to get it up, she'll have to use her mouth:

> quod ut superbo provoces ab inguine
> ore allaborandum est tibi.   (*Epodes* 8. 19–20)
>
> (Which (my penis), if you want to summon from my proud groin,
> you'll have to work at with your mouth.)

Ore (with your mouth) is echoed in *allab**or**andum* (you must work at it, *ad-laboro*). A couple of metrical elisions in the second line mean that the first three words are pronounced as a single unit, *orallaborandest*, and one can hardly read this line without feeling that one's mouth is being made to work.

Nearly a hundred and fifty years later, Catullus' greatest imitator, the epigrammatist Martial, wrote a poem which revolves around a subtle joke about the relation between reader and writer. Martial mocks a certain poet who proudly parades a taste for rough, ancient poetry, as opposed to the smoother, softer, more metrically refined type that, presumably, Martial writes himself. Chrestillus implies that his literary tastes attest to his virility, and in the last line of the poem Martial articulates Chrestillus' implied claim, but with a devastating insinuation:

> Dispeream ni scis mentula quid sapiat.   (*Epigrams* 11. 90)
> (Damn me if you don't know a virile style when you see one.)

The Latin means, literally, 'Damn me if you don't know what (a) prick tastes like.' *Mentula* (prick) is an obscene term that would not appear in decorous love elegy. *Sapiat* is a metaphor for knowledge whose literal sense means 'taste'. The metaphorical use is best known in the phrase *Homo Sapiens*. Martial deprives Chrestillus of the benefit of metaphor. More interestingly, he questions what Chrestillus' taste for virile poetry tells us: that he is virile himself, or that he wants to consume virility? Chrestillus is humiliated not because Martial insinuates that he is homosexual (homosexual practices carried no stigma as such) but because Martial insinuates that he has a taste for degrading sexual practices. Fellatio was degrading for the person who defiled his, or her, mouth to pleasure another, but the other partner in the act might be asserting his phallic dominance, his virility. The same goes for anal sex, which is degrading for the person who is penetrated but might be an act of domination for the other partner. The fact that sexual imagery was used to figure such a wide variety of relationships and activities makes it a thought-provoking metaphor for the activity of literature itself.

One of the lesser, and lesser-known, gods of the Greco-Roman pantheon is Priapus, instantly recognizable in ancient representations by his enormous, erect penis. Statues of the well-endowed god were placed in gardens and orchards, which he guarded against theft and trespass, threatening rape for transgressors. Priapus gave his name to a genre of poetry. The anonymous poet, or poets, of the Latin collection known as the *Priapea* often have the god speaking in his own voice. They display considerable ingenuity fitting into a single couplet the different violations that await thieves of different sex and age.

> Percidere, puer, moneo; futuere, puella;
> barbatum furem tertia poena manet.   (*Carmina Priapea* 13)

(You'll be buggered, boy; I warn you, girl, you'll be fucked.
  A third penalty awaits the bearded thief.)

Femina si furtum faciet mihi virve puerve,
  haec cunnum, caput hic, praebeat ille nates. (*Carmina Priapea* 22)

(If a woman commits a theft, or a man or a boy,
  let the first present her cunt, the second his mouth, the third
    his buttocks.)

Per medios ibit pueros mediasque puellas
  mentula, barbatis non nisi summa petet. (*Carmina Priapea* 74)

(Through the middles of boys and middles of girls
  my prick will go; with bearded men, it will reach only for the
    heights.)

Ovid could not have put it more elegantly! The swaggeringly phallic god Priapus has been taken by one scholar as the model for all Latin poets of invective and satire, whose hypermasculine and aggressive persona is quite different from the feminized persona that the elegiac poets adopt.

Social mockery

Not all Latin invective was sexual in nature. After the disruption of the civil wars, and the change of political system that brought in the emperors, social mobility became one of the most common targets of satirists and epigrammatists. In this epigram by Martial the poet attacks a cobbler who has made enough money to become a local benefactor, and so to put on, at his own expense, a public gladiatorial combat. In the ancient world, a great deal of what would nowadays be funded by public money, raised from taxes, was presented by rich citizens as a gift to the community. Theatre, gladiatorial shows, and chariot races were free events funded by individuals. In return, the benefactor would garner all-important prestige and respect, which might be parlayed into political office or, as in this case, social recognition.

> Das gladiatores, sutorum regule, Cerdo,
>   quodque tibi tribuit subula, sica rapit.
> ebrius es: neque enim faceres hoc sobrius umquam,
>   ut velles corio ludere, Cerdo, tuo.
> lusisti corio: sed te, mihi crede, memento
>   nunc in pellicula, Cerdo, tenere, tua.   (*Epigrams* 3. 16)
> (You're giving a gladiatorial show, Cerdo, little king of cobblers.
>   So what the awl afforded you, the dagger takes away.
> You must be drunk. Sober you'd never have wanted to do this,
>   to play, Cerdo, with you own hide.
> You've played with your hide, then. But, trust me, you must remember
>   now to keep yourself in your own skin.)

Cerdo, whose name means 'profit' in Greek, is trying to convert money into status, but Martial refuses to allow Cerdo his metamorphosis. The wit of this epigram consists in bringing the victim relentlessly back to the material realities of his trade, and particularly the raw material of his shoes: animal hide. Colloquial expressions that use words for skin or hide in a figurative sense are reduced to their literal meaning. So the phrase *de corio suo ludere*, 'to risk one's own skin' (literally, to play for one's own hide) is stripped of its metaphor: the cobbler is indeed risking his own hide, namely the money he has made from the raw materials of his trade. But why is he said to be *risking* it? Cerdo would have rented his gladiators from a *lanista* (think Peter Ustinov in *Spartacus*), and was required to compensate the *lanista* for any deaths. So (line 2), what the awl brought in for Cerdo the cobbler the dagger takes away from Cerdo the public benefactor.

Awl or dagger, animal hide or gladiator's flesh—can Cerdo change his spots?

A further level of punning in the phrase (*de*) *corio* (*suo*) *ludere* raises the same question. The word for a public show is *ludus*, and the verb *ludere* can mean 'to take part in a public show' as well as 'to risk'. Once again, Cerdo's attempt to parlay the profits of his sordid occupation into social status is stymied by a pun that brings him back to his roots: he is not giving a public show but, once again, speculating with hide. In the final couplet, Martial shifts to a second colloquial expression that makes figurative use of the word for skin. He warns Cerdo to 'confine himself to his own skin', that is, not to get ideas above his station. But a more literal meaning interferes with this metaphor, for Cerdo has indeed transferred his attention from one kind of skin to another—a wrong turning, as Martial warns him.

This is an unpleasant poem. We hear the taunting chant of the schoolyard in Martial's repeated *corium*, and our pleasure in the skill with which the poem triumphantly returns to the same raw spot is a tainted pleasure. Few modern readers would sympathize with Martial's snobbery, and we may be more inclined to baulk at the poet's casual reference to gladiators as 'hide' or 'skin' than at Cerdo's quest for social respectability. But it is a fine poem, nevertheless. Its sharp wit cuts to the essential vectors of social life and at the same time uncovers the material world that subtends it. We do not have to buy into its social attitude to be surprised and enlightened by its vision. Martial is the great Latin master of epigram, and he defined the form as we know it: the short, witty poem with a sting in its tail. Wit is a broader concept than humour. In the eighteenth century it referred to 'the imaginative or striking figure, the flash of verbal intuition, the marmoreal phrase, the pointed dictum'.[2] Essential to wit in this sense is the ability to surprise by finding similarities in the disparate, an ability that this poem displays abundantly. By the nineteenth century, when 'imagination' took on the senses of discovery and invention formerly included under 'wit', the meaning has been reduced to our current sense, humour. In the first poem of his first book (see above, p. 31), Martial refers to his epigrams with the adjective *argutus*, meaning 'quick-witted, clever'. The root meaning of the adjective is 'producing sharp or clear sounds', but it is derived from the verb *arguo*, meaning 'prove' or 'convict'. How does wit as humour relate to the broader senses of wit? Let's take another epigram of Martial:

> Heredes, nolite brevem sepelire colonum:
>> nam terra est illi quantulacumque gravis.   (*Epigrams* 9. 14)
> (Heirs, don't seek to bury the short farmer
>> For earth in however small a measure is heavy to him.)

Epigram is a form closely related to the epitaph, the form that condenses a life into the span of an elegiac couplet (the usual metre of the epitaph). In Martial's twelve books of epigrams there are many epitaphs, some for real individuals and some more generic, in which the identity of the deceased serves as an opportunity for wit. This one belongs to the second category. It is almost an anti-epitaph, and it follows a typical epigrammatic structure, in which the hexameter makes a paradoxical statement that the pentameter explains (*nam*, for) with a witty point, concentrated here in the poem's last word, *gravis* (heavy). Epitaphs are a very conventional form, and the most conventional of all epitaphic expressions is the wish that the earth rest lightly on the

---

[2] Alex Preminger and T. V. F Brogan, eds., *The New Princeton Encylopedia of Poetry and Poetics* (New York, 1993).

dead person. The expression *sit tibi terra levis*, 'may the earth be light for you', was so conventional that it was sometimes abbreviated to STTL. Another conventional epitaphic thought is that life is (too) short, *brevis*. This farmer is not so much short-lived as simply short. For the diminutive farmer, all earth is heavy, and so two allusions to epitaphic convention are drawn into a witty relation in Martial's perverse epitaph, and this relation is underlined by the similarity between the words *brevem* (accusative of *brevis*) and *gravis*. The little farmer who has had trouble with earth all his life is probably meant to be comic. When ancient literature deals with those on the bottom of the social heap it is more often than not to laugh at them. Anyone whose life was tied to the material world was deprived of the opportunities for *virtus* that would make him or her worthy of consideration (see Cerdo above). But, for the modern reader, this poem may come across as a poignant, even sensitive, response to the materiality of the farmer's life. For him, earth cannot be merely figurative, and the circumstances that pit him against it are as unavoidable as death itself. Even the minimal expression of piety on the part of his survivors, the scattering of a handful of earth on his corpse, will extend the harsh realities of his life into the grave. Much of the poem's weight falls on the word 'quantulacumque', a long word signifying a minimal amount: *quantus* = how much; quantuscumque = however much; quantulus (*quantula* in the feminine) is the diminutive of *quantus*, so *quantulacumque* = however little. The rhythm and distribution of emphasis in this line could be conveyed in a sort of English as follows: 'For earth is to that man, however-little-it-may-be, too much'. Is the modern reader wrong to hear a sympathetic intelligence in these lines, which would probably have evoked a guffaw in the original audience? Are we reading a different poem? I don't think so. Epigram is a performance that in turn requires the reader to perform it, to make it work. Halfway between an improvised sally of wit on a particular occasion and an inscription for the ages, it requires the reader to bring its wit to life. The long word *quantulacumque,* whose form clashes with its meaning, is the climax of the poem, and it requires the reader to decide in what tone of voice it is to be spoken. We could make it pathetic or we could read it as the triumphant punchline of a joke. The choice is ours.

Satire: voice and vice

The poetry of insult and mockery could be a weapon directed at real, live targets. Julius Caesar complained that the poetry Catullus directed against him had left 'everlasting blots' on his name. But it was not only recognized poets who wrote poems of insult. They might be written and circulated by anyone: poetry was not just for poets. In a letter to Cicero, his friend Trebonius, not otherwise known as a poet, encloses a poem, unfortunately lost, about which he says this:

> During the sea passage, however, I did snatch a bit of free time and have put together one of my patented little gifts for you. I have recast in verse a witticism of yours that included a handsome compliment to me (it is written out at the end of the letter). If some of the language in these verse strikes you as a bit outré, I take refuge in the scabrousness of the individual against whom my rather blunt assault is directed. You will also excuse the rancorous tone as appropriate to persons and citizens of that ilk. And anyway, why should Lucilius be entitled to express himself more freely than I? Even if he could match me on hating those he assailed, he certainly did not have targets who were more deserving of such outspoken vituperation.
>
> (Cicero, *Ad Familiares* 12. 16, trans. Peter White)

Lucilius was the father of Roman satire. He was famous for the fearlessness with which he named and attacked members of his own society. Later writers of satire, a genre that the Romans claimed (rightly) to have invented, would draw back from Lucilius' policy of naming and shaming as too dangerous, especially under an emperor, and satire became a more general ethical discourse attacking the vices and follies of humanity, urging reformation, and reflecting on the principles of right living. The Romans were proud of the fact that, although most of the literary genres in which they wrote had Greek precedents and models, the genre of satire was their own invention. In fact, for the earliest of Rome's satirists, writing satire, with its plain-speaking abuse of folly, vice, and fashion (read, Greek influence), was a way of being Roman. Its mixture of moralizing and abuse was distinctive to Roman culture.

Roman verse satire is written in hexameter, the metre of epic. So is it a high genre? In some ways it is, for the satirists tell us that satire, not epic, deals with the really important stuff: what humans actually do (and why they shouldn't). It may adopt a high, hectoring tone to shame us into mending our ways, or it may prefer to win us over with laughter directed in equal measure at ourselves, the outside world, and the author. But for some satirists the game is already lost, and there's no point in trying to reform a corrupt world; for satirists such as Juvenal, the only genuine or appropriate voice is one of anger, fearless to speak what nobody else dare say. Whatever attitude it takes to human imperfections and the vices of society, satire is the realm of the bodily and the material, and in this lies much of its claim to deal with what is real, unlike the 'higher' genres. Satire is always *exposing* something or somebody, and there is no better way to give that impression than to cut through to the physical realities that underlie our moral lives. Does satire *reduce* us to the physical and at the same time revile it? Does it revel in what it reviles so compendiously? Does satire expose itself as well as its targets? These are some of the questions that it raises.

There are three canonical satirists of antiquity, Horace, Persius, and Juvenal. We will be looking at Horace's lyric poetry, his *Odes*, in the next chapter. They are the work by which he has been known in modern times, but it was not always so. For the Middle Ages and the Renaissance, Horace was a satirist, and his ironic, autobiographical 'conversations', as he describes his satires, were his main claim to fame. Juvenal is at the opposite extreme to Horace. He's mad as hell and he won't take it any more. For Juvenal, there is no question of reformation; apocalypse is around the corner and it's a magnificent theme. Persius is the least known of the satirists and the most difficult to read. In fact, he is one of the most difficult of all Latin authors. His poetry is awkward, jagged, obscure, and at times surreal in its imagery. Of the three satirists he is the one who makes the most use of philosophy, and his Stoicism takes the form of a sustained assault on our conscience in the conviction that virtue is the only good for humans. I am going to take a close look at Persius' third satire, which begins with a vividly concrete scene, in which a student describes his daily routine, beginning with the moment he wakes up with a hangover and tries to get down to work:

> Nempe haec adsidue. iam clarum mane fenestras
> intrat et angustas extendit lumine rimas.
> stertimus, indomitum quod despumare Falernum
> sufficiat, quinta dum linea tangitur umbra.
> 'en quid agis? siccas insana canicula messes
> iam dudm coquit et patula pecus omne sub ulmo est'
> unus ait comitum. 'verumne? itan? ocius adsit
> huc aliquis. nemon?' turgescit vitrea bilis:
> findor ut Arcadiae pecuaria rudere credas.

86

iam liber et positis bicolor membrana capillis
inque manus chartae nodosaque venit harundo.
tum querimur crassus calamo quod pendeat umor.
nigra sed infusa vanescit sepia lympha,
dilutas querimur geminet quod fistula guttas.   (*Satires* 3. 1–14)

(It's like this all the time. Bright morning's coming through
The shutters and enlarging their narrow cracks with light.
We snore, enough to defume the fiery Falernian [wine],
Until the dial's shadow touches the fifth line [11 a.m.].
'What are you doing? The mad Dog-star has long been parching
The corn, and every herd's beneath a spreading elm.'
So speaks a comrade. 'Really? You don't say! Quick, someone.
Come here! What, no one?' Vitreous bile begins to swell
And I explode, braying like all Arcadia's flocks.
In due course book and two-tone parchment (hair removed),
Papyrus, and a knotty reed come to hand.
Then we complain that the ink is clotting on the nib.
Water's poured in and the black cuttle-juice thins out,
And we complain that the nib doubles the diluted drops.)[3]

Persius throws us into this scene with no introduction. We don't know
who is speaking or to whom, and as the poem progresses a swirl of voices
will accost us, leaving it ambiguous where one voice ends and another
takes up. A hubbub of confession, accusation, and denial pitches us into
the moral drama, and we feel like the hungover student who wakes to
find that it's already late. We've missed something, and that may be true
of us not only as readers of this poem but also as moral agents. Time is
running out, Persius insists, if we want to start living right.

The poem begins with a three-word sentence that suggests that the
speaker is giving an account of his routine. But to whom? And why?

---

[3] *The Satires of Persius*, trans. Guy Lee [modified], with a commentary by William Barr
(Liverpool, 1987).

Nempe implies an interlocutor and a conversation that is already underway ('Admittedly...'). The three words *Nempe haec adsidue* constitute a colloquial, shorthand beginning, which is very hard to catch in English: 'This (*haec*, neuter plural), admittedly, all the time'. We are never introduced to the speaker, though he seems to be a student with some similarities to Persius himself. Throughout the poem, speakers will materialize out of thin air. The main voice of this poem, which enters immediately after this passage ends, also speaks up without introduction. In the opening lines just quoted, a second voice cuts in at line 5 (*En quid agis?* What are you doing?), but is not identified until after it has spoken (*unus ait comitum*: so speaks a comrade). It comes out of the blue, and we might at first take it as the voice of conscience, or the imagined reaction of public opinion, or even the internalized voice of a mentor. We must remember that the text of an ancient poet, which was more or less unpunctuated, had none of the markers by which we distinguish direct speech from narrative, or one speaker from another. Persius makes us speculate on a scenario, and the variety of punctuation in modern editions of this satire suggests that there may be no right way to imagine it. Some take the words *Nempe haec adsidue* to be a critical voice, rather than part of the confession of the student; others take everything from the beginning down to 'So speaks a comrade' to be the speech of the companion. Disagreements among modern commentators over how to distribute the speakers continue throughout the poem. There is, I think, no point in trying to come to a definitive answer to this problem. Persius' text deliberately presents us with a babble of voices. We must decide whether to hear it as a quarrel within the divided self, the contending of different voices in the closely packed world of the megalopolis, or the clash of cultural clichés floating in the air. How many different voices can we

hear in a given passage, and what does it mean for a voice to be differ-
ent, or to belong to a different person? In Persius' *Satires* the arena of
ethical striving and strife is a world of voices that are hard to distin-
guish from each other. There are genuine voices, and voices that are
just mouthing off; worthy clichés are thrown as sops to the conscience,
or used to summon up courage for the struggle ahead; the desperate
cry of a drowning man makes itself heard in the distance, or perhaps it
wells up from inside us; well-wishers urge us to reform, and so do
enemies who know that we won't. Perhaps we should give up on the
effort to distinguish individual speakers and just listen to the swirl of
contending voices, whether they are all in one head or come from dif-
ferent speakers. The drama, either way, is the same: that of the conflict
between denial and crisis. If the first three words introduce us to the
question of who's speaking to whom, and why, they also introduce us
to the nub of the moral issue, habit and habituation: 'this, now is rou-
tine' (*adsidue*, continuously; cf. assiduously).

Persius' morning enters with a concreteness unusual in Latin poetry,
but the language is not purely descriptive: as the sun rises, it is the
cracks in the shutters, rather than the light itself, that widen. The trans-
ference discreetly insinuates the moral dimension of the satire: faults
magnify over time, as we miss the moment for correcting them. It is 11
o'clock, and yesterday's unmixed (*indomitum*, untamed) Falernian is
still being slept off. Another student wakes up the companions with a
sudden switch of scene to the countryside, where the working day is
long advanced (the flocks have already taken shelter from the sun). The
rhythms of country life are splendidly inappropriate to this urban
scene, and so are the language and mood of pastoral, which colour the
student's words (more on pastoral when we get to Vergil). A different
genre, signposted by the 'spreading elm' that signals pastoral, has

broken in on the satire, like interference from another radio station. Pastoral, which conjures up an ideal world of shepherds in harmony with the countryside, is in effect the opposite of satire, the form that castigates humans out of tune with themselves and corrupted by their urban environment. The nearest these students get to the world of pastoral is with the 'flocks of Arcadia' (famous for its donkeys), braying in the speaker's hungover head. But, like pastoral, satire anchors its characters in a physical world: the Falernian that is having its fizz neutralized; the greenish bile that is swelling in the angry student's body; the ink that hangs from the nib too thickly or flows too fast when diluted. These liquidities represent the material of the moral life.

On waking, the student calls immediately for a slave to bring him pen and paper. Nobody answers at first, but finally pen and ink 'come to hand', an expression characteristic of the attitudes of Rome's slave society. Instead of the slave, it is the main critical voice of this satire that now makes its presence felt, responding to the narrator's procrastinating complaint about the ink: 'It's *you* who are flowing away. The leaky vessel sounds false when struck; but you're still soft clay, to be turned again and again on the potter's wheel. There's still time. Aren't you ashamed to behave like Natta, stupid with vice? Fat has so overgrown his nerves that he no longer registers his own faults. Soon he won't even send bubbles to the surface' (20–24, paraphrased). The images succeed one another swiftly, constantly changing and yet constantly circling back on each other: on the one hand, the Falernian fizzling away, the ink flowing too fast, the bubbles gradually giving out; on the other, the swelling bile, the ink hanging thick on the nib, the nerves overgrown with fat. Persius gives us two different physical images for the ways in which the moral self might weaken over time, either diluted by dissipation or thickened by habit.

Who owns this voice that speaks at the eleventh hour? We never learn, but this is the voice that will take us to the end of the satire, at line 118. 'I know you inside and out' it says, *intus et in cute* (inwardly and in your skin, 30). Then it circles back to a scarier version of this intimate knowledge:

> magne pater divum, saevos punire tyrannos
> haud alia ratione velis, cum dira libido
> moverit ingenium ferventi tincta veneno:
> virtutem videant intabescantque relicta.
> anne magis Siculi gemuerunt aera iuvenci
> et magis auratis pendens laquearibus ensis
> purpureas subter cervices terruit, 'imus,
> imus praecipites' quam si sibi dicat et intus
> palleat infelix quod proxima nesciat uxor?   (35–43)

> (Great father of the gods, be it thy will no otherwise
> To punish cruel tyrants when malignant lust
> Dipped in fiery venom has disturbed their mind:
> Let them have sight of Virtue and pine at having left her.
> Did the brazen bull of Sicily bellow more with pain,
> Or sword hung from gilt-fretted ceiling strike more fear
> Into the purple necks beneath than if 'We're sunk,
> Sunk headfirst' Someone were to say, turning inwardly
> Pale at what the closest wife must never know.)   (trans. Lee, modified)

Even worse than being seen through is the loneliness of guilt that cannot be shared. The word *'intus'* (inwardly) comes back, but now it refers to the inner life that cannot be spoken ('turning inwardly pale') rather than to the transparency of the sinner to the critical observer ('I know you inwardly and in the skin'). If even your closest must not know what makes you pale, then is this voice that is speaking perhaps your own?

We reach the intimate domestic scene of husband and wife from a more generalized and grander starting point. The tyrant was the standard figure, in rhetoric and philosophy, of the man who has lost his self-control and become, through too much power, *impotens* (out of control, raging; rather different connotations from those of our 'impotent'!). Persius prescribes the tyrant's punishment in a magnificent four-word line that seems to conflate the fate of Tantalus in the underworld with Christian conceptions of the torments of the damned:

> virtutem videant intabescantque relicta   (38)
> (literally, Virtue, let-them-see-it and-let-them-waste-away
>   because-it-has-been-abandoned).

It is the five-syllable *intabescantque*, a long word for a protracted torment, which carries the emotional weight of the line. *Tabeo* means 'waste away' or 'rot', and to that root has been added an inceptive suffix (-sc), which conveys the notion of beginning (adole*sc*ent = beginning to grow up). Before the root there is an intensive prefix (in-; cf. *in*tense), while the *que* tacked on at the end is equivalent to 'and' before it.

Persius now alludes to two of the standard stories about tyrants. First, that of the the tyrant Phalaris, who had his victims roasted in a bull of bronze invented and made for him by Perillus, who then became its first victim (cooperating with tyranny is dangerous!). Then Persius alludes to the story of the tyrant Damocles, who suspended a sword by a single hair over the head of a courtier reclining at dinner to demonstrate that the life of a king was not as pleasant as the courtier supposed. But once again, direct speech intervenes suddenly to change the scene from the tyrant's court to something much more intimate. The ancient reader would not have been warned of this by the opening of inverted commas. What he would be expecting, from the *magis* (more) in the fifth line of the passage above, would be an answering *quam* ('did the bronze of the Sicilian tyrant's bull and the sword of Damocles...cause *more* terror *than*...'). Persius' answering clause, when it does come, is phrased asymmetrically to the *quam* clause ('did the sword of Damocles cause more terror than *if someone would say to himself*...') and it pits one very obvious kind of physical terror against something more abstract. At first, we do not know what to make of *imus, imus praecipites* (we are going, going headlong), especially since *imus* could mean 'lowest', as well as 'we are going'. 'Lowest' might be quite a plausible guess, given the context (the fear of tyrants), but *praecipites* (headlong, cf. precipitous) clinches the meaning 'we are going'. It is a further surprise that these three words, with their rhetorical repetition, are spoken by someone to himself. A complete change of register has taken place before we have quite realized it, as conventional moralizing about tyrants, fearful and fearing, has dissolved into the panicked interior monologue of a man whose fear isolates him from his own wife. What it is that haunts him we do not know. But the language of his exclamation echoes previous images of flowing, bubbling, and fizzling out. While we speak, Persius implies, something momentous is happening: moral inertia has become the inertia of a moving body, and is gathering speed along the path of least resistance, downwards. The speed of this development is conveyed by the speed with which the new drama interrupts the hackneyed commonplace about tyrants, assembles its components, and is gone.

Procrastination, aimlessness, passivity—these are the faults with which the main voice of the satire castigates the student who woke up in the opening lines:

Have you an objective? A target for your bow?
Or do you everywhere chase crows with crocks and mud,
Not caring where you're carried, living extempore?

(60–62, trans. Lee)

The same voice goes on to tell of his own childhood training in rhetoric and how he used to shirk the tasks that were set him. But his addressee, the student, no longer has the excuse of being a child, and he knows some philosophy, which, in the list of the speaker comprises:

Just what we are, what life we're born to lead, what place
Allotted, where and whence we gently round the turn,
How limit silver, what to rightly choose, the use
Of newly minted coin, how much we should disburse
To country and our near and dear, the person god
Has bidden you be, where in the human world you're
        posted.   (67–72, trans. Lee)

The speaker lists some characteristically Stoic concerns and positions, and this sally into professional philosophy provokes, as if by reflex, the appearance of another voice, an imaginary centurion who delivers an amusing speech on the irrelevance of philosophy. 'My own native wit is enough for me...I don't need these learned disquisitions about nothing ("that nothing can come of nothing and nothing return to nothing"). Is it for this that philosophers are pale and miss their meals? (*hoc est quod palles* | *cur quis non prandeat hoc est?*)' (78–85). Is he right? Is philosophy a pedantic enquiry into nothing? As an answer we are plunged immediately into another scene in which, as we gradually make out, a sick man is talking to his doctor:

'Inspice, nescio quid trepidat mihi pectus et aegris
faucibus exsuperat gravis halitus, inspice sodes'

qui dicit medico, iussus requiescere, postquam
tertia compositas vidit nox currere venas,
de maiore domo modice sitiente lagoena
lenia loturo sibi Surrentina rogabit.
'heus bone, tu palles'. 'nihil est'. 'videas tamen istuc,
quidquid id est. surgit tacite tibi lutea pellis'.
'at tu deterius palles, ne sis mihi tutor.
iam pridem hunc sepeli; tu restas'. 'perge, tacebo'.
turgidus hic epulis atque albo ventre lavatur,
gutture sulpureas lente exhalante mefites.
sed tremor inter vina subit calidumque trientem
excutit e manibus, dentes crepuere retecti,
uncta cadunt laxis tunc pulmentaria labris.
hinc tuba, candelae, tandemque beatulus alto
conpositus lecto crassisque lutatus amomis
in portam rigidas calces extendit. at illum
hesterni capite induto subiere Quirites.   (88–106)

('Examine me. My chest has got this throbbing, my throat
Is sore, my breath unpleasant. Please examine me',
Says someone to his doctor, and is told to rest.
But when the third night finds his veins are running steady,
He's round at a rich friend's with a jar of modest thirst,
Requesting mild Surrentine to drink while at the Baths.
'You're pale, dear boy'. 'It's nothing'. 'Well, whatever it is,
Best get it seen to. Your skin's yellow—quietly swelling'.
'I'm not as pale as you are. Kindly don't play the tutor.
I buried him long ago. You're next'. 'Right. I'll keep quiet'.
So he goes bathing, stuffed with rich fare, belly white
And pharynx slowly exhaling a sulphurous mephitis,
But with the wine the shakes come over him and knock
The hot glass from his hand and bare his chattering teeth.
Then fall from those loose lips the oil and the hors-d'œuvre.
Hence trumpet and wax tapers and last our poor dear friend
Laid out on the high couch, thickly bedaubed with balms,
Extending rigid heels towards the gate. But him
Yesterday's new Romans, heads covered, shouldered high.)
(trans. Lee)

In the middle of this little scene comes an argument about which of the disputants is paler. Pallor is here a symptom of illness rather than a mark, almost a badge, of the philosopher's ascetic lifestyle. 'Is it for this that philosophers are pale?' the centurion asked. The centurion is answered: better to be a pale philosopher than pale with a mortal illness. Physical health and illness were common Stoic metaphors for the moral life, and they appear frequently in satire. In one of his rare positive pronouncements, the satirist Juvenal declared that the only legitimate request to the gods was for *mens sana in corpore sano* (a healthy mind in a healthy body, *Satires* 10. 356). Sanity, for us, is a mental state, but the primary sense of the Latin word *sanus* is physical, and indeed we can hardly imagine mental wellbeing except through the metaphor of physical health. We might ask of Persius' little drama whether it is an allegory in which a familiar reality (going to the doctor) figures events that are no less real or important but less apparent: we are sicker than we think, but not in the obvious way; spiritual death is an all too real possibility. Or is the moral content contained in the terms of the scene itself? Perhaps what Persius describes in this scene is a moral event to which our age has given a name of its own—denial.

Once again, direct speech cuts into the poem, without us knowing who is speaking or even, unless we are reading a modern text, that a new speaker has been introduced at all; the scene does not become clear until the third line. At the same time as we learn that we have been listening in on a patient speaking to his doctor we also realize that the two lines of quoted direct speech ('Examine me...') are all part of the subject of this sentence. A better way of representing what happens in the Latin would be: 'the person who (*qui*) says to his doctor 'Examine me...', when ordered to rest, then goes to his rich friend and . . .' This is not so much a narrative ('first he says this and then that happens') as a generalization that the sick man is acting out, whether he knows it or not. The sick man goes to a patron to request a light drink for his visit to the Baths, and a little interchange takes place that echoes the main confrontation of this poem. The patron advises his client to have his health seen to, but he is told not to play the guardian (*tutor*, a person who keeps another safe, *tutus*). 'I've seen my guardian buried, you're next.' This remark is recalled at the end of the scene when the sick man dies and his bier is hoisted by 'citizens as of yesterday' (*hesterni* . . . *Quirites*). It was a Roman custom for a man of substance to free some of his slaves on his death, a display of generosity that cost him nothing. Slaves who had been formally freed became Roman citizens. So it is a nice irony that the man who spoke of burying his tutor is buried by his own manumitted slaves. And there is a similarity between the two events: burying his tutor, the speaker proves that he is no longer a minor, and the new citizens cease to be slaves when they bury their master.

The build-up to this ironic climax is brilliantly controlled and characteristically rooted in the physical world. Death coming to the sick man is described as the eruption of a volcano. Sulphurous exhalations are followed by a tremor that shakes the cup from his hands, and finally the oily relishes dribble from his lips. With a swift change of scene (*hinc*, hence) we are introduced to the appurtenances of the funeral (horn, candles, corpse), listed in a tricolon crescendo that culminates with the corpse itself, laid out in accordance with Roman custom, smeared with perfume to disguise the smell of decay, its feet pointing to the door. The deceased is elevated by the word '*beatus*' (blessed; cf. beatific) and at the same time mocked by the diminutive form in which it appears (*beatulus*).

The student responds to this anecdote with a protest that it doesn't apply to him: 'Examine me, then. I'm fine. No symptoms of ill health.' To which the voice replies 'Maybe, but how's your heartbeat when the neighbour's girlfriend smiles at you, or cash is in the offing? And how's your throat? Let's test it with a healthy dinner of raw veg' (107–12, paraphrased):

> temptemus fauces; tenero latet ulcus in ore
> putre quod haud deceat plebeia radere beta.   (113–14)

> (Let's test your throat: that tender mouth conceals a septic
> Ulcer which no plebeian beet must irritate.)   (trans. Lee)

The critical voice pretends to have found the student's hidden ulcer, but of course that isn't the problem; either he is anticipating the student's excuse or the ulcer is a metaphor. Is the student's moral fibre (to switch metaphors) so degraded that he can't endure a simple life? From here the satire comes to a close with a precipitate upping of the ante:

> Alges, cum excussit membris timor albus aristas.
> nunc face supposita fervescit sanguis et ira
> scintillant oculi, dicisque facisque quod ipse
> non sani esse hominis non sanus iuret Orestes.   (115–18)

> (You're chilled when white fear lifts the stubble on your limbs.
> At other times your blood boils at the touch of anger's
> Torch, your eyes flash, and you say and do what even
> Lunatic Orestes would swear was lunacy.)   (trans. Lee)

Non sanus (not healthy/sensible) quickly becomes equivalent to *insanus*, as the morally flawed student is told that his raging would shock the mad Orestes of the stage. In its most extreme form, Stoicism claimed that all vices are equal, and that only the Stoic sage is sane. Persius' satire leaves us with this absurd conclusion as it summons the last of its voices, a stage character (Orestes) who enters to swear an oath about a real person. After all the vivid direct speech in this satire we end with a speech we are asked to imagine, and it's very hard to do so. We are as far removed from the colloquial, realistic world of the opening as we could be.

The image of the (proverbially soft) beet scraping the ulcerated throat of the fussy student is an echo of Persius' description of his satiric writing in the first of his satires. There an imaginary objector asks him why he insists on making it so unpleasant for the reader.

> sed quid opus teneras mordaci radere vero
> auriculas? (*Satires* 1. 107–8)

> (But what is the need to scrape with biting truth
> Their little ears?)

The same verb is used here for 'to scrape' (*radere*) as in the third satire. It's harder to imagine an ear scraped by what it hears than a throat by what it swallows. A tender throat is a physical reality, but what is a tender ear? Is *tener* here proleptic (anticipatory)? The truth bites, and so *makes* your ear feel tender, which is a sign that the satire has done its work. Or is someone with a tender ear simply unable to hear the truth, as the student is unable to tolerate rough fare?

Satire often describes itself as rough, biting speech, and Persius will become the prime model, in the European satiric tradition, for the harsh, difficult style appropriate to a genre that speaks uncomfortable truths. In the first satire, Persius contrasts his unpopular but truthful, free-speaking satire with the kind of smooth, sexy verse that packs in the audience at public recitations. This poetry scratches us too, but in a different way:

> scilicet haec populo pexusque togaque recenti
> et natalicia tandem cum sardonyche albus
> sede leges celsa, liquido cum plasmate guttur
> mobile conlueris, patranti fractus ocello.
> tunc neque more probo videas nec voce serena

ingentis trepidare Titos, cum carmina lumbum
intrant et tremulo scalpuntur ubi intima versu.   (*Satires* 1. 15–21)

(This (of course) to the public, combed and in clean toga,
Wearing (at last) a birthday sardonyx, white faced,
You'll read from the platform, having rinsed the supple throat
With liquid roulade, languishing the orgasmic eye.
Then, in no seemly manner, nor with voice serene,
Huge Tituses are seen to thrill as poems enter
Their loins and vibrant verses scratch their intimate parts.)

(trans. Lee)

The passage is perhaps the most lurid example of the first satire's very
Roman obsession with effeminacy and its equally Roman use of sexual
imagery to describe matters of style and taste. The decadent poet who
is conjured up to represent the taste of the times is feminized, but so is
the audience he excites. It is a Roman commonplace that effeminate
men appeal to women. This speaker is turned on by his own gargling
and by the sight of the audience's reaction to his poetry. It is a love-fest
become kinky orgy, compared to which Persius' aggressive relation to
his readership looks downright decent. Just how metaphorically are we
to take the final two lines? If you can associate a sensation with Persius'
image of the poetry entering via the nether regions, or at least scratch-
ing an orifice that is not the ear, then you are already compromised. But
if there is a real sensation involved then surely the poet who describes
it knows it himself. Satire has a tendency to turn on the satirist who is
getting into a lather about all this depravity. Persius distinguishes satire
from the feminized, crowd-pleasing kind of poetry that is its oppo-
site in terms of the different kinds of scraping they perform. Both
scrape tender parts. But suppose that we don't shy away from satire.
Suppose we enjoy this stuff, what then? We remember what Martial
said to the reader who likes poetry to give him a bumpy ride:

Dispeream ni scis mentula quid sapiat.

3

....

HORACE: THE SENSATION OF MEDIOCRITY

Golden mediocrity

Daniel Defoe's *Robinson Crusoe*, published in 1719, is one of the great adventure stories. Robinson Crusoe is shipwrecked on a desert island but survives, by dint of endurance and ingenuity, for several years until he is finally rescued and returns to England. When he announces to his father, at the beginning of the novel, that he plans to go to sea, his father delivers a long sermon on the perfections of the middle station in life. Only the desperate or the overly ambitious go to sea, and Robinson should take proper satisfaction in the fact that, being of the upper echelon of the lower middle class, he has landed in the ideal situation. He should settle into it, not run away. Crusoe senior waxes lyrical about the advantages of the middle estate and the disadvantages of what lies on either side; he enlarges on his theme for a good page, pouring out sentiments that are profoundly alienating to a modern reader. Contentment no longer has a ring to it; fulfilment and achievement are the terms we deal in, even revenge ('Living well is the best revenge,' as the slogan of the eighties had it). After all, if Crusoe had listened to his father there would have been no adventure to recount. The speech of

Crusoe's father sounds to us like stale moralizing that comes from a book, as lifeless as the virtues it prescribes. And indeed it does come from a book, or several books, all of them ancient. But, as the speech goes on, the contemporary reader may gradually begin to feel the emotion that Crusoe's father invests in the idea of happy mediocrity—'feel' in the sense of 'appreciate', for few of us can share it. Anyone familiar with classical literature will recognize bits and pieces of Horace, Seneca, and others, commonplaces that are too common for comment. But here they are deployed in a dramatic situation and applied to a specific social context far removed from anything those classical authors knew. They are ideas that have had a very long life.

Probably the most famous ancient version of Crusoe senior's tirade is one of Horace's odes (*Odes* 2. 10), and it is surely not a coincidence that, when Horace urges the addressee of that poem (Licinius) to steer a middle path in life, he uses a string of nautical metaphors. Horace's poem is an entirely appropriate point of reference in a book about a castaway. In the Licinius ode, Horace coins the phrase that would stick to him, for better or worse, more than any of his memorable coinages: *aurea mediocritas* (golden moderateness), an oxymoron that seems even more paradoxical if we translate the second word with its English derivate 'mediocrity'. In the accusative form in which it appears in this ode it is a very long word (*mediocritatem*), and one that is custom-made for the metre in which this ode is written, and for none other. So it is not surprising that this phrase has become an emblem of Horace's œuvre. The whole ode, in fact, is one of Horace's most famous. Victorian schoolmasters liked the fact that it is heavy in moral pronouncements (nine in twenty-four lines), but modern readers have found that a stumbling block rather than a recommendation. If modern readers find it hard to love *mediocritas*, as Horace urges ('whoever loves golden *mediocritas* ...'), can we respond to a poetry of *mediocritas*? It may help to stress that the Latin word doesn't have the same connotations of insignificance as our 'mediocre'. Aristotle defined virtue as a mean between two vices, and the Latin word *mediocritas* is sometimes used to allude to this notion of virtue as middleness. In another poem (*Epistles* 1. 1. 41), Horace expresses the dynamism of the Aristotelian principle when he says that *virtus est vitium fugere* (virtue consists in *fleeing* vice).

If *mediocritas* is the point between two extremes, we can expect a poetry of *mediocritas* to feature a good deal of the antithetical forms of expression that the Roman poets so favoured. We are not disappointed. In the second stanza of the ode to Licinius, Horace writes that whoever loves golden *mediocritas* avoids the extremes, on the one side of sordid poverty and on the other of the splendid palace. This is how he puts it:

> auream quisquis mediocritatem
> diligit tutus caret obsoleti
> sordibus tecti, caret invidenda
>   sobrius aula.   (*Odes* 2. 10. 5–8)

> (Whoever loves golden *mediocritas*
> safely lacks the squalor of a tumbledown house,
> soberly lacks an enviable palace.)

Many of Horace's odes are written in stanzas of four lines, which gives them a very different quality from poetry written in couplets or in hexameters. The stanza is a more complex unit than any of the verse forms we have looked at so far, and the antithesis that is distributed over the second, third, and fourth lines is more sinuous than what we find, for instance, in Ovid's elegiac couplets. All the lines in this stanza are enjambed, and the sense tumbles from one line to the next in unpredictable ways. The main verb, 'loves' (*diligit*), comes, as usual, at the end of its clause, but it is emphatically enjambed to underline the oxymoron of loving middleness, and Horace's word order places love and lack into close proximity (*diligit*, loves; *caret*, lacks). What follows now are two parallel clauses telling us what the lover of *mediocritas* avoids: he lacks the squalor (*sordibus)* of a tumbledown house (*obsoleti tecti*) and he lacks an enviable palace (*invidenda aula*). Two adjectives, *tutus* (safe) and *sobrius* (sober) attach safety to the avoidance of one extreme (squalor) and sobriety to the avoidance of the other (splendour); the first adjective comes before the verb *caret* and the other after it, an example of chiasmus (*abba*). But Horace's calculated asymmetry of expression between these parallel clauses complicates the picture: 'the squalor of a tumbledown house' is opposed to 'a palace to be envied'. With the gerundive *invidenda* (to be envied, enviable) Horace introduces the fear of the evil eye (*video* = I see), always a worry for the fortunate or successful in the ancient world. *Tutus* (safe), then, could just as well go with the avoidance of luxury as with its opposite, and that is how we take it, until we come to the fourth line and read *sobrius*. What motivates the avoidance of splendour, then? Are we being sober or just safe in refusing it? The art of reading a Horatian poem is the art of giving each word its proper weight, or rather of distributing the weight appropriately between the words, and here Horace's dynamic word order makes us very conscious of how we are doing this.

The Licinius ode opens with a nautical metaphor advising Licinius neither to take the shortest line between two points, and so brave the open sea, nor to hug the dangerous shore in fear of storms. If he observes this advice he will live *rectius*, which means 'more properly' (cf. rectitude), or, literally, 'more straight'. *Rectius* is one of those words that we forget are metaphors, but poetry likes to remind us of how steeped our language is in metaphor, and Horace want us to notice the paradox that the 'straighter' way is to avoid the most direct way. He points out that one of our most common moral metaphors (straight-dealing, rectitude, straightforwardness) is too static for the business of living well. The pursuit of Aristotelian virtue, like sailing, requires a constant adjustment according to the changing geography and weather. When we are doing well we must be prepared for a change in fortunes, and when things are going badly we must hope for one. Alternation is the name of the game. The ode revels in antithesis and variation, letting out the sail and drawing it in, so to speak, as the length of the contrasting units of meaning expands or contracts in a constant stream of carefully controlled asymmetries. The final stanza brings back the nautical metaphor:

> rebus angustis animosus atque
> fortis appare; sapienter idem
> contrahes vento nimium secundo
>   turgida vela.   (2. 10. 21–4)

> (In difficult circumstances show yourself
> spirited and brave; you would be wise too
> to pull in your swollen sails in a wind that is too favourable.)

This stanza is made up of two parallel elements, uneven in length, which pivot around a chiasmus: *fortis appare* (be seen to be brave) is the emphatic climax of the first element, which begins with 'in strait-ened circumstances' (*rebus angustis*); but *sapienter idem* (wisely, you (will) also…) leads off the second element, and the circumstances come *after* (*vento nimium secundo*: in a too favourable wind). *Fortis* (brave) and *sapienter* (wisely) represent different kinds of virtue, and the contrast between them, emphasized by the chiasmus, is rendered slightly asymmetrical by the change from adjective (*fortis*) to adverb (*sapienter*). The adverb gives dynamism to the second part of the stanza, urging us on towards the verb (*contrahes*: you will draw in), which, being transitive, draws us towards its object, the final phrase of the poem (*turgida vela*: swollen sails). This stanzaic form, known as the Sapphic, after the Greek poet Sappho, ends with a short fourth line, filled here by the words 'billowing (lit. swollen, turgid) sails'. The metrical rhythm of this line is equivalent to the rhythm of the English phrase 'shave and a haircut', and it rounds off the stanza neatly. But the meaning of the phrase fights against the rhythmical effect, leaving us with a tense combination of letting out and drawing in. As a closural phrase, *turgida vela* suggests reserves of energy yet to be expended. *Mediocritas* in this poem is a tensile quality. The fact that circumstances are changing continually demands a flexible response from the human agent. Horace's own poetic response to the basic idea conveyed by the poem varies as he delivers in quick succession a dense series of pronouncements to the same general effect, but with an extraordinary variety of expressive means.

This poem, as the tirade of Robinson Crusoe's father attests, has been taken as a general statement about the human condition, but it may not be quite as Olympian as it appears. Almost all Roman poems are addressed to someone. Horace's Licinius is probably Licinius Murena, closely related to Horace's patron Maecenas, adviser to Augustus (on whom more below). Licinius was outspoken and headstrong, and is known to have defied Augustus at least once. When the emperor appeared as witness for the prosecution at a trial where Licinius was acting for the defendant he is reported to have said, 'What are you doing here, and who sent for you?' (Dio 54. 3), an extraordinary way to speak to the emperor. This incident happened the year after Horace published his first three books of odes (22 BC); later that same year Licinius was found guilty of joining a conspiracy against Augustus and executed. In this context, Horace's poem looks like advice about political survival to a man who sails close to the wind, advice that was not to be heeded. Bland generalities begin to look like political tact on the part of Horace, who avoids specificity so as to disguise an awareness of the more brutal aspects of power under the guise of wisdom. Horace's patron, Maecenas, would have welcomed the fact that his poet had publicly laid a steadying hand on the shoulder of his potentially embarrassing relation. So, to the immediate addressee, Licinius, we can add a secondary addressee, namely Augustus. A great deal of Augustan literature can be thought of in this way: poetry written to be read by the emperor over the shoulders of the addressee. Or, to come at it from another angle, poetry that is read by a readership which imagines the emperor's response. The poem is not only addressed, obliquely, to the ultimate power, it also represents to the reading public (a small elite, it must be remembered) the kind of thing the emperor might be thought to approve. Horace's tact, in other words, is credited to the regime. In Horace's poem, the realities of the emperor's power can be glimpsed beneath the commonplaces of the third stanza, where Horace elaborates the idea that it is the highest trees that are struck by lightning, and so on. We can also read 'Augustus' for Jupiter when Horace says that Jupiter brings on the grim winter and then dispels it (so the wise man will be prepared for a change in fortune). General and specific flicker in readers' minds, as we move between translating philosophical generalities into veiled threats or directives and seeing political realities from a great height, where they are subsumed under a broader philosophical perspective. Horace seems to enunciate this very process when he follows the statement that Jupiter brings on and dispels the winter with an equivalent statement about Apollo: 'Sometimes Apollo stirs the silent Muse with his lyre. He does not always bend his bow.' Apollo's two attributes, bow and lyre, both in their different ways dependent on tension, might represent the vision and the power of Augustus respectively. In fact, Apollo's bow and lyre might be the duck and rabbit of this poem.

A mosaic of words

Horace's poetry has been admired by many readers who would not have responded warmly to the gospel of 'golden *mediocritas*', among them Friedrich Nietzsche, who wrote a famous description of Horace's style:

> Up to the present I have not obtained from any poet the same artistic delight as was given me from the first by an Horatian Ode. In certain languages that which is here obtained cannot even be hoped for. The mosaic of words in which every word, by position and meaning, diffuses its force right, left, and over the whole, that minimum in the compass and number of signs, that maximum thus released in their energy,—all that is Roman, and if you will believe me, it is noble par excellence. All other poetry becomes somewhat too popular in comparison with it—mere sentimental loquacity.
>
> ('What I learned from the Ancients', in *The Twilight of the Idols*)

Nietzsche's use of the language of class to distinguish the noble Horatian style from the sentimental loquacity of other poets may have been influenced by another well-known Horatian tag, *Odi profanum vulgus* (I hate the profane mob, *Odes* 3. 1. 1). Hardly a democratic sentiment! Others have had less flattering descriptions of the class associations of Horace's poetry than Nietzsche's 'noble par excellence'. One critic has called Horace's 'the poetry of comfortable stipendiaries', a characterization that has more to do with the content of Horace's poems, their gospel of contentment (which is all very well if you're comfortably off), than with their poetic texture. For Nietzsche, the nobility of Horace's poetry lies in the way that it finds something more concrete in language than a tone of voice, releasing the potential energy in the words to strike sparks off one another. Like many other commentators, he stresses Horace's economy of means, and he figures Horace as a general deploying his forces, tactical rather than tactful.

Nietzsche's characterization echoes ancient descriptions of Horace's poetry, of which the most famous occurs in Petronius' *Satyricon* (118. 5), where one of Petronius' characters refers to the *curiosa felicitas* (careful aptness/felicity) of Horace. The phrase is an oxymoron worthy of Horace himself, for the primary sense of *felicitas* is luck, while the root of *curiosa* is *cura* (care). 'Careful felicity' perfectly captures the sensation of reading Horace, whose poetry seems both laboriously calculated and epiphanically right at the same time. Quintilian, the author of a treatise on rhetoric, says something similar when he speaks of Horace as being *verbis felicissime audax* (10. 1. 96, 'most felicitously daring in his vocabulary'). Horace's is a poetry in which every word counts in a way that is quite different from the elegists. Again and again we are made aware of the fact that the *mot* is *juste* and has been placed for the maximum effect, often to produce a striking juxtaposition. Horace himself contributed to the criticism of his own poetry when he discussed the subject of diction in his didactic poem *The Art of Poetry* (*Ars Poetica*). There he recommends the cunning juxtaposition (*callida iunctura*, 47–8) that rejuvenates a well-known word. Words, he says, are subject to entropy and decay, just like everything else. But the effect of any word can be refreshed by clever juxtaposition to another.

It is not just on the level of individual words or clever combinations that Horace's poetry produces its characteristic sensation. In modern times Horace's poetry has often been called the poetry of transitions. Donald Davie, in a very Horatian poem called 'Wombwell on Strike', speaks of

> His sudden and smooth transitions
> (as, into a railway tunnel,
> then out, to a different landscape).

This seems to conflict with Nietzsche's comparison of Horace's poetry to a mosaic. But both descriptions are equally apt, and if you put them together you get a sense of the bifurcated physicality of Horace's poetry. We glide seamlessly from one topic or point to another, but we also watch a picture gradually come into focus.

A perfect example of this bifurcated sensation is provided by the most famous and most translated of Horace's *Odes*, the Ode to Pyrrha, as it is sometimes known (1. 5). In 1955 Ronald Storrs claimed to have found at least 451 translations in twenty-six languages (nearly half of them published in his *Ad Pyrrham*).[1] By now the count must be well over 500. This is the fifth poem in Horace's first book of odes.

Love, Horatian style

Quis multa gracilis te puer in rosa
(What slender boy hugs you in a bed of roses,

perfusus liquidis urget odoribus
drenched in liquid perfumes,

grato, Pyrrha, sub antro?
Pyrrha, beneath a pleasant cave?

cui flavam religas comam,
For whom do you tie back your blond hair,

[1] Ronald Storrs, *Ad Pyrrham* (Oxford, 1959).

simplex munditiis? heu quotiens fidem	simple in your toilette? Alas, how often will he
mutatosque deos flebit et aspera	bewail a change in your affections and the gods
nigris aequora ventis emirabitur insolens,	and wonder at seas rough with black winds, unused to it all,
qui nunc te fruitur credulus aurea,	who now enjoys and trusts golden you,
qui semper vacuam, semper amabilem	who hopes you'll always be loveable, always
sperat, nescius aurae fallacis! miseri, quibus	available, ignorant of the changeable breeze! Wretched are those
intemptata nites. me tabula sacer votiva paries indicat uvida	to whom you shine, untried. As for me, the sacred wall with its votive tablet shows
suspendisse potenti	that I've dedicated my dripping clothes
vestimenta maris deo.	to the sea's powerful god.

(1. 5)

The subject matter of Horace's odes is extremely varied, but love is a major theme, and this is the first poem dealing with love in the first of the four books. Already in this first love poem of the collection Horace speaks from a position of retirement, and with the detached voice of experience, slightly self-mocking in tone—a far cry from the masochism of the 'wretched' love elegists. It is a voice that is in many ways defining of the Horatian persona. But only at the end of the poem are we introduced to Horace the lover at all. Latin poetry did not use titles to orientate the reader's expectation, and so Latin poets can play with the reader's sense of what the poem is about, of what is central and what peripheral. Is this poem about Pyrrha, the boy, or Horace himself? We begin perhaps by assuming that it is about Pyrrha, then we shift our attention to the boy, and finally we realize (though perhaps we have suspected this all along) that Horace himself is a player in this scenario.

The poem is sometimes referred to as *Ad Pyrrham* (To Pyrrha), which is a convenient way of naming it, since Latin poetry is almost always addressed to someone. In Horace's case the addressee is often a real contemporary, and sometimes an important figure, such as the emperor Augustus himself or his aide Maecenas, but a host of distinguished Roman men receive an ode, and they would have been proud (and solicitous) of the honour. The women of Horace's poetry are another matter. In most cases they have Greek names and cannot be identified with anyone we know from the historical record. Pyrrha's name is derived from the Greek word for fire, and it could also mean 'golden-haired'. It is translated into Latin in Horace's 'cui *flavam* religas comam' (for whom do you bind your *golden* hair?). Names such as Pyrrha's would conjure up the world of Greek poetry, which Horace boasts of having brought to Rome. His appropriating of Greek metres for the Latin tongue is an act of cultural imperialism whose material equivalent was the plundering of Greek works of art for display in Roman villas. In English poetry, the Corinnas, Glyceras, Phyllises, etc. that people the love poetry of the Renaissance and beyond are similarly generic figures, reminding us that the conventions of Latin poetry are being rehearsed and given new life in their modern context, just as in the original Horatian context these names allude to a prestigious Greek poetry. But the name of Horace's Pyrrha does not have exclusively literary resonances. Roman slaves were frequently given Greek names, and the name Pyrrha might suggest a freed slave who had become a courtesan.

The question lingering in our minds as Horace slips from (jealous? exasperated? amused?) questions, through exclamation to magisterial pronouncement is 'What is Pyrrha to you?' As sympathy for Pyrrha's new lover gathers to culminate in the cry 'wretched are those to whom you glitter, yet untried' (*miseri, quibus // intemptata nites*) the question of Horace's interest in this scenario becomes unavoidable. But he does not answer in the first person. Rather he points to the evidence of the 'sacred wall' where his deliverance from the sea is celebrated by a votive tablet to Neptune. 'It's all on record', Horace tells us, 'over there. I'm *hors de combat*.' Horace forestalls our question, gliding from the *intemptata* (untried, unattempted), which applies to the boy's naive perspective, to the evidence that *he*, Horace, speaks from experience. Horace has retired, safely, from his fling with Pyrrha, which is here figured as a shipwreck. Like a sailor grateful to Neptune for his deliverance, Horace has hung up his wet clothes in the temple and recorded his gratitude in a picture on a votive tablet. We have passed directly from the moment before disillusionment, when the young man gazes at Pyrrha glittering deceptively like the sea, to the moment of resignation and recovery after experience.

Horace's poetry is particularly rich and complex in its closural effects. Typically Horace avoids the kind of ending that brings a poem resoundingly to a close; many of his poems end by opening out onto a new vista, or fading off in a poignant diminuendo. This one seems to be an exception, as Horace turns from Pyrrha and the boy to himself, dismisses our suspicions and signs off, revealing in the final stanza the secure position from which the poem has been spoken. But the ending is more complex than it might at first seem. Appealing to the evidence of the votive tablet, Horace claims that, as far as Pyrrha is concerned, he is no longer in contention. But does a picture outweigh the words he has spoken? Appealing to the votive tablet may be a figurative way of saying 'Look at the facts: we're history', but can it register

Horace's attitude? Do his words perhaps betray a bitterness that belies the tablet's claim? It is a typically Horatian irony that, in claiming to be out of the picture as far as Pyrrha is concerned, Horace completes the narrative implied by the sea imagery that has been deployed throughout the poem (glittering sea, storm, shipwreck, and deliverance). The final gesture is both outside and inside the picture of Pyrrha and her lover.

Let's now think about the movement of this ode as an example of Horace's 'art of transition'. Horace manages both to keep the focus steady and to engineer a series of dissolves by keeping our ear attentive to a succession of key words beginning with q or c. This is not just a sound, but the characteristic beginning of relative and interrogative pronouns. The first word of the poem, *Quis* (which?), is an interrogative pronoun. The second sentence begins with another interrogative pronoun, *cui*, but this one is in the dative (for whom?). The following sentence leads off with the interrogative adverb, *quotiens* (how many times? cf. quota), or at least it would if Horace hadn't prefaced it with the exclamatory *heu* (alas!), which shifts the utterance from question to exclamation (how often will he…!). There follow three relative pronouns: a repeated *qui* (who), and then *quibus* (to whom). It is only with the final sentence that we escape these q/c sounds with the personal pronoun *me* (me). As the key pronouns with their distinctive opening sounds mutate from the interrogative to the relative, via the exclamatory *quotiens*, Horace's voice becomes more authoritative. By the end of the poem he is no longer the curious voyeur but the retired lover who knows the story. In addition to the change in grammatical function of the q/c words there are changes in grammatical case. Not surprisingly, this is an effect that is particularly suited to the Latin language, and the Romans had a word for it. Polyptoton (many-casedness) refers to the repetition of the same or similar words in different cases. But it is not just an ornament here. Horace comes at the same scene from different angles, changing the perspective from which it is seen. We begin with the importuning boy (but which one is it now? *Quis*?) and then move to the subtle seductions of Pyrrha's toilette, which is *for* someone (but for whom? *cui*?). Later, Horace laments the predicament of those *to whom* (*quibus*) Pyrrha glitters—another dative, but with a different shade of meaning. Each of these words approaches the scenario from a different angle.

Moving in now to a closer look at the first stanza, we can see that there is a nice contrast between the complicated, crowded scenario of the first two lines (boy, girl, roses, perfume, cave) and the straightforward question that neatly fills the last line of the stanza. As Pyrrha ties up her hair, Horace wraps up the stanza. Or so it seems, until we get to the next stanza, which begins with two words in apposition to Pyrrha, extending the question we thought was complete in the previous stanza. *Simplex munditiis* means something like 'simple in your toilette'. The phrase is an oxymoron (and a 'cunning juxtaposition'), since *munditiis* is a plural form of the noun and it implies elegance; we might translate 'simple in your refinements'. Pyrrha's simplicity is deceptive, just as Horace's extension of the sense unit into the second stanza is unexpected.

Enjambement, the continuation of sense across the break between lines or stanzas, is the most important feature of Horace's art of transition. Unlike the usually self-contained elegiac couplet as written by the elegists, Horace's stanzas are very fluid. Reading the elegists, we usually know at any given point how close we are approaching to the completion of a sense unit. A large part of the pleasure of reading Horace, by contrast, is that, just as we think a sentence is wrapping up, it unexpectedly acquires new energy, delving into a byway or tributary (or emerging from a tunnel into a new landscape, as Donald Davie puts it). In this poem not a single stanza is self-contained in sense, and there are some striking enjambements. For instance, in the second stanza the sense is complete at *flebit* (Alas, how often will he *bewail* your promise and the changed gods), but the words *et aspera* (and the rough...) at the end of the line open the sentence up again. It could end again at *ventis* (and [he will bewail] the sea rough with black *winds*), but the following line subordinates the object *aspera aequora* to a new verb, *emirabitur* (*he will marvel* in his inexperience at the seas rough with black winds), and this grammatical rearrangement neatly reflects the inexperienced boy's wonder. But even now we're not finished with this sentence, as the relative pronoun that begins the next stanza indicates (the boy, *who* now...). With this further extension we're returned from the future to the present, where the poem began, with the difference that then the boy was an object of conjecture, of jealous curiosity, whereas now he is an example of a pattern of which the poet is well aware. Horace's poem does not construct an argument (for instance, 'Who's kissing you now? That boy may think he's lucky, but soon enough he'll know...I can speak from experience'). Instead, the transitions effect a continuing metamorphosis, as the constantly evolving syntax and repetitions-with-a-difference change our perspective on the scene and our sense of where the poet speaks from. This poetry is at the opposite pole to Sulpicia's awkward struggle to say what she means.

We will leave this poem with a very close look at the first two lines, which are a good example of Horace's art on the smallest scale:

> Quis multa gracilis te puer in rosa
> perfusus liquidis urget odoribus...?

The first two lines of this stanzaic form (called Third Asclepiad) are metrically identical, but in this case they feel quite different in rhythm because of the different patterns of the words. The metre of these two lines can be represented sonically as

dum dum / dum da da dum / dum da da / dum da da.

Substituting the symbol – for a long syllable (dum) and the symbol ∪ for a short (da), we have (the slanting lines divide the feet):

$$- \quad - / - \cup \cup \; -/- \; \cup \cup / - \cup -$$
Quis multa gracilis te puer in rosa

Similarly

$$- \quad - / - \cup \cup - / - \cup \cup / - \cup -$$
perfusus liquidis urget odoribus

There is no verb in the first line, which reads, literally: '**what** *much* **slender** you **boy** *in roses*'. Or, in something more like English: 'what slender boy [somethings] you in much roses)'. The pronoun *te* (you) in the accusative is the object of a verb for which we must wait. Around this *te* Horace interweaves two phrases *Quis...gracilis...puer* (what slender youth) and *multa...in rosa* (in much roses). But he does so in such a way as to create concentric circles around the *te*: *Quis **multa** gracilis* TE *puer **in rosa***. *Multa...in rosa* forms the outer circle and *gracilis...puer* the inner, with Pyrrha (*te*), appropriately, in the centre. The effect is as much visual as aural: Pyrrha is embraced by the boy, and both are surrounded by roses. Horace accentuates the tendency of all Latin poetry to allow each word to hold its own and achieve an almost tangible individuality, often emphasized by juxtapositions of incompatible words, such as *multa* (much) and *gracilis* (slender).

The second line completes the sense left dangling at the end of the first line, but not immediately. Instead of telling us what the boy is doing to Pyrrha in all those roses, Horace puts the boy in the passive (*perfusus*, drenched). We are grateful when an active verb puts in an appearance (*urget*, presses), but it doesn't dispel the atmosphere of stifling enclosure ('drenched in perfume he presses on you in a bed of roses'). The other component of the line is the adjective–noun phrase *liquidis…odoribus*, which combines two different sensations, the oiliness of the perfume and its scent. But the phrase is split up so as to suggest that one word goes with *perfusus* (the liquidity) and the other with *urget* (the scent). The boy is drenched in the oily liquid and presses his perfumed attentions on Pyrrha. We should remember that luxury to the Romans felt oily: to anoint your head with scented oil at a dinner party was for them what opening a bottle of champagne is for us.

When the verb *urget* enters to impart some dynamism to the scene, it does so at a particularly strategic point in the metrical line, to which we must now turn. The lines of Horace's lyric metres are composed of different combinations of a variety of feet, and the stanzas themselves are composed of different kinds of line. This gives the Horatian stanza a very intricate music. The stanza of 1. 5 (Third Asclepiad) has three different metrical lines: the first two are identical, but the third and the fourth are different from the first two and from each other. The main foot of this metre is the choriamb $- \cup \cup -$ (dum da da dum). In the first two lines of the stanza it is preceded by a preparatory spondee (dum dum; $- -$) to impart a rather conclusive effect to the first half of the line: $- -/- \cup \cup -$; i.e. dum dum/ dum da da dum (*quis mul/ta gracilis*). But the dactyl that begins the second half of the line gives it a fresh shot of energy ($- \cup \cup/- \cup -$; dum da da/ dum da dum [*te puer/ in rosa*]). In the second line of 1. 5 that surcharge of energy coincides with the arrival of the verb *urget* (*urget o-/doribus*). The same kind of effect occurs at the first line of the third stanza, *qui nunc te fruitur credulus aurea* (who enjoys you now, trusting [that you are] golden). Here *aurea* does double duty: since the adjective *credulus* is derived from a verb (*credo*, I believe), we hear *credulus aurea* (believing in your goldenness) as well as *te fruitur... aurea* (he enjoys golden you). The rhythmic dynamism of the second half of the line energizes the verb in the root of the adjective *credulus*. Another notable metrical effect occurs at the same position of the next line with the words *qui semper vacuam, SEMper amabilem*. The second *semper* (always) has a different rhythm from the first because the initial consonant of *vacuam* makes the second syllable of *semper* long by position. So the line goes *qui semPER vacuam, SEMper amabilem*. The effect is to give the second pair of words an expansive, almost ecstatic lift, helped by the two dactyls at that point of the metre. It nicely conveys the boy's credulous swooning.

Horace's stanzas often end with a shorter line rounding them off. This particular stanzaic form follows the two identical longer lines with two different shorter lines, the first of which feels more conclusive than the second. The rhythm of the first of the short lines is

Dum dum / dum da da dum / dum
(*grato, / Pyrrha, sub ant / ro*).

It is followed by a line that adds a short syllable before the final long: Dum dum / dum da da dum / da dum (*Cui fla / vam religas / comam*). The tying back of Pyrrha's hair is an appropriate way to end the stanza, so that Horace seems to be producing an image of poetic closure itself. But, as we have seen, this stanza has a false ending and the sentence continues at the beginning of the next.

Horace's oblique introduction of himself in the final stanza of 1. 5 puts the little scene he has conjured up into a fresh light. It is not unusual for a Horatian poem to take more radical twists when the poet enters in person. A famous example is the poem (*Odes* 1. 22) that begins with the line *Integer vitae scelerisque purus* (the man whose life is upright and who is free of wrongdoing . . .). That man, Horace tells his addressee Fuscus, needs no weapons, however dangerous the territory through which he passes, for he will be protected by the gods. The opening line of this poem, with its sonorous endorsement of moral pride, became one of the most well known of Horatian tags. Eduard Fraenkel, one of the twentieth century's great Horace scholars, tells us that the opening stanza was sung to the tune of a hymn at funeral services in Germany.[2] David West reports that there is a setting of this ode in hymn style in the *Scottish Students' Song Book* of 1897.[3] Horace's lyric stanzas, with their complex rhythmical effects, became the preferred form for Latin hymns and school songs, and his frequent use of 'improving' maxims influenced the content of these songs enormously. But many of Horace's worthy tags look quite different when read in their context, and this poem needs to be severely cropped if it is to be set as a hymn. Its beginning is impeccable: the man of blameless life walks safely without weapons, protected as he is by the gods. After these worthy generalizations Horace turns, as he so often does, to something particular and, more particularly, himself. The proof of these lofty pronouncements is that, when he was wandering in the woods and singing of his girlfriend Lalage, Horace encountered a savage wolf, which promptly turned tail and ran. 'Put me in the burning deserts and I'll love my Lalage, who speaks and laughs so sweetly,' Horace concludes. We have been misled by the worthy opening, and now Horace pulls the rug from under our feet. But in return for our lost 'hymn' he gives us a more delicious

---

[2] Eduard Fraenkel, *Horace* (Oxford, 1957), 184.
[3] David West, *Horace, Odes 1: Carpe Diem* (Oxford, 1995), 104.

music. The poem is in the Sapphic metre, whose first three lines run
−◡− −/−◡ ◡/−◡−◡ (dum da dum dum / dum da da / dum da dum da);
this complex rhythm is followed by the breezy rounding off of the final
short line −◡ ◡ − ◡ (dum da da dum da: 'shave and a haircut').

In this poem the last two lines read:

> dulce ridentem Lalagen amabo,
> dulce loquentem.

> (I will love my sweetly laughing Lalage,
> sweetly talking.)

The verb, *amabo* (I will love), stands at the end of the first line, with its
object preceding it (sweetly laughing Lalage) and following it (sweetly
speaking [Lalage]). So the last, short line of the poem is 'sweetly talk-
ing', an appropriate phrase with which to end a poem. It is a typically
Horatian 'feminine' ending, which does not contain any crucial infor-
mation nor complete any syntactical unit; the two words are simply a
variation of *dulce ridentem* (sweetly smiling), and the fact that there is
only one different sound between them gives the effect of an echo.
Rhythmically, the two phrases are contrasted: the first puts on the
brakes (dum da dum dum dum: *dulce ridentem*), while the second
flows smoothly and swiftly (dum da da dum da: *dulce loquentem*). The
poem dissolves rather than ends.

Horace's ending is beautiful, but it may not be entirely serious.
Horace the 'moderate' lover (see *Odes* 1. 5) is mocking the intensities
of Latin love poetry, from Catullus to the elegiac poets, for whom the
idea that the lover is specially protected by the gods is conventional.
For one thing, the generic Greek name that Horace has given his mis-
tress, Lalage, means 'prattler'. Horace has taken the two ls of her ono-
matopoetic name and distributed them between the two words *dulce*

loquentem of the last line, which are in effect a Latin translation of the Greek Lalage. Her name stands in the Greek form of the accusative (-en), surrounded by the two Latin forms of the accusative echoing each other (-em). Horace claimed to have introduced Greek metres and subjects to Rome in his *Odes*, which play constantly with the mixing of the Greek and the Roman. All the love objects of the *Odes* have Greek names.

Love is one of the main themes of Horace's *Odes*, and its first appearance, as we have seen, provides a complete contrast to the poses struck by the love elegists. In the first elegy of Propertius, for instance, his love for Cynthia is the beginning of a new life, and Cynthia, he stresses, is the first (Cynthia *prima* suis miserum me cepit ocellis . . . tum *primum*, Propertius 1. 1. 1–3). By contrast, from the first love poem of the *Odes* on, Horace will often take the position of the wry observer of love's ironies and perversities. Horace published the first three books of *Odes* together, and in the poem fifth from the end of the three books (i.e. corresponding to 1. 5, fifth from the beginning) we find the following (in David West's translation, n. 3):

> Till now I have lived my life without complaints
> From girls, and campaigned with my share of honours.
> Now my armour and my lyre—its wars are over—
>   Will hang on this wall
>
> Which guards the left side of Venus
> Of the sea. Here, over here, lay down my bright torches,
>   The crowbars, and the bows that threatened
>   Opposing doors.
>
> O goddess, who rules the blessed isle of Cyprus,
> And Memphis never touched by Sithonian snow,
>   Lift high your whip, O queen, and flick
>   Disdainful Chloe, just once.   (3. 26)

This poem is very similar to 1. 5, except that here Horace's retirement from love, marked by the dedication of the tools of his trade to Venus, is announced from the beginning, only to be put into question by the ending. The prayer to the goddess of love in the last stanza is not what we have been led to expect. Does Horace, himself retired from love, want the satisfaction of seeing Chloe feel love's pain, just to bring her down (is she the reason why he retired?)? Or can he not quite bring himself to be love's retiree (just one last fling, one last challenge)? Does the word 'once' in the last line mean that this is to be just a fling, or does it remind us that a single touch from the goddess of love's whip can cause major havoc? It is a typically Horatian open ending.

Horace begins this poem by speaking of love as a military campaign. Conventional comparisons of love to war took on particular importance for the poets of the Augustan age. Augustus came to power at the end of a traumatic sequence of civil wars, and many Romans who were not sympathetic to his de facto monarchy were nevertheless grateful for the peace that his reign brought to Italy. For the elegists, love and war were sometimes viewed as opposites (If we had all been lovers, there would never have been a civil war) and sometimes as equivalents (You think I'm not a real Roman? Love, too, has its campaigns). The connection between love and war was bolstered by the fact that love, to the ancient mind, was not an ennobling experience but a violent passion; images of sickness and madness abound. If civil war was *furor* (raging madness), then so was love. When Horace casts himself as love's ironic retiree, this persona may have as much to do with his political biography as with his amatory career. Horace had fought on the losing side in the civil wars that led up to the reign of Augustus. As a young student in Athens (the equivalent of university for a Roman) he had been recruited by Brutus and

Cassius, the assassins of Caesar, who claimed that they had liberated Rome from the threat of monarchy. It was an idealistic cause, and Athens, whose own history of democracy had included a famous tyrannicide, was a good place to advertise it. Caesar's lieutenant, Antony, and his heir, Octavian (who would be renamed Augustus), followed the assassins to Greece and defeated them at the battle of Philippi in 42 BC. Horace benefited from the clemency of the young Octavian, and later his talent would make him an intimate of the emperor. So Horace the retired lover, standing on the sidelines and observing the tragi-comedy with an ironic smile, parallels, supports, and possibly figures Horace's retirement from politics, republicanism, and a passion for great causes.

The relation between love and politics is made quite explicit by another poem from *Odes* 3 (3. 14). It is one of Horace's political poems, or at any rate so it seems at the beginning, where Horace takes on the persona of a public herald announcing the triumphant return of Augustus from three years of campaigning in Spain. After urging Augustus' family and the girls and boys of Rome to turn out for the welcome, Horace makes a transition, in the central stanza, to himself. With Augustus in charge he need fear no civil discord or violent death, and he too, in his own way, will celebrate this occasion. He goes on, in the second half of the poem, to give his slave a shopping list for the dinner. After the procuring of wine and perfumed oil (remember Pyrrha's boyfriend!) there is procuring of another sort:

> dic et argutae properet Neaerae
> murreum nodo cohibere crinem;
> si per invisum mora ianitorem
>   fiet, abito.

> lenit albescens animos capillus
> litium et rixae cupidos protervae;
> non ego hoc ferrem calidus iuventa
> > consule Planco.   (3. 14. 21–8)

> (And tell the mellifluous Neaera to hurry,
> binding her perfumed hair in a knot.
> If the surly doorkeeper blocks you
> > leave and desist.

> Greying hair makes gentler spirits
> of those who looked for fights and brawls.
> I would not have borne this in my hot youth
> > when Plancus was consul.)

The short fourth line of this Sapphic stanza has a strong closural effect ('shave and a haircut') that here cuts off the expected train of thought with an abrupt surprise. The normal behaviour of young members of the elite when the house of a courtesan was blocked by the doorman was to remonstrate, or break and enter. But Horace tells his slave to go away (*abito*, a brusque imperative). This unexpected turn is trumped by the frisson provided by the end of the final stanza. After explaining that middle age has toned down the rowdy behaviour of his youth, Horace leaves us with the thought that he would never have put up with such rejection when Plancus was consul. The phrase *consule Planco*, which takes up the final line of the poem, is a date. It was Roman practice to name the year after one of its consuls, and Plancus' year was 42 BC, the year of the battle of Philippi. Hot youth is the time for wrangling and mêlées, whether it be in the name of love or of politics. Horace has put that behind him. The political subtext of these two stanzas is that Augustus' firm hand, coupled with a citizenship weary of civil war, produces welcome peace. It is conveyed by the parallel images of the knot that controls (*cohibere*, cf. inhibit) Neaera's locks and Horace's own greying hair. But this translation of the language of politics into that of love allows Horace to express regret for the heady republicanism of his youth in a safer mode. The trailing afterthought with which the poem ends leaves us free to speculate. *What* would he not have tolerated back in 42 BC?

A *fin de siècle* Horace?

Towards the end of his life Horace produced a fourth book of odes. According to an ancient biographer, Horace was commissioned by Augustus to write celebratory odes on the military victories of his sons-in-law Drusus and Tiberius, and he wrote a short book of odes to feature them. The book opens with a love poem. Horace has for a long time been immune to love, but now he feels its stirrings again. He asks Venus to spare him (a man of fifty, after all!); she should persecute a more suitable lover, young Paulus Maximus, for instance. As for himself, he has given up love—why, then, does he dream persistently of the beautiful Ligurinus? Clearly, the return of love to Horace at the beginning of this new collection parallels, or figures, the fact that he is taking up again the poetic genre that he had so definitively established six years ago. For Venus, perhaps, read Augustus. But this is nothing so crude as an allegory. Its tone and music, which are new to Horace, seem more appropriate to the agenda of love than of poetry. They made an impression on the *fin-de-siècle* poet Ernest Dowson (1867–1900), who used a phrase from this poem as the title of his most famous poem (more on that below). Horace begins

> Intermissa, Venus, diu,
> rursus bella moves? parce precor, precor.
>   non sum qualis eram bonae
> sub regno Cinarae. (4. 1. 1–4)

(Interrupted for a long time, Venus,
are you waging war again? Spare me I beg, I beg.
I'm not what I used to be under the rule
of my good Cinara.)

The phrasing is simple and straightforward. Venus' return is nicely echoed in the unusual, pathetic, repetition of *precor* (I beseech you), a word that is almost an anagram of *parce* (spare me). More subtly, the renewal of love brings a rearrangement of syntax, as the opening word *intermissa* (inter-rupted, let fall) migrates from *Venus* to *bella* (wars): the inflected ending of *intermissa* could be either feminine singular (interrupted love (Venus)) or neuter plural (interrupted wars). We first assume that it is feminine singu-lar and agrees with *Venus*; without the capital letter (the distinction was not made in an ancient manuscript) the word *venus* can mean, simply, sex. *Venus*, sex or goddess, has been interrupted for a long time (*diu*). But over the line break we read that Venus is stirring up war again. Perhaps *inter-missa* modifies *bella* (you set in motion wars that have long been dor-mant), a reassessment that gives new energy to the syntax, stirring up what seemed to have been settled. As with *Odes* 3. 14, the image of love as war imparts a particular urgency to Horace's words for his contemporary readers. The ever-present possibility of war's return hovers behind the other agendas of this poem, amatory and poetic. As in *Odes* 3. 14, Horace is not what he was, but this time the point of reference is a previous love affair ('under the rule of my good Cinara'), not a consulship. A pathetic echo of the final sound of *bonae* in the noun it modifies, *Cinarae*, comes close to the effect of modern rhyme, for *Cinarae* is placed at a significant break in the metrical line. The sentence has a dying fall.

So, who was this Cinara? Her name, like that of all Horace's women, is Greek. It means 'artichoke', which is not very promising to the mod-ern ear, though it has erotic associations in Greek. Most of the women in Horace's poetry, with their generic Greek names, seem inter-changeable, but Cinara is an exception. She is mentioned twice in Horace's *Epistles* (1. 7. 28 and 1. 14. 33), published in 20 BC, and she comes back again later in the fourth book of odes. That in itself is not significant, since other female names occur more than once in Hora-ce's œuvre. But in all these passages Horace is looking back, half regretfully, on his younger self. The name Cinara has a particular role to play for Horace's persona, though whether or not there was a real Cinara we can never know. Ernest Dowson seems to have thought there was. His poem 'Non sum qualis eram bonae sub regno Cinarae' uses Horace's Cinara as the frame for a story of doomed love and bro-ken lives:

> Last night, ah, yesternight, betwixt her lips and mine
> There fell thy shadow, Cynara! thy breath was shed
> Upon my soul between the kisses and the wine;
> And I was desolate and sick of an old passion,
> Yea, I was desolate and bowed my head:
> I have been faithful to thee, Cynara! in my fashion.

> All night upon mine heart I felt her warm heart beat,
> Night-long within mine arms in love and sleep she lay;
> Surely the kisses of her bought red mouth were sweet;
> But I was desolate and sick of an old passion,
> When I awoke and found the dawn was gray:
> I have been faithful to thee, Cynara! in my fashion.

The famous line 'I have been faithful to thee, Cynara! in my fashion' has something of Horace's irony and 'mediocrity', but is there a case to be made for a 'decadent', late-romantic Horace?

Dowson is responding to something very distinctive in Horace's fourth book of odes. The final lines of this poem, in particular, have a pathos and impressionism that was profoundly congenial to Dowson's sensibility.

me nec femina nec puer
    iam nec spes animi credula mutui
nec certare iuvat mero
    nec vincire novis tempora floribus—
sed cur heu, Ligurine, cur
    manat rara meas lacrima per genas?
cur facunda parum decoro
    inter verba cadit lingua silentio?
nocturnis ego somniis
    iam captum teneo, iam volucrem sequor
te per gramina Martii
    campi, te per aquas, dure volubilis.   (4. 1. 29–40)

(As for me, neither boy nor girl,
    nor credulous hope in mutual feelings,
nor matching others drink for drink gives pleasure,
    nor binding my head with fresh flowers.
But why, Ligurinus, alas, why
    does a stray tear fall down my cheeks?
why does my eloquent tongue trail off
    mid-speech in embarrassing silence?
In my dreams at night
    I seem now to have you, now to chase you, elusive,
chase you across the grass of the Campus
    Martius, through the waters, cruel boy, as they flow.)

The repeated *cur* (why) and the rhyming effects (*meas...genas; decoro...silentio*) in the second stanza are characteristic of Horace's fourth book of odes, but it is the final image that is most memorable. The young Ligurinus exercises in the Campus Martius, and in his dreams Horace pursues him. The stanzaic form of this poem is unusual for Horace, for the last of the four lines is not shorter but longer than the preceding line. Horace capitalizes on this to leave us with the poem still reaching for Ligurinus as it ends. After the first line has situated us in Horace's dreamworld, the rest of the final stanza consists of two dicolons, each articulated by anaphora (*iam...iam; te...te...*). The second line is symmetrically divided into two with the same components in the same order ('now captured I hold you, now flying I follow you'). But the two *te* (you) clauses that complete the stanza, while of the same length (ten syllables), cut across the line division and are composed differently. The final clause adds a vocative, *dure* (literally, hard one) to conclude the poem with an oxymoron, juxtaposing the adjective describing the boy (*dure*) to that for the waters (*volubilis*, flowing; cf. voluble). Though opposed in meaning, these words both express the unattainability of the boy. His resistance to Horace's advances is compounded by the fluid intangibility of the dream in which he appears. The opposed tactile sensations with which the poem ends leaves us with a love object suspended between fantasy and reality.

All the Roman love poets write poetry to or about boys, and Horace's casual 'neither girl nor boy' is a common expression that is intended to cover the expected erotic field for a Greek or Roman male. It is, however, unusual for a Roman poet to give his male beloved a Roman name. The most appropriate homosexual love object for an elite Roman male was a slave boy. This is because sex was thought of as an asymmetrical relationship, and any male who performed a 'female' sexual role would be degrading himself. Sex between two male Roman citizens, then, would inevitably compromise one of them. But Ligurinus (Ligurian) is clearly a Roman name, and his activities on the Campus Martius, Rome's parade ground, mark him out as a Roman citizen rather than a slave. This makes him a problematic love object. Ligurinus is the only boy who is given a Roman name in the *Odes*. He is anomalous, like Cinara.

Ligurinus does not feature much in *Odes* 4, which turns out to be a book about poetry as much as love. But the very specific erotic pathos attached to the name prevents him from becoming simply a device by which Horace speaks about his poetic career. The figure of Ligurinus has struck many of Horace's readers, including Tom Stoppard, who refers to him prominently in his play *The Invention of Love*, about the great Latin scholar and poet A. E. Housman (1859–1936). In Stoppard's play, the recently dead Housman looks back on his life, and particularly his great, unrequited love for a contemporary at Oxford. The dreamlike pathos of Horace's poem is associated with Housman's regret for a love that remained unfulfilled. Through the figures of Cinara and Ligurinus, Horace the 'past-it' lover takes on a pathos that associates him with the late-romantic, end-of-the-century world of Dowson and the young Housman.

A dinner invitation

To end this chapter I will turn to a very different sort of relationship, but one that is central to Horace's œuvre. A major theme of Horace's poetry is the business of dealing with the great and powerful, and in this poem Horace invites one of the most powerful men in Rome to dinner:

> Vile potabis modicis Sabinum
> cantharis, Graeca quod ego ipse testa
> conditum levi, datus in theatro
>   cum tibi plausus,
>
> clare Maecenas eques, ut paterni
> fluminis ripae simul et iocosa
> redderet laudes tibi Vaticani
>   montis imago.
>
> Caecubum et prelo domitam Caleno
> tu bibes uvam: mea nec Falernae

temperant vites neque Formiani
   pocula colles.   (1. 20)

(You will down cheap Sabine from plain
goblets, a wine that I laid up and sealed myself
in a Greek jar, when you were acclaimed
   in the theatre,

Maecenas, distinguished knight, when the banks
of your ancestral river and the playful
echo of Mount Vaticanus rendered
   praise to you.

Caecuban and grapes that have been squeezed
in Cales you can drink at home. Neither Falernian
vines nor Formiae's hillsides take the edge
   from my cups.)

Many types of Latin poem are based on everyday utterances or communications: prayer, insult, letter, oath, etc. One of the poetic types that the Romans invented is the invitation poem, of which this is a prime example. We are immediately struck by the fact that this is not a very gracious invitation. It begins with the word *vile* (cheap) and ends with a negative. Hardly a tempting offer. But, surprisingly enough, this churlishness is typical of the Latin invitation poem. A famous version by Catullus (Poem 13) even tells the invitee that he will have to bring the wine and the dinner himself! Why such grudging hospitality? To answer this we must first take account of the fact that the invitation poem is in itself something of a paradox. It is really the poets who expect to be invited to the tables of the high and mighty, where they vouch for the culture and humanity of their host, and may be called upon to sing for their supper by reciting, or even improvising, a poem or two. The exchange of poetry for dinners is one way that poets represented the relation between poet and patron. But when they did so they were presenting a self-consciously cynical version of a much more complex reality. Roman society was permeated by informal personal relations between inferiors and superiors. These relations, nourished by the exchange of favours and marks of respect, pertained at every level of society, and ran the gamut from material dependence to deferential respect. Expressed in the baldest terms, the superior would be called the *patronus* (from *pater*, father) and the inferior the *cliens* (from *clinatus*, leaning on). Strictly speaking, *patronus* meant 'legal advocate', and advocacy was one of the commonest ways that a member of the Roman elite would gather clients. Barristers were not allowed to receive pay, and so a successful advocate such as Cicero accumulated favours owed to him by grateful clients, which could be called in when he was running for office or needed a loan. It is from this relation between advocate and the person he represented that English 'client' has come to mean (paying) customer rather than dependant, as in Latin. For the most part, the Roman poets avoided the word '*cliens*', which was demeaning, and instead '*amicus*' (friend) would be used for both parties. The fiction of equality was maintained in the face of what both parties knew was an unequal relationship.

Which brings us back to Horace. Maecenas, whom Horace here invites to dinner, was the second most important man in Augustan Rome. A supporter of Augustus from the beginning of his climb to power (when he was still known as Octavian), Maecenas became the intermediary between Augustus and the poets, and without him there might never have been that flowering of poetic genius that is the main legacy of Augustan Rome. Propertius, Horace, and Vergil all acknowledge his patronage, though just what that involved remains unclear. Horace speaks of gifts from Maecenas, but he is keen to emphasize that there has been no quid pro quo. Naturally, Maecenas and Augustus hoped that the poets would be moved to sing the achievements of the regime and to announce the coming of a Golden Age. The pressure to write something of appropriately grand scope on this theme can be felt in the 'refusal poems' (*recusationes*) that dot Augustan literature. Protesting that his talent is too slim for the mighty task of adequately hymning the Augustan age, the poet has it both ways. But finally Vergil would answer the call and write the definitive Roman epic to rival Homer. Opinions differ as to whether Augustus got more, or less, than he bargained for, as we will see in the next chapter.

Horace, too, wrote his political poems, addressing the renovation of Roman moral and religious traditions that Augustus vaunted as central to his Golden Age. But this is not one of them. What is on show here is an exemplary relationship between the great man of affairs and the humble poet, one that is intended to do credit to them both. As intermediary between Augustus and the poets, Maecenas allowed the relationship between poetry and power to be expressed as reciprocal and personal. Horace speaks to the great man as an equal, and in the process he flatters them both. But the first few words of this poem seem to register the underlying tensions that are being controlled in the way these words jostle each other for space. *Vile* (cheap) is an odd word with which to begin an invitation, and we know that we are reading an invitation from the second word *potabis* (you will drink). *Potabis* connotes boozing rather than sipping, so the very Horatian word that follows it, *modicis* (modest), has an oxymoronic effect. The boozing may be immoderate (as between friends) but the cups themselves will be plain—Maecenas is no snob. *Sabinum*, the final word of the last line, tells us that the wine comes from Horace's Sabine farm, which was a gift from Maecenas.

Like Cinara, the Sabine farm is a recurring character in Horace's poetry and, more often than not, this rural retreat serves to represent

Horace's independence from the worldly Rome and its power-brokers. Horace has not been bought, or so he claims, and in the rural farm he can escape from the pressures and demands of the big city. The oblique thank-you contained in the name of the wine with which Horace will entertain Maecenas also suggests that Maecenas comes to Horace's world on the poet's terms, but that, in turn, is just the way that Maecenas would want it to seem. What Maecenas has given Horace is a place from which the poet can recognize the great man's culture and humanity in an informal setting: together, they will swig away at cheap wine in ordinary vessels. *Cantharis*, at the beginning of the second line, is a Greek word for a large drinking vessel, and so clashes nicely with *Sabinum*, a word redolent of solid, rural Italian virtue. Horace bottled this Sabine wine, he tells us, in a Greek jar, to improve the flavour. But the Sabine wine in a Greek jar also makes us think of Horace's claim to have been the first to put Latin poetry into Greek lyric metres, of which this poem is itself a witness. Horace bottled the wine to mark the occasion when Maecenas was greeted on his appearance in the theatre by a standing ovation. He seems to be alluding to an occasion on which Maecenas made his first public appearance after recovering from a serious illness. It was customary for the crowd at a Roman theatre to make its feelings known by the reception it gave to important figures when they took their place in the theatre. The jar marks an occasion in Maecenas' life and in his public career. But Horace's poetry, the Roman wine in the Greek jar, will last longer than the ephemeral applause that erupted in the theatre. It is a more adequate way to preserve Maecenas' fame. Or perhaps we could put it another way: Horace's poetry allows that applause to be 'uncorked' again and again, as the central stanza of this poem will prove.

Two contrasting impressions linger in our minds at the end of the first stanza: the wine sealed up and stored away in jars and the applause that erupts in a theatre. But this first stanza, so self-contained and condensed, is in fact incomplete, for the next stanza opens with a vocative that identifies the addressee. The sense spills over into the second stanza, and from line to line within the stanza, just as the applause ricochets off the banks of the Tiber and the Vatican Mount. Maecenas' moment of glory in the theatre is ratified by the surrounding natural world. But that nature is itself marked by Maecenas. The Tiber is described as the river of his fathers because Maecenas was of Etruscan extraction and, according to another poem of Horace, descended from Etruscan kings. Sometimes known as the Etruscan river, the Tiber marked the eastern border of Etruria. In spite of his regal descent and eminent position, Maecenas modestly chose to remain a knight, the second social rank in Rome, under the senators. When Horace addresses him as *clare* (distinguished) he uses an honorific title that was associated with senators, so to call him a *clare... eques* is a typically Horatian oxymoron. It reveals Maecenas himself as the model for the tensions we have seen in the first stanza. When Maecenas took his place in the theatre, it would have been in the rows reserved for the knights, so the applause may have been partially in recognition of his self-restraint.

Montis imago (echo of the mountain), which makes up the shorter line of this stanza, provides a nice icon of the echo itself, for an echo truncates the sound it repeats. Though *imago* means 'echo' in this case, it is a word of broad meaning that covers all kinds of copy or imitation. To close the stanza with the phrase *montis imago* is to remind us that what we are reading is an imitation, to throw us back again to the relation between the poem and what it celebrates. Horace wants to refer us to a real event, a spontaneous outbreak of joy, doubled by the playful echo of a surrounding nature, and he wants his poem to capture something of the contingency and one-offness of the occasion. But if he captures it in his poem (just as he 'bottled' it in his wine), doesn't that betray the nature of the event? Perhaps it does, but an essential part of the event was its reverberation, its *imago*, and the poem is a continuation of that reverberation.

In the Roman invitation poem it is traditional to imply that the poor fare the poet has to offer is more than compensated for by other advantages of higher value: friendship, good conversation, poetry, congenial company. Horace's version of that compensation is the friendship and intimacy expressed by the fact that the wine he will serve is associated with an event in Maecenas' life. But in the final stanza Horace returns to the defiant pose of the first stanza. We could think of the poem's structure as bipartite, leaving out the middle stanza: 'at my place you will drink Sabine from simple vessels; at home you can drink fancy wines, but not here'. The third stanza seems to forget the second and simply returns to the poem's beginning. It can do that because, syntactically, the second stanza is a subordinate clause, a parenthesis. It is as though the window of a quiet sitting room had been suddenly opened, allowing the raucous city to intrude on the interior for a moment, only to be quickly shut so that the conversation can continue.

Horace ends his poem with a contrast between the wine that is available to 'you' and the wine that is available to 'me'. Symmetry is avoided by assigning different parts of speech and different cases to the constrasting words: **tu** *bibes* (you will drink [better wines]), **mea**...*pocula* ([no fancy admixture softens] my cups). But accompanying the obvious contrast between me and you is the more interesting antithesis of *domitam* (tamed) and *nec... temperant* (do not soften). At home Maecenas will drink a wine that has been crushed in the press, but at Horace's he will drink wines that have not been softened or 'restrained'. The implication is clear: Horace's turf is his own.

This ending may remind us of the restrained aggression behind the ending of *Odes* 3. 14, with its reference to the year of the battle of Philippi. We admire the deftness with which the lowly Horace negotiates his conflicting commitments; the glancing revelation of underlying tensions; the combining of agendas, which fall into different configurations at each reading. Horace is an elusive poet, revelling in the sheer finesse that allows him to 'get away with it'. It is ironic that the poetry of the son of a freed slave became a model for the conversational elegance of the English gentleman, and that Friedrich Nietzsche saw it as paradigmatic of 'noble' speech. Horace is, as the translator James Michie describes him, 'master of the graceful sidestep'. But his poetry is too variegated, its verbal texture too multifaceted and kaleidoscopic to be read simply as elegant speech displaying a deft command of manners. And it is the conflict between the elegant utterance and the play of light and energy between written words that accounts for the unique sensation of reading Horace.

There are many aspects of Horace that we have not explored in this chapter. The poets of archaic Greece, whose metres and manner Horace claimed to have imported to Rome, were intensely engaged in the politics of their time, and Horace does not neglect this side of the lyric genre. He was one of the two great poets of the Augustan age, and he addressed its momentous events and grandiose projects, especially in the sequence of six odes at the beginning of the third book known as the Roman Odes. In the Greek poet Pindar he found an examplar of the high lyric style suited to the celebrations of great achievements and of the mythical traditions of great cities, though he was careful to underline the danger of imitating Pindar. At the other end of the literary spectrum, Horace wrote *Satires* and *Epistles* (verse letters) in a deliberately casual, conversational style, which 'talks us into sense', as Alexander Pope put it (*An Essay on Criticism*, 654). In the *Epodes*, a collection inspired by the Greek genre of 'iambic' invective, or insult poetry, Horace allows himself a wide range of diction, and especially an obscenity that is totally absent from the *Odes*. Finally, his *Ars Poetica*, a didactic poem that laid out some of the most important principles of ancient poetics, was probably his most influential work. So this chapter has focused only on a portion of Horace's œuvre. By contrast, in the next chapter we will consider passages from all the works of Horace's great contemporary, Vergil. With Vergil we come to the first poet of antiquity whose œuvre is quite self-consciously composed as a whole.

4
....

VERGIL: THE UNCLASSICAL CLASSIC

Vergil's *Aeneid* became a classic almost immediately after it was written, and it has retained that status ever since. Part of the reason for this is the status of the Roman empire itself, both in terms of the influence it has exerted over European history and of the model it has provided, positive or negative, for every subsequent empire in the West. For the *Aeneid* is the epic of empire. It is also the epic of tradition, not just of *a* tradition but of tradition itself, in the original Latin sense of 'handing over', 'transmission'. On various levels the *Aeneid* is the story of a handing down, or over, from Greece to Rome, in which the torch both of empire and of culture passes from one civilization to another. Aeneas is a minor hero from Homer's *Iliad* who escapes from a Troy defeated by the Greeks and makes his way to Italy, under the guidance of the gods, to found a new race. Vergil self-consciously set out to write *the* Roman classic under a regime that was eager to define itself as the incarnation and culmination of Roman tradition, and he succeeded.

Canonical status of this magnitude is not always kind to an author. The *Aeneid* was a school text within generations of Vergil's death, and for hundreds of years schoolchildren all over the world struggled to construe passages from Vergil and learn them by heart. Henry Miller speaks for many:

I am one individual who is going to be honest about Vergil and his fucking *rari nantes in gurgite vasto*. I say without blushing or stammering, without the least confusion, regret or remorse, that recess in the toilet was worth a thousand Vergils, alway was and always will be.[1]

Miller alludes to Vergil's line *apparent rari nantes in gurgite vasto* (scattered men appear, swimming in the vast swell, *Aeneid*; 1. 118), which, no doubt, he had been cajoled to admire. It is a description of shipwreck from the beginning of the first book of the *Aeneid*; in it, I suspect, Miller saw depicted his floundering attempts to orientate himself in the sea of Vergilian grandiloquence while Vergil looked on, fat and famous. Other detractors of Vergil have emphasized his secondary, derivative quality, especially in relation to Homer, making a vice of the fact that the *Aeneid* is the epic of tradition; others still have castigated Vergil as a propagandist for Augustus and a notable example of the collusion between art and power. It comes as a surprise to those who think of Vergil as 'the classic of all Europe' (T. S. Eliot's description)[2] that he was described by one ancient critic as 'the inventor of a new form of bad taste' (Donatus, *Vita Vergili* 44). Despite the sonorous lines and rolling paragraphs, Vergil's style and sensibility can often seem anything but classic.

The first step: pastoral

The shape of Vergil's career is straightforward, and it has come to define the trajectory we expect of the classic author. His three extant works, the *Eclogues*, the *Georgics* and the *Aeneid*, succeed one another as steps up the ladder of genres, from pastoral to didactic and on to epic. Each

---

[1] Henry Miller, *Black Spring* (Paris, 1936), 56–7.
[2] T. S. Eliot, *On Poetry and Poets* (London, 1957), 70.

work is longer than the last and tackles a higher theme. But the three works also allude to each other, so as to suggest that the whole œuvre is, in some says, a single work. All three, also, are written in the same metre, the hexameter. This is a Roman œuvre not only in its oblique reflections on the political revolution brought about by the first emperor, Augustus, but also because each work is modelled on the example of a Greek predecessor, leading to the ultimate challenge— to produce a Latin classic to rival the epics of Homer. The *Aeneid* manages to comprise in its twelve books a story that echoes both the *Iliad* (war) and the *Odyssey* (a journey), alluding to Homer continuously, in detail and in broader narrative pattern. Vergil's didactic poem about agriculture (*Georgics*) looks back towards the *Works and Days* of the archaic Greek poet Hesiod. His first work, the *Eclogues*, is based on the *Idylls* of the Alexandrian Greek poet Theocritus (third century BC), sophisticated poems written by a city-dweller about rustic life. In the *Eclogues* Vergil narrows the focus of Theocritus' *Idylls* to the lives of herdsmen (*pastores*) as they converse and sing about their life and loves in an idealized landscape, and in the process he invents the pastoral genre. After Vergil, other poets will find it appropriate to launch their poetic careers with a collection of pastoral poetry.

Pastoral poetry can seem a very artificial genre, and indeed Vergil's *Eclogues* have a lot to answer for. The Clorises, Amaryllises, and Corydons that pepper Renaissance poetry and madrigals; the porcelain shepherds and shepherdesses arrayed in museum cabinets that we pass on the way to the 'real' art; the 'swains' of arch conversation: all derive ultimately from the *Eclogues*. But Vergil's *Eclogues* are not as unreal as they might seem, for though they conjure up an idyllic world of love and song, the realities of the turbulent period in which they were written make themselves felt in the lives of these shepherds. Like the life of love in the poetry of the Augustan elegists, the 'irrelevant' pastoral world of the *Eclogues* provides a safe place from which to take a perspective on contemporary politics, and on the grand projects of Roman imperialism and of the Augustan regime. On the one hand, then, the *Eclogues* exercise the privilege of art not to notice or be concerned with the greater world around it, and they make the case for a protected 'elsewhere'. But, on the other hand, they acknowledge that this very possibility depends on the indulgence of the powers that govern the greater world. As with love elegy, the reader wavers between a charmed commitment to the other world (the life of love, the life of shepherds) and doubts about its viability. In the case of the love poets, it is the ambiguity of their persona that holds the balance: we can't quite take the leap into the lover's obsessive world because we suspect that he may be just a little ridiculous. With the *Eclogues*, it is the artificiality of this world that makes us uneasy. Where would this place exist, where shepherds sing of their loves in such exquisite poetry against an idyllic scenery compounded of Greece and Italy?

But harsh realities hover on the horizon of this never-never land. The first *Eclogue* is a dialogue between two shepherds, one of whom has lost his farm and must emigrate. Vergil himself, so the ancient biographies tells us, lost his farm in the confiscations that followed the civil war, as the victors, Antony and Octavian (soon to become Augustus), found land for their demobilized veterans. In the first *Eclogue*, Tityrus has been spared the confiscations, thanks to the help of a mysterious young man (Octavian?) whom he approached on a visit to the big city. But the opening words go to Meliboeus, lamenting his tragedy and contrasting his lot with that of Tityrus, who is a little insensitive to the suffering of his friend. The shepherds speak in a manner that is both sophisticated and rustic, and they deliver some of the most mellifluous Latin verse that has ever been written. The first *Eclogue* ends with an offer of hospitality from Tityrus:

> hic tamen hanc mecum poteras requiescere noctem
> fronde super viridi: sunt nobis mitia poma,
> castaneae molles et pressi copia lactis,
> et iam summa procul villarum culmina fumant
> maioresque cadunt altis de montibus umbrae. (*Eclogues* 1. 79–83)

> (But you could rest here with me for the night
> on green rushes; I have ripe apples,
> soft chestnuts and plenty of cheese,
> and already far off the roofs of the villas give off smoke
> and lengthened shadows fall from the high mountains.)

Smoke on the horizon and spreading shadows hint at the encroaching of civil war and confiscations of land on this literary haven, and the balance between escapist fantasy and the oblique representation of current realities has been a defining feature of the pastoral tradition ever since. In his final speech, Meliboeus rather hyperbolically imagines his life after dispossession as exile to some very remote and forbidding places: Africa, Scythia, and even Britain, a whole world away. Will he ever see his native land again, or the smoking chimney of his turf hut and his fields? All this will go to a brutish soldier:

> impius haec tam culta novalia miles habebit,
> barbarus has segetes? (1. 70–71)

> (Shall a wicked soldier have these fallow lands so beautifully tilled,
> a barbarian these crops?)

This line and a half may be a bitter *cri de cœur*, but it is also one of the most melodious and fluid passages of Latin poetry in the whole canon (pronounce: impius hike tam culta nowahlia meelehs habaybit). It is, first of all, highly dactylic: only one spondee (dum dum: *haec tam*) breaks the flow of dactyls (dum da da), the basic metrical feet of the hexameter. But another metrical effect is even more striking. Though Latin metres depend on the distinction between long and short syllables, they also recognize the existence of stress accent, which was a feature of spoken Latin. There are then two kinds of emphasis that a syllable might have: the emphasis that falls on the beginning of each metrical foot and the emphasis caused by word stress. Hexameter Latin poetry tends to create conflict between these two kinds of emphasis in the first part of the line and coincidence in the last two feet, which run – ◡ ◡/– – ('munching a beanstalk' in the schoolchild mnemonic for the rhythm of the hexameter: 'Down in a deep dark hole sat an old pig munching a beanstalk'). In the first line quoted, the only place where there is conflict is on the word *tam*, which as a monosyllable has a stress accent, but is positioned in the weak second half of its foot. In the sequence *culta novalia miles habebit* not only do metrical and stress emphasis (ictus and accent, as they are known) coincide, but they coincide, in all but the final foot, on the consonant l, which the Romans recognized as the most euphonious of the consonants. The musical effect is enhanced by the variation of vowels preceding the l (-ul, -al, -il). When the soldier (*miles*) comes in to supply the noun for the adjective *impius* he completes a melody that seems to betray the meaning of the words. The next half line, which completes the sentence, is extremely condensed: it consists solely of an adjective in the nominative and a noun (with demonstrative pronoun) in the accusative, a subject and an object. From the previous line we supply the noun that goes with *barbarus* (a barbarian **soldier**) and the verb that governs *has segetes* (**will have** these crops). This line and a half presents a typically Vergilian theme and variation, where the expectation of symmetry allows Vergil to leave out the important words from the variation. The first two words of the half line echo the first two words of the previous line: an adjective in the nominative and a demonstrative pronoun in the accusative. It is an answering phrase, a dying cadence that completes a glorious bel canto melody, but one that pivots on the words *impius* and *barbarus*, which one would expect to be spat out rather than sung. There is an alarming disjunction between the sound of these words and their meaning. We read them again and try to inject desperation into the repeated sounds falling on a heavy emphasis in *culta novalia miles*, but the desperation competes with the melodious flow of the line. Perhaps we are to think that the 'fallow land so beautifully tilled' will civilize the brutal soldier who will take possession of them. More likely we are brought up against the propensity of the pastoral genre (as Vergil is shaping it) to *contain* suffering, and perhaps even to betray it. The opening lines of the *Eclogue* announce this propensity, as Meliboeus finds beautiful and melodious symmetries in which to cast the poignant contrast between his own situation and that of Tityrus:

> Tityre, tu patulae recubans sub tegmine fagi
> silvestrem tenui Musam meditaris avena;
> nos patriae finis et dulcia linquimus arva.
> nos patriam fugimus; tu, Tityre, lentus in umbra
> formosam resonare doces Amaryllida silvas.   (1. 1–5)

> (Tityrus, you reclining under the shade of a spreading beech,
> give thought to the woodland Muse on your slender pipe.
> I am leaving the boundaries of my country and the sweet fields.
> I am fleeing my country; you, Tityrus, at ease in the shade,
> teach the woods to resound with the name of Amaryllis.)

Vergil introduces us to the pastoral life represented by Tityrus, reclining in the shade and singing of his love, through the perspective of Meliboeus, who must relinquish it. The pastoral fantasy of shepherds with time on their hands will come in later ages to represent the leisured life of the poet or the scholar, but the fragility of this protected idyll in a troubled world is acknowledged by Vergil from the start. Tityrus' languid pose is the object of a resentful gaze. But possibly we should think of Meliboeus, not Tityrus, as the representative pastoral figure, for the pastoral world is always on the point of dissolving; it is visited rather than inhabited.

Dialogue, duet, and echo are the characteristic forms of pastoral, and the contrasted fates of Tityrus and Meliboeus together make a typically pastoral music in these opening lines. Meliboeus' potentially bitter complaint comes out in a neat chiasmus: 'Tityrus, you ... we ... we ... you, Tityrus'. The same contrast is made twice, with elegant variation: 'you are reclining in the shade and singing; I am leaving'. In the lines describing Meliboeus' suffering we again have theme and variation, long line and short. Again, we have the mellifluous ls and the coincidence of ictus and accent (*dulcia linquimus arva*). The verb that conveys Meliboeus' misfortune and governs the objects *patriae finis* (boundaries of the homeland) and *dulcia arva* (sweet fields) is positioned between the noun and adjective. As a unit, *dulcia linquimus arva* (we leave the sweet fields) is smoothly euphonious, and the poignant verb is absorbed into the beauty of the 'sweet fields'. We glide over the meaning of the phrase in order to enjoy the overall beauty of sound. The symmetry of Meliboeus' opening utterance is pleasantly 'distressed' by the fact that, after the two lines introducing Tityrus, each player is given a line and a half, instead of two. Meliboeus cuts into his own situation mid-verse to complete the line with a brief picture of Tityrus, lounging in the shade, a painful contrast to the haste of *nos patriam fugimus* (I am fleeing my country). Tityrus is *lentus*, a word that means 'slow', 'pliant', or, as here, 'secure', 'unconcerned', verging on '(emotionally) cold'. Unconcern and ease have been uncomfortably combined.

The descriptive emphasis of the first *Eclogue*'s opening lines is on Tityrus' pastoral life, with its key ingredients of shade and song, the latter featured prominently in the second and fifth lines. Pastoral song is integrated into its environment. Tityrus practises a 'woody Muse' on an 'oat' and teaches the woods to resound with Amaryllis' name. The very sound of the line makes her name, *Amaryllida* (⌣ ⌣ – ⌣ ⌣: da da dum da da), into an echo, picking up the metrical shape of *resonare* (⌣ ⌣ – ⌣) but adding another short syllable to sweep the line onward. In a different kind of echo effect, Vergil contrives to put the two accusatives, *Amaryllida* and *silvas*, next to each other. These accusatives are objects of different verbs, *resonare* (to echo Amaryllis) and *doces* (you teach the woods). However Meliboeus may resent the contrast between the fates of the two shepherds, his suffering is gathered into the resonance of Tityrus' woodland song, whose music Meliboeus wants to prolong, even as he relinquishes it.

In Vergil's *Eclogues* we are constantly made aware of the artistic frame: the mellifluous writing; the convention that allows rustic shepherds to speak in a sophisticated, even learned, style; the unreal landscape; the intimations of contemporary politics in this never-never land: all these draw our attention to the licence of poetry to create its own world. It is with good reason that these poems have been said to have art as their subject. But they raise questions. What is the balance between the crucial *difference* of art, the fact that it is *not* reality, and its need to take on real, potentially intractable content if it is not to be merely escapist? The

Eclogues measure the pressure of the true on the beautiful. Protectedness, peace, pleasure, fantasy, utopianism, reconciliation: all find their place in what art means for us, but they can tip over into irrelevant escapism if they do not take on any grit. To be *lentus in umbra* (relaxed in the shade) is an ambivalent condition.

The *Eclogues* mostly take the form of dialogue: shepherds meet and talk, and sometimes their talk gives way to competitive or cooperative song, sometimes to insults. In this opening *Eclogue* Tityrus explains to Meliboeus how he has come to retain his farm, and this prompts a lengthier description by Meliboeus of the very different futures that await the two of them. Finally, Tityrus suggests that Meliboeus spend the night with him. The poem ends with the word *umbra*, so prominent in Meliboeus' opening lines, in which he describes Tityrus' enviable ease beneath the shade (*umbra*, cf. umbrella) of the beech tree. But now the same word in the plural (*umbrae*) means not shade, but 'shadows' (*umbrae* can also mean 'ghosts', or 'shades' in the older English sense). Tityrus speaks:

> et iam summa procul villarum culmina fumant
> maioresque cadunt altis de montibus umbrae. (1. 83–4)

> (And already in the distance the tops of the villas' roofs are smoking, and bigger shadows fall from the high mountains.)

In these lines, Vergil juxtaposes the smoke that rises from the tips of the villas with the shadows that fall from the high mountains. The smoke of cosy sociability (Tityrus invites Meliboeus to spend the night with him) is contrasted with ominous shadows, in which we can read the encroaching affairs of great men, played out at the expense of those at the foothills. Hyperbaton (the separation of the noun–adjective pair *maiores…umbrae*) gives emphasis to the final word, whose resonances are prolonged in the silence that ensues on the poem's ending. The final word of this first *Eclogue* looks forward to the end of the final *Eclogue*, which reads:

> surgamus: solet esse gravis cantantibus umbra,
> iuniperi gravis umbra; nocent et frugibus umbrae.
> ite domum saturae, venit Hesperus, ite capellae. (10. 75–7)

> (Let us rise: shade can be unpleasant for singers.
> The shade of the juniper is unpleasant; shadows harm the crops also.
> Go home now you're full, evening has come, go home, my goats.)

Umbra is repeated twice, but this emblem of pastoral comfort, and of its protected environment, has now become equivocal. The statement that 'shade tends to be unpleasant to singers' (*solet esse gravis cantantibus umbra*) reminds us that the pastoral's shaded enclosure is not without problems as an image of the seclusion within which poetry is written. We might think of the anxieties of modern poets and writers who work in the groves of academe and worry that they are losing their edge. It's an appropriate connection, for the academic world has been often been examined through the lens of pastoral. We want to ask what exactly Vergil means by *umbra* (patronage? leisure?), but the pastoral terms of these poems cannot always be translated unequivocally into a real-world equivalent, and this is another way in which the *Eclogues* reflect on art. We expect literature to be about something more than its apparent subject, to be exemplary of something broader, and yet we also want it to create an engrossing and coherent other world. 'Let us rise and go home with the goats who have grazed their fill' makes a final statement that seems to enclose the collection in its pastoral world, but the association of singing shepherds with sophisticated poets throughout the *Eclogues* encourages us to put more weight on *surgamus*: 'let us rise' to a more ambitious genre, perhaps. The young Milton ends his pastoral poem *Lycidas* with a more emphatic intimation of greater things:

> And now the sun had stretched all the hills,
> And now was dropped into the Western Bay;
> At last he rose, and twitched his mantle blue:
> Tomorrow to fresh wood's and pastures new.   (*Lycidas* 192–3)

Nature, toil, and culture: the *Georgics*

It is a very different natural world that confronts us in Vergil's next work, a didactic poem on farming known as the *Georgics*. Vergil begins his account of the farmers' work, appropriately, with spring:

> vere novo, gelidus canis cum montibus umor
> liquitur et Zephyro putris se glaeba resolvit,
> depresso incipiat iam tum mihi taurus aratro
> ingemere et sulco attritus splendescere vomer.   (*Georgics* 1. 43–6)

> (In early spring, when the cold water on the white mountains
> melts, and the crumbling sod breaks up under the west wind,
> I would have the bull begin to groan as the plough is dug in,
> and the ploughshare, rubbed by the furrow, begins to shine.)

Nature is no longer the responsive, echoing bower which the shepherd fills with the sound of his mistress's name. The suspended turning point of day, in which Tityrus reaches out to Meliboeus, is replaced here by the moment of seasonal change, which must be grasped by the farmer who would subdue the earth and force it to serve his purposes. There is a stark contrast between the release of nature from the grip of winter and the beginning of work for the bull, yoked to the plough. But this contrast implies that there is a connection between the loosening of the sod, crumbled by the westerly wind (*Zephyro*) and the groaning of the bull when the plough is plunged (*depresso...aratro*). The phrase *depresso aratro*, like *Zephyro*, displays the terminal -o of the ablative case, making the phrase 'when the plough is dug in' an ablative absolute. The ablative absolute is a syntactic construction consisting of noun and participle (the plough having been plunged) which conveys the circumstances attending the action of the main verb. It is as though ploughing were a seasonal circumstance, like the blowing of the Zephyr, to which other parts of nature respond. But, of course, it isn't. In these lines, human culture grafts itself onto natural processes to produce a strange hybrid, in which the instruments of agriculture (plough and ploughshare) are assimilated to the mountain rivers, the crumbling sod, the bull, and the furrow. The aggressive incursion of humanity into natural processes is marked by the emphatic downbeat of **de**presso: in the midst of the loosenings of spring something bears down, hard: the pressure of human work and need. Echoing this word, in the equivalent position of the next line, comes *ingemere* (to groan aloud). The emphasis falls on the two prefixes, *de-* (down) and *in-* (an intensive), the bite of the plough and the effort forced from the bull. There is very little sign of humanity in this scene. The workman who bears down on (*depresso*) the plough has been elided by the impersonal syntactic construction, and the only human agent appears to be the didactic author himself, introduced in the dative in the third line 'let the bull begin to groan *for me*' (i.e. 'I would have the bull groan'). The lack of a human perspective allows ploughing to take on an alien aspect, in which the sinking of the plough acts not on the earth but the bull, while the furrow works on the ploughshare rather than vice versa. As the bull groans, the ploughshare, polished by the furrow it cuts, gleams in the spring light. Is the purpose of all this effort to produce a shining ploughshare? There is an ecological tone to these connectivities and reversed perspectives: energy is converted as the loosenings of spring summon the work of the plough, which in turn produces the brilliance of the gleaming ploughshare. Are humanity and its activities part of nature or an alien excrescence? That depends on whether we read Vergil's assimilations of the human to the natural as beautiful, grotesque, or ironic.

By ending the passage with the detail of the polished ploughshare, Vergil suggests that there is something beautiful about labour itself. Gerard Manley Hopkins must have remembered this passage when he wrote (in *The Windhover*) 'Sheer plod makes plough down sillion shine'. Vergil's 'poem of the earth' wavers between an optimistic confidence in the effectiveness of hard work and a despairing sense of futility in the face of the random violence and sheer cussedness of nature. Later in this first book, after describing, in language studded with military terms, the battle of the farmer with the earth (for its own good, of course), Vergil adds a brief coda on the miscellaneous natural pests that obstruct the labours of man and bull: the goose, the crane, the endive, and the shade itself. This leads straight into the statement that Jupiter himself did not want agriculture to be easy, and he deliberately 'sharpened human minds with care' so that his kingdom would not grow sluggish and slothful. Before Jupiter there was no tilling: life was easy until he hid the means of sustenance from mortals. But this had the providential effect of whetting human ingenuity, and necessity spurred the development of culture:

> tum variae venere artes, labor omnia vicit
> improbus et duris urgens in rebus egestas.   (1. 145–6)

> (Then the different arts arrived, toil conquered/invaded everything relentlessly, and need bore down in harsh conditions.)

The phrase *labor* (toil) *omnia* (all things) *vicit* (conquered) is a famous Vergilian ambiguity. Did toil overcome everything, or did it invade everything? And in which of its possible senses should we take *labor*: the sense that is more like English 'toil/labour' or another more like English 'difficulty' (a sense still active in our use of 'labour' to refer to the travails of childbirth)? Vergil is either saying that everything became difficult for us or that humanity prevailed through hard work. If we take the phrase with the rest of its line we will be inclined to an optimistic reading: the arts came and human labour won out. But the enjambement casts the word '*labor*' in a new light by attaching to it the emphatic adjective *improbus*, which makes up the first foot (a dactyl) of the next line. *Improbus* has two components, the negative prefix *im-* (cf. immobile, impotent, etc.) and the adjective *probus* (upright, righteous, cf. probity). *Improbus* is the same word that is applied to the goose in the list of pests, where it means something like 'shameless'. That settles it in favour of the negative reading, then? Not necessarily. *Improbus* could also carry the sense 'relentless'. Toil might be 'shameless' in the sense that it is dogged, ruthless, and blinkered. Those who argue that the meaning 'toil overcame all (obstacles)' is impossible because *improbus* never carries a positive meaning are thinking too crudely. Toil triumphs because its nature is to persist heedlessly; it triumphs, and it's good for us, but it isn't necessarily attractive. The arts and crafts (*artes*) are multifarious (*variae*), but *labor* is always the same damn thing. We might think of it as humanity's answer to the brute instinct of the goose, which does what comes naturally, but is shameless (from our point of view). The rest of the line that begins with the enjambed *improbus* seems to complete a typical Vergilian dicolon: two phrases joined by 'and' making a theme and variation. The whole dicolon is enclosed by the two nouns *labor* and *egestas* (need), an effect enabled by the chiasmus (*abba*) in which the sequence noun (*labor*) adjective (*improbus)* is reversed in the phrase *urgens...egestas*. But is *egestas* (need) equivalent to *labor improbus*? If so, the two phrases would produce a common Latin rhetorical structure in which the same thing is said twice in different ways. Alternatively, the two elements could be related causally, with *egestas* the providential incentive for *labor* (roughly, 'necessity is the mother of invention'). Compounding our problem, but reinforcing the same alternatives, is the question of whether *urgens* mean 'bearing down upon' or 'spurring on'.

These speculations constitute a complex reflection on the role of scarcity and toil in human life, and I think Vergil intended us to be caught up in them. Clearly the enjambement of *improbus* makes us think again about how we are to take the words *labor omnia vicit*, and such reassessments are a common effect of enjambement in Latin poetry. Equally, the dicolon, on one level simply a rhetorical device to produce abundance of expression, offers a range of possible functions for the word 'and'.

'The classic of all Europe': the *Aeneid*

The hard slog of farming is good preparation for the harder slog of empire-building in the *Aeneid*, a task that makes a deeper psychological demand on its agents. Having described the archetypally Roman activity of farming, one closely connected in the Roman mind with war, Vergil moves up the generic ladder once more to the highest of genres, epic, for his final work. The prologue to the *Aeneid* begins with the confident words *Arma virumque cano* (I sing of arms and the man). Ancient poems were often known by their opening words, and these words, which found their way into many an ancient graffito, signified

Vergil as surely as Da Da Da Dum means Beethoven. But the prologue of the *Aeneid* builds to a statement that says it all:

tantae molis erat Romanam condere gentem.   (*Aeneid* 1. 33)

(It was such an effort to found the Roman race.)

It is the word '*molis*' (effort) that carries the weight of this line. As so often, the English derivate has changed the quantity of the vowel. Our 'molest' has a short o, and it is hard for us to feel the sheer tonnage of the Latin word *moles* (two syllables), which carries also the meanings 'vast undertaking', 'boulder', and 'massive structure'. So *molis* describes the massiness of what will be founded—the city of Rome and the vast reach of the Roman empire—as well as the effort required to found them. The trisyllabic *Romanam* (Roman (race)), made up of three long syllables, seems to extend the long o of *molis* and to be heaved into the middle of the line like a capstone. But *molis* also alludes to a commonplace of pessimistic Roman thinking about the power of the empire at its height: Rome has reached such a pitch of power that it threatens to collapse under its own weight. The line expresses awe at the solidity of the Roman achievement, certainly, but at the same time it seems to ask whether the colossal effort that the epic will describe has been repaid, and on its periphery hovers a trepidation about the stability of this groaning edifice (*moles*), which may revert to the dead weight of a heap (*moles*).

In the *Georgics*, Vergil looked forward to the epic he would write, as though he were planning the ascent of his tripartite career. The poem to come is there described as a temple, and at its centre will stand Augustus and his conquests. But the epic that he did write tells a story that never gets as far as Augustus. In fact, it doesn't even reach the foundation of Rome. Instead, it tells how a minor Trojan hero from

Homer's *Iliad* escaped from the destruction of Troy and made his way to Italy, following a succession of prophecies and revelations that he was to found a glorious empire. After a diversion by way of the newly founded Carthage, where he falls in love with queen Dido, and then abandons her at the behest of the gods, he visits his deceased father in the underworld, where he is given a bracing vision of Rome's future and its calling. Finally, in spite of the implacable enmity of the goddess Juno, he arrives at his destination, Italy. There, after a promisingly peaceable start, he is drawn into a war with the Italians, and kills their champion, Turnus, in single combat. In the last lines of the *Aeneid*, the defeated Turnus asks for mercy. Aeneas hesitates, and then, overcome by fury and lust for revenge (for Turnus has killed his charge, the young warrior Pallas), Aeneas sinks his sword into Turnus' chest:

> hoc dicens ferrum adverso sub pectore condit
> fervidus; ast illi solvuntur frigore membra
> vitaque cum gemitu fugit indignata sub umbras.   (12. 950–2)

> (Saying this he sinks his sword into the chest of his adversary
> in a rage; but Turnus' limbs are loosened in chill death
> and his life flees down to the shades, protesting.)

It is no coincidence that the word used when Aeneas sinks his sword into Turnus is the same as the word for founding the Roman race (*condere*) in the line I quoted earlier. This final act of founding, though, is not so much a burdensome effort (*moles*) as a heady release of the emotion that Aeneas has been called on to repress throughout the *Aeneid*. To many readers, he has seemed a pallid hero. Doggedly devoted to a duty that has been imposed on him, rather than chosen, he has had to repress his emotions throughout. Here, at last, he is *fervidus* (blazing). The word stands in emphatic enjambement, drawing energy from the sound of words in the previous line: *ferrum* (steel) and *adverso* (facing him). Some readers may feel relieved that Aeneas has claimed from Turnus the heat that he sadly lacked as a lover of Dido; now it is Turnus who is cold (*solvuntur frigore membra*).

But this is not how most modern readings of the *Aeneid* see the final scene. In the underworld, Aeneas' father, Anchises, had told him that the Romans, as rulers of the world, were to 'spare defeated peoples and defeat the proud': *parcere subiectis et debellare superbos* ('proud' not 'superb'). Has the whole laborious edifice collapsed in the face of human passion? Or has Vergil acknowledged the ruthless energy that will drive the Romans forward on their world-historical way? The last word of the epic has resonances too, for *umbra* is the same word that brings both the first and the last of the *Eclogues* to a close. Vergil's poetic career comes full circle on this equivocal word. The stakes are higher now than at the end of the first *Eclogue*; as Turnus' life flees 'down to the shades' (*sub umbras*) the word *umbra* takes on a meaning that it often has in the plural, namely 'ghosts'. The line *vitaque cum gemitu fugit indignata sub umbras* is swift and almost entirely dactylic. One word stands aloof from the dactylic (dum da da) pattern of this line, and that is *indignata* (dum dum dum da), a long word that blocks the swift flow of the line and seems to encapsulate the resistance of the losers, who won't go gently into the new world order. It resonates in the air after the *Aeneid* has ended. Were Hollywood to film the *Aeneid*, this word would point the way forward to a sequel (*Turnus Returns?*), and in some ways Milton's *Paradise Lost*, which begins with the defeated angels in hell plotting their revenge, takes up the hint. As it is, there would be no sequel to the *Aeneid*, and this remains one of the most abrupt and puzzling last lines in literature. Vergil was reputed to have been a slow worker and a perfectionist. According to the ancient lives of Vergil, he was intending to spend three more years perfecting the *Aeneid* and then to devote himself to philosophy, but he died of disease after a trip to Athens. He regarded the *Aeneid* as unfinished and asked his executors to burn it, which fortunately they refused to do. Some have seen the sudden, violent, and puzzling ending of the *Aeneid* as a mark of incompletion. One of these was the Renaissance poet Maffeo Vegio, who wrote, in Latin, a thirteenth book of the *Aeneid*, beginning where Vergil left off. Vegio neatly tied up Vergil's 'loose ends' and concluded his expanded *Aeneid* with the appropriate ceremonies of funeral and wedding. Whether or not this was a good idea, it reminds us how unorthodox Vergil's ending is.

The killing of Turnus is not the last event that the *Aeneid* represents, and Vergil is as good as his word in putting Augustus at the centre of his epic, though he is no part of its narrative. The *Aeneid* achieves much of its grandeur by looking forward, in prophecies, similes, and descriptions of works of art, to what, for the original Roman reader as for us, has already happened. The grandeur of Rome becomes even grander when it is seen from a distance, fated to come about. But the human actors of the story do not share the perspective of an audience that knows what is to happen. This applies most particularly to Aeneas himself, who follows a series of divine directives telling him that it is his duty, and destiny, to survive the fall of Troy (rather than to die nobly) and to found a new and glorious race. Gradually he discovers that it is not a second Troy that he is called upon to found, but that he and his band of Trojans are to recognize a common ancestor with the Italians and merge their identity in a new race. The way forward will be the way back, or vice versa, a principle that was crucial to Augustan propaganda. Augustus' revolution, his virtual reinstatement of monarchy after five hundred proud years of the Roman Republic, was cast by him as a rebirth of tradition. Almost the whole of Roman history up to this point finds its way, by hook or by crook, into Vergil's epic. In the last lines of the *Aeneid,* one brief moment of irresistible passion and violence quivers in the foreground, while through it we see the history of Rome's future as it has gradually accumulated over the epic's twelve books.

Like the *Odyssey,* the *Aeneid* starts *in medias res* and later recaps the story so far in a narration delivered by the wandering hero to his host. In Homer's *Odyssey,* it is the sybaritic Phaeacians who offer Odysseus hospitality at a crisis in his journey, and listen to his story. In the case of Aeneas, it is Dido who hosts him in her newly founded Carthage. The episode foreshadows the wars with Carthage, which will be Rome's decisive entrance onto the scene as a Mediterranean super-power. But Vergil casts the first contact between the two nations as a love story. Aeneas and Dido, both leaders of a people in exile, will recognize each other as kindred souls, and fall in love (with a little help from the gods). But Aeneas will be ordered by Jupiter to move on, and his desertion will precipitate Dido's suicide and inspire the curse she will deliver on her funeral pyre, invoking an avenger. Several hundred years later, Hannibal will answer her call.

The narrative of the *Aeneid* begins with a storm, with which the goddess Juno, antagonist of Rome and patron of Carthage, drives the Trojans off their course just as they are about to reach Italy. They wash up at Carthage, and there Aeneas recounts to Dido the story of the fall of Troy and his subsequent travels, together with the gradual revelation of his duty to find Italy and make a dynastic marriage with the Italian princess Lavinia. This will be the origin of the Roman race.

I am going to take two very different passages from the first book; together they provide a contrast that goes to the heart of the experience of reading the *Aeneid.* I begin with Jupiter's announcement of Rome's destiny, which comes towards the beginning of the first book, in a reassuring speech to Venus, mother of Aeneas. The first climax of Jupiter's speech rings with the word *Romanos*:

> Romulus excipiet gentem et Mavortia condet
> moenia Romanosque suo de nomine dicet.   (1. 276–7)

> (Romulus will continue the race and found the martial
> walls and will name the Romans after himself.)

The dactyl *Romulus* (dum da da) becomes the much more weighty molossus (three longs) *Romanos* (dum dum dum) after Romulus has founded the walls of Mars. Perhaps the most impressive feature of these two lines is the confidence with which they sweep away the existence of Romulus' brother, Remus, and the fratricide that accompanied the founding of those walls. This is a ruthlessly positive version of the founding of Rome, convenient for a regime that had installed itself after winning a bloody civil war. Jupiter then delivers the most resounding lines in the whole of the *Aeneid*.

> his ego nec metas rerum nec tempora pono:
> imperium sine fine dedi. quin aspera Juno
> quae mare nunc terrasque metu caelumque fatigat
> consilia in melius referet, mecumque fovebit
> Romanos, rerum dominos gentemque togatam.   (1. 278–82)

> (For them I set no turning posts nor term to their power.
> I have given them empire without end. Even harsh Juno,
> who now troubles the sea, the land, and the heavens with fear,
> will change her plans for the better, and with me she will favour
> the Romans, masters of the world, the race that wears the toga.)

The passage begins with a typical Vergilian theme and variation: first the negative (I have set no limits) and then the positive (I have given…).

Metae, in the first line, are the turning posts in a chariot race. So Jupiter is not necessarily speaking about limits, but rather change: Rome will not be subject to the wheel of fortune. In the next line, endlessness is made audible in the pairing of *sine fine* (without boundary/end), where the same sound is repeated, but the i changes from short in *sine* (like *cine*ma) to long in *fine* (pronounce feeneh). *Imperium*, the capacity to command (*imperare*), was the supreme administrative power, vested originally in the kings, but then, under the Republic, in the consuls and certain other magistrates. But consuls and magistrates held an *imperium* that was limited both by time (office could only be held for a year) and by the checks and balances ensured by collegiality (there were two consuls) and powers of veto. *Imperium sine fine*, then, confers on the Roman people what no Roman individual could claim, though by the time Vergil was writing these words Augustus had done so.

There would seem to be nowhere further to go from *imperium sine fine*. But there is more. The word '*quin*', which continues this line and opens a new sentence, means something like 'indeed' or 'what's more'. The harsh resistance of Juno, itself imperial in scope (covering land, sea, and heaven), is introduced only to be swept away as Juno is joined with Jupiter in the project of nurturing the Roman people. *Romanos* returns, this time in the emphatic first position and supported by an internal rhyme with *dominos* (lords). Another dicolon characterizes the Romans as both 'lords (*dominos*) of the world (*rerum*)' and 'the togaed people'. The second phrase is no quaint reference to Roman fashion, but rather one half of a polarity, for the toga was the non-military dress of the Romans. They are to be both conquerors of the world and men of peace. The extraordinary resonance of this line is imparted by a rhythm that Vergil particularly liked: the hexameter has been divided into three parts, each longer than the last (*Romanos—rerum dominos—gentemque togatam*). Vergil extends the molossus (dum dum dum) of *Romanos*, first by inserting two shorts (dum dum da da dum: *rerum dominos*), and then by adding another short to the end of that (dum dum da da dum da: *gentemque togatam*). The line stands on its own, as though it were made to be quoted, and so it was, not long after it was written. Suetonius (*Life of Augustus* 40) reports that Augustus quoted this line to express his disgust that Romans were no longer wearing the requisite toga at theatrical events during public festivals. The toga was the national dress, but it was cumbersome and hot, and many had abandoned it for more comfortable alternatives. Augustus' sarcastic quotation shows that Vergil's line had achieved iconic status within a generation of its composition.

After this climax Jupiter rounds off the first part of his speech with a lordly *sic placitum* (that's my decision). He then works up to a second climax, but this one is much more problematic. The second half of Jupiter's speech announces the coming of Augustus. Defeated Troy, Jupiter announces, will enslave Greece, and from the Trojan stock Caesar will be born, whose *imperium* will be bounded by the Ocean and his fame by the stars. This Caesar will be called Julius, after Aeneas' son Iulus. Whether Vergil is referring to Julius Caesar or his adoptive son Augustus, also known as Julius Caesar, is not clear, but he is endorsing the Julian family's claims to descent from Aeneas and, through him, Venus. This Caesar, Jupiter announces, will be received into Olympus as a god. No doubt this is why Vergil makes it ambiguous as to which Caesar is meant: Julius had been apotheosized after his death, but it was quite another thing to make the same claim about a living Roman. Finally, Jupiter announces the coming of a Golden Age, whose crowning feature will be the closing of the gates of the temple of Janus. This was Augustus' proudest claim. The gates of the temple of Janus were ceremonially closed when Rome was not at war. Janus was the god of the door (*ianua*), and was depicted looking both ways, like a door, which also made him the god of beginnings—January is the first month of the year. In this ceremony of the opening or closing of the door of Janus, Rome represented its relations to the outside world. After the battle of Actium (31 BC), the decisive battle of the civil wars through which Augustus came to power, they had been closed for the first time since 235 BC.

> cana Fides et Vesta, Remo cum fratre Quirinus
> iura dabunt; dirae ferro et compagibus artis
> claudentur Belli portae; Furor impius intus
> saeva sedens super arma et centum vinctus aenis
> post tergum nodis fremet horridus ore cruento.   (1. 292–6)

> (Grey-haired Trustworthiness and Vesta, and Quirinus with his brother
>   Remus,
> will dispense justice; the grim gates of War, with their tight iron frames,
> will be closed; within, ruthless Fury,
> sitting on brutal weapons, her arms bound behind her back
> with a hundred knots, will roar, bristling, with bloody mouth.)

The Golden Age is sponsored by some impressive figures. *Fides* (trustworthiness) was one of the prime virtues to which the Romans laid claim. She is hoary because of her antiquity, for her association with Rome goes far back. Vesta is the goddess of the hearth, and her temple symbolized the permanence of Rome. It contained an undying fire, tended by the Vestal Virgins. An elegant variation of construction introduces the next pair: Fides *and* Vesta; Quirinus *with his brother* Remus. Romulus is identified by the name given to him on his apotheosis (Quirinus), and this name was associated with the term by which the Romans might be ceremonially addressed as a group assembled in peacetime

(*Quirites*). During the long period of civil wars that culminated in Augustus' victory at Actium, the fratricidal story of Romulus and Remus at the very foundation of the city was taken as a symbol of things to come. Here, though, the brothers appear together, giving laws, a sign that civil wars are at an end. As are all wars. The dread gates of War enclose the next sentence, with adjective (*dirae*) and noun (*portae*) emphatically separated in hyperbaton. In this case the hyperbaton has a visual effect, enclosing the sentence like the doors themselves. These gates are kept shut 'with iron and tight-fitting frame'. Instead of saying the same thing twice, as he usually does, Vergil here says one thing by means of two ('hendiadys' is the Greek word for that): the gates are kept closed by a tight-fitting frame *of* iron. But something is wrong with this picture. The closing or opening of the gates of Janus symbolized Rome's relation with the world outside, but in this version the temple acts as a prison. Inside, viciously restrained, sits Vergil's bête noire, *Furor*.

Furor (madness, rage, passion) appears throughout Vergil's œuvre as the enemy of all human enterprise, waiting to break out, in nature or the human soul, to destroy the hard-won achievements of civilization. So this image could refer to the Roman claim to have brought peace to the world it has conquered. *Furor* is described as *impius*, the negative of the word *pius*, which is used to characterize Aeneas throughout the poem. *Sum pius Aeneas* (I am *pius* Aeneas, *Aeneid* 1. 378) are the words with which he introduces himself to his mother Venus, when she appears to him, incognita, in the first book of the *Aeneid*. *Pius* cannot be translated by one English word (and certainly not 'pious') but a *pius* person has the right, dutiful emotions towards gods, country, and family. So the negative *impius* here may allude to civil war: juxtaposing *impius* with *intus* (within), Vergil makes a closely connected phrase of these words, whose similar sound causes one to overlap with the other. Civil war is indeed both 'immoral' and 'within'. But what Jupiter is saying is that Rome is safe from war precisely because *Furor* is restrained within the temple of Janus. The result is a striking ambiguity: it is both sinister and reassuring that *Furor* is *intus*. But even more ambivalent is the elaborate picture of *Furor's* imprisonment, which is as savage as the prisoner himself: the roaring mouth of *Furor*, bloodied by an iron bit, brings Jupiter's speech to a close. Yes, *Furor* is restrained, but he is not pacified, and the restraining power must exercise a savagery worthy of the victim himself. As the culmination of a speech forecasting the glorious future of Rome and the extent of its domination abroad, this picture of barely contained violence 'within' is disturbing to say the least. Is this *Furor* to be held in reserve, ready to be unleashed on the recalcitrant?

Auden was certainly thinking of Jupiter's speech when, in his poem 'Secondary Epic', he ridiculed Vergil's trick of disguising hindsight as foresight in the prophetic moments of the *Aeneid*. Why, he facetiously asks, does the history of Rome suddenly stop with the Golden Age of Augustus' reign? Why does Vergil not go on to prophesy the destruction of Rome by the barbarians? It's all too neat, too convenient for Vergil's patron, Augustus. But Vergil did not have the same hindsight about Augustus' reign as Auden had. The modern reader knows that Augustus' reign continued up to AD 14 and that he founded a dynasty under which Rome enjoyed a cessation of civil wars until AD 69. The imperial system, too, was to last for the rest of Rome's history, another four hundred years. Vergil, who died in 19 BC, knew none of this, and the picture of *Furor* raging within that brings Jupiter's prophetic speech to a close is not a picture of stability but of the threat that hangs over the Roman world. It clashes violently with the first climax of Jupiter's speech, the one that concerns the broader sweep of

Roman history and ends with *imperium sine fine*. At this point in Augustus' reign the future is uncertain. The gates of the temple of Janus have indeed been closed, but how long will this state of affairs last? What will happen if Augustus should die?

From another angle, though, the picture of *Furor* brings the second half of Jupiter's speech to a satisfying close. Jupiter begins his speech by declaring that Troy's descendants will turn the tables on their old enemies, the Greeks, who will be conquered by the new race, as indeed they were. Among the plunder that was brought to Rome from Greece was a painting, by the great Apelles, of War sitting on a pile of weapons with its arms bound behind its back. Augustus exhibited this painting prominently in his forum, along with other famous works of Greek art. Vergil has transferred it to the temple of Janus and given it an application to Roman history, a good example of the Roman appropriation of Greek culture. *Furor* imprisoned in a Roman temple is itself an image of Greek culture (in the form of Apelles' painting) made to speak of Roman issues.

On many levels the *Aeneid*, like much of Roman literature, is concerned with defining the complicated relation between Greece and Rome. Aeneas is a figure from Greek literature, but he's an enemy of the Greeks. When Anchises meets his son in the underworld he distinguishes between the unmatched cultural achievements of the Greeks and the political and martial arts that will be the contribution of the Romans. Vergil's Roman epic is heavily influenced by Homer, and it carries on a persistent dialogue with the values and ideals that underly the Homeric poems. Throughout his wanderings, Aeneas' responsible art of leadership is contrasted with the more swashbuckling leadership of Odysseus, who does not manage to bring any of his men home with him alive. Achilles and Odysseus, the heroes of Hom-

er's *Iliad* and *Odyssey*, were magnificent egotists, fascinating, charis-
matic, and, in the case of Odysseus, many-sided (hence his standard
epithet *polytropos*—'man of many turns'). By contrast, Aeneas is a
man moulded by his experiences and fitted to a role. Looking back
regretfully to the Troy he has lost, and looking forward hopefully to
the future that he will enable (though never know), Aeneas has no
settled place in time. He is defined as much by what he must sacrifice
as by what he does. This makes him the archetypal imperialist hero,
for the imperialist project appears altruistic in proportion to what has
been sacrificed for it by its agents. Aeneas, the uncharismatic and self-
denying hero, also provides the right ideal in the aftermath of the civil
wars, which had come about when strong, self-assertive personalities
such as Caesar, Pompey, and Mark Antony had subordinated the com-
mon good to their own personal honour.

Another aspect of imperialist ideology in the *Aeneid*, along with its
self-sacrificing hero, is the fact that the Roman empire is not repre-
sented as the triumph of a particular nation or race. It is the Trojans
whose fortunes the story follows with hope and fear, but the heroes of
this story are destined (so Jupiter declares) to lose their cultural iden-
tity and be absorbed into the Italians. Of course, Vergil's readers would
identify themselves as Romans more than as Trojans, but Italy is a
broader concept, and one that had only recently taken hold in Vergil's
times. Vergil deliberately confuses ethnic identities in the *Aeneid* by
undermining the oppositions on which identity is founded. Anchises'
speech to his son in the underworld distinguishes the Roman art of
ruling from the aesthetic and scientific arts of the Greeks. But when
Aeneas visits the future site of Rome (though he does not know it) in
Book 8, he finds that it is inhabited by Greeks from Arcadia, and their
king, Evander, delivers a speech urging Aeneas to spurn riches and

make himself worthy of a god, a very Roman idea. Furthermore, the reader who looks back proudly to Trojan ancestry must also see the Trojans from the perspective of the *Aeneid*'s Italians, as effeminate Easterners. Once or twice we are rudely reminded that Aeneas is probably wearing a funny Phygian hat. National identity, in the *Aeneid*, is under construction: Aeneas becomes a Roman as he takes on the project to which Jupiter guides him. This reflects the realities of the Roman empire. Unlike the more exclusive citizenship of Athens, Roman citizenship was not dependent on birth, and was widely granted to people from all over the empire, according to what the Romans regarded as merit. The *Aeneid* is imperialist in its vindication of the Roman right to rule, but it emphasizes that the Romans themselves originate from a merging of peoples in a world where identity is constantly being revised or questioned.

The poet of pathos

I want to turn now from imperialism to a different aspect of the *Aeneid*, for which we move from Jupiter's speech to a scene later in the same book. It is a scene that concerns the past rather than the future, and it features an Aeneas who has no inkling of what Jupiter has just told Venus about the future. After his speech, Jupiter despatches the divine messenger, Mercury, to prepare the Carthaginians and their queen to receive the shipwrecked Trojans. At the break of the next day Aeneas sets out to reconnoitre and runs into his mother Venus, who has disguised herself as a huntress. She tells Aeneas where he is and how Dido and her people have come to settle there, driven from their Phoenician home by Dido's brother, who murdered her husband. Venus reassures Aeneas that his ships and comrades are safe, and then disappears, just as he recognizes her. Aeneas then makes his way to the city, surrounded by a protective cloud that his mother has cast on him. The city, or city-in-the-making, is Carthage, Rome's great antagonist to be, but now a hive of building activity. Aeneas the wanderer envies those whose walls are already rising. He sees a Carthaginian temple to Juno decorated with paintings of—the Trojan War. This was the moment, the narrator comments, when Aeneas began to hope for a change in his fortunes. But as he marvels at the representation of his recent past, Aeneas speaks for himself:

> consitit et lacrimans 'quis iam locus,' inquit, 'Achate,
> quae regio in terris nostri non plena laboris?
> en Priamus. sunt hic etiam sua praemia laudi,
> sunt lacrimae rerum et mentem mortalia tangunt.
> solve metus; feret haec aliquam tibi fama salutem.'
> sic ait atque animam pictura pascit inani
> multa gemens, largoque umectat flumine vultum.   (1. 459–65)

> (He halted and, weeping, said, 'What place is there now, Achates,
> what region on earth that is not full of our suffering?
> Here is Priam. Even here there are rewards for what is praiseworthy,
> there are tears for human action, and mortality touches the mind.
> Let go your fears; this fame will bring you some deliverance.'
> Thus he spoke, and fed his soul on an empty picture,
> groaning deeply and bathing his face in freely flowing tears.)

We might compare the feelings with which a Roman reader would have reacted to Jupiter's prophecy with the emotions that are expressed by Aeneas as he looks at the tragic events that have made him an exile. Jupiter's prophecy is, for the Roman reader, a tableau representing the past, just as the paintings on Dido's temple are for Aeneas. Each of these visions marks out a different level on which we engage with Aeneas' story. The discrepancy between the pathos of Aeneas' words and the grandeur of Jupiter's prophecy marks the difference between the story as it unfolds for Aeneas and the history of Rome as it is recalled by the contemporary Roman. In his words, Aeneas gives an ironic equivalent of Jupiter's vision of imperial rule, unlimited in space or time, when he asks '*Quae regio in terris nostri non plena laboris?*' (What region of earth is not full of our suffering?) He means that everyone has heard of the Trojans' travails, but his phrasing suggests that the Trojans have occupied the thoughts of the world's peoples just as the Roman legions would occupy their territory: 'What place is not *full* of our travails?' The story of the Trojans becoming Romans will indeed become THE story. At the same time, the phrase allows us to understand 'what place is there where we have not suffered?' It depends on whether you are looking from the perspective of Aeneas or of the contemporary Roman. Aeneas' wanderings have covered a good swathe of the Mediterranean world, and this confused wandering contrasts sharply with the projection of Roman power across the globe that is to come. But from the limited perspective of Aeneas himself, at this particular moment, there are no contrasts between present and future to be drawn. The confident claim to reputation and renown (*fama*) that one might expect of any ancient epic hero is pathetically muted in the words 'this renown will bring you *some* deliverance' (*feret haec* **aliquam** *tibi fama salutem*). The two modifiers *haec* (this, sc. fame) and *aliquam* (some, sc. security) precede their respective nouns, and this lays a significant emphasis on *aliquam*. Aeneas comforts Achates, but with more pathos than conviction.

What sort of deliverance or *security* could *fama* bring the Trojans? Is the very knowledge that one is known a comforting knowledge? Probably so, but Aeneas is also reassured that he has washed up on a civilized shore, where what is praiseworthy is recognized and rewarded.

So perhaps he can hope that the Trojans, celebrated on the Carthaginian temple wall, will be received with respect. He is also encouraged that the paintings indicate a capacity for sympathy. In the line and a half beginning *sunt hic etiam...* (Even here there are...) we have three elements, each with a similar meaning. The first two are expressed with the same syntax: 'due rewards for honour' and 'tears for human affairs'. The third is expressed differently: *mentem mortalia tangunt* (mortality touches the mind). This clause is parallel in meaning to *sunt lacrimae rerum*, but the verb (*tangunt*, touch) takes us further into the realm of pure emotion and away from the idea of due rewards. To say that '(here) mortality touches the mind' is to make a more general statement than 'here there are rewards for honour and tears for human affairs'. This is another example of the subtle effects that can be achieved by saying the same thing another way. The phrase *lacrimae rerum* might be seen as comparable to either of the two flanking expressions, and depending on how we pair it the emphasis shifts. In fact, the line *sunt lacrimae rerum et mentem mortalia tangunt* has often been quoted, isolated and out of context, as a key to the Vergilian sensibility. Without the parallel *sunt hic etiam sua praemia laudi* (even here what is praiseworthy gets its reward), the phrase *sunt lacrimae rerum* has often been taken to mean 'there are tears in things' (i.e. something like 'tears are inherent in life'). This translation corresponds to a widespread view of Vergil as the poet of 'the tears of things', the pessimistic poet of pity and sympathy. It is a far cry from the image of Vergil the grand celebrant of Augustan rule and Roman imperial domination, wielder of 'The stateliest measure ever moulded by the lips of man' (Tennyson). But both views of Vergil have been held, and sometimes by the same people.

Classical scholars have been keen to point out that to take the phrase *sunt lacrimae rerum* as 'there are tears in things' is a misinterpretation, making something more general and vague out of what has a specific meaning in this context. Aeneas consoles Achates with the thought that the Carthaginians are civilized people, for they recognize valour and experience grief for human suffering: *rerum* (the genitive plural of *res*, thing) is probably an objective genitive, and so *lacrimae rerum* should be translated 'tears *for* things'. A large part of the vague, generalizing pathos that has been heard in this line comes from the word *rerum*. The Latin word *res* is one of the most difficult of words to translate. The *Oxford Latin Dictionary* lists nineteen senses, starting with 'property' and 'wealth' and moving through 'that which can be conceived as a separate entity', 'that which actually exists', to 'a deed or act, that which occupies one's attention', 'a matter at issue', 'the affairs of state', and 'the state of affairs'. The *OLD* does not hazard an opinion as to which sense fits this passage. Two versions of *rerum* in this line, picked at random from current translations, are 'men's lot' and 'passing things'. 'Thing' is the usual crutch of students translating *res*, the same word that is used to translate the neuter plural in *mortalia* (mortal *things*). Since the Latin adjective has three genders, an adjective can stand on its own where it is clear which noun we are to supply. In the case of the adjective *bonus* (good), for instance, the masculine *bonus* on its own would be taken to mean a good man, *bona* a good woman, and *bonum* a good thing. *Mortalia* is the neuter plural of the adjective *mortalis*, mortal. So, 'mortal things'? Students are usually discouraged from using 'things' to translate either *res* or the neuter plural. Often, *res* is combined with another word that gives it a specific meaning: *res publica*, 'the public *res*', is the usual way to refer to the state (cf. republic) and Augustus' *Res Gestae* (things done) is his account of his 'achievements'. But Vergil's usage here, like the neuter plural *mortalia*, cannot definitively be pinned down to one specific meaning, and translations that produce elegant phrases to get around the clumsy 'things' risk betraying the vagueness, which is an essential component of the emotion. The edges of the word are fuzzy, blurred by tears.

If Aeneas' statement is pathetic, then so is Vergil's comment. Aeneas, he says, 'feeds (*pascit*) his mind on an empty (*inani*) picture'. It is hard to say whether we should emphasize *pascit* or *inani*. Is it wonderful or ridiculous that Aeneas finds mental sustenance in what is only a picture, a mere imitation? The picture decorates a temple to Juno, the goddess who opposes the Trojans throughout the *Aeneid*, so it is quite plausible that it is there to celebrate her triumph over the Trojans. Aeneas, then, reads counter to the intentions of the picture's creators. Does that invalidate his reactions? Does he, in fact, feed only off his own emotions when he wets his cheeks with a 'generous flood' (*largo flumine*) of tears? The English word 'large' has now lost the connotations of generosity (*largesse*) and liberality (set at large), that it used to have, connotations derived from the Latin *largus*. The verb *largior*, for instance, means 'I lavish'. Do these connotations of *largus* give a self-indulgent tinge to Aeneas' tears? W. R. Johnson comments on this scene: 'Here, as often, the emotions of the characters are not ways of revealing the characters, who in turn reveal the *muthos* [story, plot] in their words and actions [as in Homer]; here both the characters and *muthos* exist to reveal emotions and meditations on emotions.'[3]

Vergil the poet of pathos is just about compatible with Vergil the classic of all Europe, in T. S. Eliot's phrase, but what about Vergil the poet of the eros of death?

---

[3] W. R. Johnson, *Darkness Visible: A Study of Vergil's Aeneid* (Berkeley, CA, 1976), 101.

volvitur Euryalus leto, pulchrosque per artus
it cruor inque umeros cervix conlapsa recumbit:
purpureus veluti cum flos succisus aratro
languescit moriens, lassove papavera collo
demisere caput pluvia cum forte gravantur.   (9. 433–7)

(Euryalus rolls in his death, and his blood flows
down his beautiful limbs, and his slack neck rests on his shoulders:
just as a crimson flower cut by the plough
goes limp in its death, or poppies with weary neck
bow their heads when they are weighed down by rain.)

Nisus and Euryalus are young Trojan warrior-lovers in the Greek
tradition exemplified by the *Iliad*'s Achilles and Patroclus (at least as
Greeks after Homer saw them). They have volunteered for a danger-
ous mission to pass through the camp of the Italians, who are besieg-
ing the Trojans, and to bring word to Aeneas that his help is needed.
On the way they decide to slaughter and despoil some of the sleep-
ing enemy, and it is the glint of a plundered helmet in the moonlight
that gives them away to an enemy patrol, which hunts them down
and kills them. The episode, which started so heroically, devolves
into a cowardly slaughter of defenceless enemies, and this leads to
the death of the lovers. But as Euryalus dies our attention is focused
on the languid beauty of his body in the moment of death, which the
double simile replays in slow motion. The neck that lolls on Eury-
alus' shoulders is his own, but taken out of context it might have
been a lover's; an English translation cannot omit the possessive,
but Vergil's Latin can, allowing our minds to stray. Two phrases
expressing languorous collapse echo each other at the end of the
second and fifth lines: *conlapsa recumbit* (having collapsed, leans)
and *languescit moriens* (grows slack, dying). An elegant chiasmus

reverses the respective positions of the main verb and participle in the two phrases. *Languescit* is an inceptive form of the verb, which implies process (compare our putrescent, etc.), a sense that is doubled by the present participle *moriens*. Vergil lets the scene unroll in slow motion, encouraging us to linger over the beauty of this young death.

In his book on the *Aeneid*, W. R. Johnson examines characteristic moments like this under the category of 'dissolving pathos'. Contrasting the death of Euryalus with passages from Homer to which Vergil's lines allude, Johnson says that 'we are locked into a sweet, tainted melancholy', adding '*Languescit moriens* and *lasso collo* (with his tired neck) create a stifling, mesmerising stasis; their sentimentality sidesteps the fact of disaster, so that what is fearful about this death lingers—beautified, unresolved, and corrupt' (ibid. 64–5).

Here are the passages from Homer to which Vergil alludes:

He spoke, and from his bowstring shot another arrow direct at Hector, and his heart yearned to wound him. Hector he missed, but Gorgythion, the fine son of Priam, his arrow struck, the chest pierced. Him Castianeira bore, Priam's wife, a woman from Aisyme—the beautiful Castianeira, like a goddess in form and figure. As a poppy in a garden lolls its head to one side, heavy with seed and spring rain, so, weighted with its casque, to one side dangled his head.   (*Iliad* 8. 300–8, trans. Johnson)

And

And he fell with a dull clang, and his armour rattled about him as he fell, and his hair, lovely as the hair of the Graces themselves, and his braids, clasped with gold and silver, were soaked with his blood. And like a flourishing young olive tree that someone tends in a quiet place where fertile water gushes, a tree that flowers in beauty, and it is shaken by every windy current, and it thrives in the whiteness of its blossoms—then a sudden wind with great whirling beats down and uproots it from its trench, flings it on the ground; even so was Euphorbus of the stout ashen spear, he, the son of Panthous, whom Menelaus, son of Atreus, killed and fell to despoiling.

(Iliad 17. 50–60, trans. Johnson)

Vergil's lines carry along with them memories of these Homeric passages, well known to the Roman reader, and they invite the reader to compare their different character. But there is more. Vergil's death of Euryalus also echoes the end of one of Catullus' love poems, where Catullus bitterly accuses Lesbia of having destroyed his love:

> nec meum respectet, ut ante, amorem,
> qui illius culpa cecidit velut prati
> ultimi flos, praetereunte postquam
>   tactus aratro est.   (Poem 11. 21–4)

> (…and she should not look for my love, as before,
> which by her fault has collapsed like the meadow's
> last flower, touched by the plough
>   as it passes.)

This dense allusive web is typical of Vergil's poetry, and here it draws together two completely different authors, with their different contexts and associations. Catullan pathos is overlaid on Homeric attention to detail and to the realities of the physical world. Johnson's description of what emerges ('beautified, unresolved, and corrupt') is provocative, and perhaps exaggerated, but it reminds us that even a classic can have a very personal style and sensibility.

It is one of the puzzles of the *Aeneid* that Vergil follows this *Liebestod* by speaking in his own person, for the only time in the whole work, to graft the memory of this dubious couple onto a vision of the Roman imperium:

fortunati ambo! si quid mea carmina possunt,
nulla dies umquam memori vos eximet aevo,
dum domus Aeneae Capitoli immobile saxum
accolet imperiumque pater Romanus habebit.   (*Aeneid* 9. 446–9)

(Lucky pair! If my songs have any power,
no day will ever remove you from the memory of the ages,
while the house of Aeneas dwells on the Capitol's unmovable rock
and a Roman father holds supreme power.)

It has been said that Vergil's deepest emotional engagement in this epic of Rome is with the victims, the losers, and the defeated. Dido, not Aeneas, is the figure who has captured the imaginations of generations of readers (including St Augustine and Berlioz). In the Renaissance, the key Vergilian value of *pietas* was identified with *pity*, which does indeed derive from the Latin word. Both Aeneas and Vergil himself were characterized by this quality. And indeed, through the powerful sentiment that suffuses much of Vergil's writing the *Aeneid* appeals to a community of sensibility as much as to a sense of belonging to the Roman world order. But perhaps the two are not so incompatible. In the *Aeneid* we have the beginning of what one critic, speaking of later ages, has called 'imperialist nostalgia', whereby a subject assuming a dominant perspective adopts, paradoxically, a nostalgic yearning for what the dominant culture has caused to perish.[4] Like it or not, Vergil has profoundly influenced the Western imperial consciousness.

Vergil's glorification of the lover-warriors Nisus and Euryalus, who contribute very little to the story of Rome's creation, claims the epic poet's traditional power to bestow fame and memory on those it celebrates. But it also claims the privilege of the poet to write against the

---

[4] Renato Rosaldo, 'Imperialist Nostalgia', *Representations* 26 (1989), 107–22.

grain of history and against the values in the name of which success is (retrospectively) seen as justified. *Fortunati ambo* (happy pair)! The power of Vergil's song can make it so. In the next chapter we will meet two poets who stretch the power of poetry to define its own reality to the limit. We will encounter an epic that seeks to take back history and a tragedy that leaves us exultant in the triumph of a monster.

5

....

LUCAN AND SENECA: POETS OF APOCALYPSE

'For all the magnificence of the *Aeneid*, one senses an enormous moral vacuum in the poem. Men do what they do because they are told that it is right or necessary, not because they believe in it.'[1] There is some truth to these words of Frederick Ahl, a scholar who did much to restore the reputation of Lucan in the late twentieth century. In this chapter we will meet two heroes who believe in what they do with the utmost conviction. They are both monsters. Nobody who reads the two works we will look at in this chapter can deny that their authors are inspired to the heights of poetic sublimity by their terrifying protagonists. Lucan's *Civil War* and Seneca's *Thyestes* can be taken as the originals of all those literary works that have been said to be 'of the devil's party', starting with Milton's *Paradise Lost*, which owes much to Lucan.

With Lucan and Seneca we jump ahead from the period of the first emperor, the Augustan Age of Vergil and Horace, to the time of the last emperor of the dynasty Augustus founded. Nero, the last of the Julio-Claudians, is known as a bad emperor, and that was the case even in his own time. His biography, in Suetonius' *Lives of the Twelve Caesars*, makes lurid reading—incest, matricide, 'marriages' to both

[1] Frederick Ahl, *Lucan: An Introduction* (Ithaca, NY, 1976), 65.

men and women (as both bride and groom), and, worst of all, public performance as a lyre player and charioteer. No wonder the dynasty came to an end with his murder! Part of what made Nero a bad emperor in the eyes of his peers was his excessive devotion to the arts. Not only did he write poetry and sponsor festivals and competitions, but he performed and competed himself, something that may have been acceptable in Greece but was incompatible with the dignity of a Roman aristocrat. During his reign (AD 54–68), shorter than that of Augustus, literature flourished: Seneca, Lucan, Persius, and (probably) Petronius all wrote under Nero. Seneca and his nephew Lucan were both close to the emperor, Seneca as tutor of the young Nero and adviser in the early years of his reign, Lucan as a brilliant young poet whose talent Nero admired and envied. But membership of Nero's inner circle was a precarious position, and both writers were forced to commit suicide when they were implicated, rightly or wrongly, in a conspiracy against the emperor in AD 65. Lucan was twenty-five years old.

Nero's reign might well have qualified as a Golden Age of literature. But Rome already had a Golden Age, the reign of Augustus, and so nineteenth-century literary historians dubbed this the Silver Age, and the name has stuck. These historians were following an ancient model of history, according to which a Golden Age is followed by decline, which runs through a series of metals until we reach our own age of iron. But, as literary historians, they were also noticing certain traits of post-Augustan, and particularly Neronian, literature: first, what they took to be an excessive reliance on rhetoric; next, a competitive urge to outdo previous poetry, often in terms of sheer extremity; and finally, a tendency towards epigrammatic expression and excerptable purple passages. All this, they thought, was encouraged by the growth of public poetic recitations, where poets jostled with each other to make the most powerful immediate effect on an audience hungry for sensation. This was incompatible with the balance, maturity, and decorousness that were taken to be characteristic of the classical, as exemplified by Vergil, Horace, and (in prose) Cicero and Livy. It will come as no surprise that there has been a reassessment of these 'Silver' writers in the last thirty years or so, and that the very traits that earlier consigned them to secondary status have recommended them to contemporary tastes. But we should remember that Seneca, Lucan, and Ovid (with whom Silver literature is usually thought to begin) were important models for our own Golden Age of literature, the Elizabethan, and that the period of English literature we usually refer to as Augustan, the age of Pope and Dryden, was not responsible for the work that we value most highly. In this chapter, I will make a case for the sensational, the sublime, the bombastic, and the excessive in the two greatest poets of the Neronian age, Lucan and Seneca. Their style, certainly, is sensational(istic), but so is their subject matter. Horror is the most important emotion, a far cry from Vergilian pathos.

Lucan's *Civil War*: an epic without a hero

We start with Lucan, because he makes a nice follow-on from Vergil. Lucan, the *Wunderkind* who committed suicide at the age of twenty-five, wrote an unfinished epic in ten books on the civil wars that led to Caesar's dictatorship and the fall of the Republic. By the time of Nero, the monarchy (in practice, if not in name) that had been established by Augustus had prevailed for nearly a century. It had been brought to birth by a series of civil wars that were profoundly traumatic for the Romans, and the always precarious problem of succession kept the spectre of civil war at the back of their minds. Both the horrors of civil war and the loss of political liberty, on which Rome so prided itself, conjured up visions of apocalypse. Lucan's *Civil War* covers the conflict between Pompey, representing the cause of the Republic, and Caesar, the founder of the Julio-Claudian dynasty, of which Nero was the last representative. Augustus (then known as Octavian) began his career as the avenger of his adoptive father, Julius Caesar. After defeating Caesar's murderers at the Battle of Philippi in 42 BC he waged war against his erstwhile ally, Mark Antony. That civil war would end in 31 BC with Octavian's victory over Antony and his ally, the Egyptian queen Cleopatra, at the battle of Actium. There is not much about the civil wars in the *Aeneid*. Augustus would not have wanted to stress that bloody part of his career. Vergil sweeps on from the mythical past through the present into the distant future of the Roman empire, but Lucan's story is confined to the origin of the losses with which he himself lives, the losses of the Republic and of liberty. The grandeur of Vergil's *Aeneid* derives from his resonant prophecies of what we (and his Augustan readers) now know has already happened, the swelling sense that where we are now was foreseen, foretold, and predestined long ago, and by the highest authority. It is the horror of Lucan's *Bellum Civile* that we know what is going to happen and there's nothing we can do about it; we will always live in the aftermath of this traumatic event. As narrator of the civil wars, Lucan wants to make time stand still, or to protract his narrative for ever, since as long as we are engaged in the final conflict that will bring Caesar to power, liberty is not yet lost (though we know that it will be). But to dwell on this moment is painful, for civil war is the ultimate monstrosity. Vergil sings of 'arms and the man' and of the transformation of Aeneas' fortunes, from defeat at Troy to the founding of an imperial people; the story that Lucan has to tell is of the defeat of the cause of liberty at the hands of a man (Julius Caesar) who claimed Aeneas as his ancestor. The 'arms' will be those that a powerful people has turned on its own entrails, as Lucan puts it in the third line of his poem. Vergil impresses on us that 'it was such a *moles* (burden) to found the Roman race', while Lucan speaks of the collapse of Rome under its own weight. But the horror of Lucan's subject is more than tinged with sublimity. There is pride in a catastrophe so complete, and a crime so terrible, that only Rome could have given birth to them.

The Republic was lost because Caesar defeated Pompey, and as a result Nero is now emperor. But isn't this a dangerous connection for Lucan to make? Augustus disguised his revolution, a virtual return to monarchy after five hundred proud years of democracy, by claiming that he had restored the Republic. This afforded him the convenience of deniability and his subjects the comforts of self-deception. But no such fig leaf covered the despotic rule of Nero. Lucan identifies the Pompeian cause with liberty, and he sees its defeat as the imposition of servitude, under which Rome still labours. He covers the obvious implication for Nero with a stroke of flattery so gross that many have suspected irony:

> But if the fates could find no other way
> for Nero's coming...
> For this reward we accept
> even these crimes and guilt... (*Civil War* 1. 33–7)

Even more interesting than the puzzle of Lucan's intentions towards Nero is his attitude to the three heroes of his epic: Pompey, Julius Caesar, and Cato. First of all, there was no precedent for a polycentric epic such as this, in which it is impossible to say where the centre of gravity lies. Pompey's is the just cause, but is he a worthy representative? Lucan makes no attempt to play down Pompey's human faults: his vanity, his passivity, and his uxoriousness (endearing though it may be to us). When he is defeated by Caesar at the battle of Pharsalus, and then killed by a treacherous Egyptian pharaoh, the uncompromisingly upright Cato continues the war. With Pompey dead, Lucan comments, Cato can be wholeheartedly a Pompeian. The name of the cause now is liberty, and Cato can incarnate it without subordinating republicanism to an individual's personal ambition. He can do this because his dedication to virtue overrides every other emotion or consideration. But Cato's *virtus* transcends politics too, and his lust to test and display it verges on the pathological. And what of Caesar, the villain of this story? If Milton was of the devil's party, then Lucan is of Caesar's party. No reader of this epic can deny that the evil genius of Caesar elicits some of Lucan's most powerful poetry. Can poetry, then, be an adequate medium for this subject, or is poetry compromised by its very nature? Lucan the narrator intervenes passionately in his story, almost becoming another character. His rhetoric pushes the position of each of his protagonists to the limit, to see what they are made of. In the process, he bounces between commitment and disillusion, horror and awe.

The two main protagonists of the civil war are contrasted in a famous passage at the beginning of Book 1. Pompey, the great general whose glory days are behind him, though his name is still to be conjured with, is contrasted with Caesar, the force of nature who cannot remain still. Pompey is like an old oak, laden with trophies, which stands only because of its own weight, offering shade with its trunk rather than its branches. And yet, although it threatens to fall at the first strong wind, and many sturdy trees stand about it, this one alone is worshipped (Lucan is not the only Roman who saw the presence of divinity in a mighty tree). This image of Pompey is summed up in the opening half line of this passage:

> stat magni nominis umbra,
> qualis frugifero quercus sublimis in agro
> exuvias veteres populi sacrataque gestans
> dona ducum nec iam validis radicibus haerens
> pondere fixa suo est, nudosque per aera ramos
> effundens trunco, non frondibus, efficit umbram;
> et quamvis primo nutet casura sub Euro,
> tot circum silvae firmo se robore tollant,
> sola tamen colitur.   (1. 135–43)

> (He stands, the shadow of a great name.
> As an oak-tree stands high in a fruitful field,
> bearing the ancient trophies of a people and the consecrated
> gifts of princes. But the roots by which it clings are not strong;
> held in place by its own weight, it spreads bare branches in the air
> and creates shade with its trunk rather than its leaves.
> And although it leans as though it would fall at the first gale,
> while around it many trees grow tall, strong and solid,
> it alone is worshipped.)

Lucan puns throughout the poem on Pompey's sobriquet *Magnus* (the Great). Pompey's great name is itself 'Great'; he is the shadow of the name *Magnus* as well as the shadow of a great name. In an English translation of this famous half line we put the key word 'shadow' first, and so spoil the bathos of Lucan's sequence: he stands, a great name's (the name Great's) shadow. The emphatic monosyllable *stat* (he stands) suggests persistence, but *umbra* at the end of the line implies that Pompey is no longer what he was (*umbra*, remember, also means a ghost). That paradox is precisely the point: reputations, names, and icons have a life of their own, quite apart from the person or thing they designate, and they persist even when they are only husks. *Umbra* refers not only to Pompey's relation to a reputation he has outlived, but also to the comfort a great name affords to others, like the shade of a tree. Pompey will be associated with the cause of freedom and of the Republic throughout, and I suspect that Lucan here hints that his followers shelter under impressive names such as *libertas* and *respublica*. Do these words still mean anything? Lucan leaves us in no doubt that he supports Pompey, liberty, and the Republic, and that he expects us to do the same, but his epic is shot through with ironies and equivocations, and it would be characteristic of him to subject his own commitment to the question.

If Pompey is an old oak, held up by its own weight, Caesar is the lightning that will strike it down. But Lucan works up to his simile from some more abstract descriptions of Caesar. The portrait of Caesar begins at exactly the same point in the hexameter as *stat magni nominis umbra* and begins by echoing the rhythm of that phrase exactly:

> sed non in Caesare tantum
> nomen erat nec fama ducis, sed nescia virtus
> stare loco, solusque pudor non vincere bello.
> acer et indomitus, quo spes quoque ira vocasset,
> ferre manum et numquam temerando parcere ferro,
> successus urgere suos, instare favori
> numinis, impellens quidquid sibi summa petenti
> obstaret, gaudensque viam fecisse ruina.   (1. 143–50)

> (But in Caesar there was not only
> the name and reputation of a leader, but a courage that did not know
> how to stand still, and only one source of shame: not to conquer
> in war. Eager and headstrong, wherever hope or anger called
> he acted, and never hesitated to defile his sword.
> He followed up his successes and pressed hard on the favour

of god, pushing aside whatever opposed him in the quest
for supreme power, and delighted to make a path for himself through
   destruction.)

All Roman authors like to say the same thing twice, but Lucan is the
master of bi-locution. This whole passage consists of pairs of expres-
sions varying a thought. Particularly striking is the line and a half
beginning *sed nescia virtus*. That phrase, as it stands, means some-
thing like 'but an ignorant (or heedless) courage', and so we take it,
until we cross to the next line where it becomes clear that we should
understand *ne-scia* (not knowing) more as a verb than an adjective:
'a courage that does not know—how to stand in place' (*stare loco*).
Pompey, we remember, 'stands' (*stat*), but under the weight of his
own bulk; by contrast, Caesar's inability to stand in place gives new
direction and impetus to the words of the previous line. The
enjambement and attendant syntactic shift in *nescia*, from attribute
(*nescia virtus*) to verb (*nescia stare*), is a brilliant icon of Caesar's
own restlessness, and yet the original concept of a 'heedless *virtus*'
sticks in our minds; as we shall see, Caesar's *virtus* is its own goal and
doesn't need to take account of anything else. The second element
of this dicolon is constructed in the same way, except with a noun
rather than an adjective performing the function of a verb. The
phrase *solus pudor*, 'his only shame', becomes 'he was only ashamed
(not to conquer in war)'. Some have found this a weak companion to
the other half of the dicolon, and have argued that we should stress
bello rather than *vincere*: Caesar regards it as shameful not to prevail
by war (rather than by any other means). Once we have become
attuned to the atmosphere of perversity that prevails in Lucan's epic
of wars 'more than civil' (*plus quam civilia*), as he puts it in the epic's
first line, we become increasingly adept at ferreting out the more

shocking reading that may lie beneath the obvious one. But it is a characteristic of Latin poetry to require the reader to *perform* the text, so that the meaning is only comprehensible once we attribute the proper weight to each word.

Two lines down, Caesar is fierce (*acer*) both 'to urge on his own success' (*successus urgere suos*) and to 'press hard on the favour of— the god (*numinis*)'. The enjambement delivers a sacrilegious frisson, and it comes hard on the heels of a paradox, for *in-stare*, 'to press (literally, stand) upon' is an action that usually strives against resistance, not support. But Caesar presses every advantage simply for the sake of pressing it; he obeys only the law of a nature that abhors a vacuum. Lucan's succession of dicolons characterizing Caesar's energy is followed by a magnificent simile comparing Caesar's progress to a bolt of lightning, and this unfolds in a single sweep with minimal redundancy:

> qualiter expressum ventis per nubila fulmen
> aetheris inpulsi sonitu mundique fragore
> emicuit rupitque diem populosque paventes
> terruit obliqua praestringens lumina flamma;
> in sua templa furit, nullaque exire vetante
> materia magnamque cadens magnamque revertens
> dat stragem late rursusque recolligit ignes.   (1. 151–7)

> (As a thunderbolt, forced out through the clouds by the wind,
> with the sound of the jolted aether and the shattering of the sky,
> flashes and interrupts the light of day, terrifying the fearful peoples
> and dazzling their eyes with its slanting flame;
> it rages against its own precincts, and since nothing solid prevents its
>   escape,
> lays waste far and wide, both as it falls and as it returns
> to collect its fires together again.)

We usually think of lightning as a violent discharge, but this simile turns it into another of nature's cyclical processes. The lightning gathers again after its rampage, just as Caesar's energy is recharged, rather than exhausted, by action. With the phrase *in sua templa furit* (it rages against its own precincts) we are reminded that lightning is not just a natural phenomenon but the instrument of Jupiter's anger. *Templa*, which I have translated 'precincts', is applied first to the divisions of the sky used for interpreting signs from the gods and second to the temples of the gods themselves. It was a notorious puzzle, and sometimes a joke, that the lightning that expressed Jupiter's will might strike his own temples. The lightning to which Caesar is compared rages against its own precincts, reminding us of this paradox. But Lucan does not mention Jupiter. His epic is, astonishingly, deprived of the 'divine machinery' that hovers above the action of ancient epic from Homer on. It is a speaking absence, a vacuum that is filled by various forms of the supernatural, culminating in a scene where the witch Erichtho resuscitates a dead man to prophesy the outcome of a battle (*Civil War* 6. 507–830).

On very rare occasions, Lucan as narrator does draw attention to the presence of the gods. The most chilling of these is a passing phrase at the beginning of Book 6, as Pompey and Caesar draw up their camps in preparation for the final battle. After the leaders, intent on war, have pitched their camps on neighbouring hills, 'and the gods saw their pair' (*parque suum videre dei, Civil War* 6. 3), Caesar decides that it is time for the showdown. The gods have become spectators at a gladiatorial combat, waiting for the matched pair that is to entertain them to take a position on the sand. When the battle is joined, Lucan berates Jupiter, who turned day into night in horror at the crimes of the mythical Thyestes (more on him later), but simply looks on at the spectacle of brothers and fathers killing each other. The gods care nothing for mortals, he cries ('But we *do*,' the gods might reply, 'we're watching this combat with great excitement'). Then, in one of Lucan's blackest jokes, he crows that humanity will have its revenge on the uncaring gods, for the civil war will make gods of men (the deified emperors), and earth will invade heaven (7. 455 ff.).

Lucan follows his character studies of the two protagonists with a different perspective, the 'public seeds of war' (1. 158–9). This is conventional Roman moralizing about the trajectory of the imperial people's history. Adversity and poverty, so the story goes, nourished virtue in the rising nation, but Rome succumbed to its own success as the growth of power encouraged greed and ambition to run rampant. Finally Rome becomes a more hackneyed version of Caesar himself:

> non erat is populus quem pax tranquilla iuvaret,
> quem sua libertas inmotis pasceret armis.   (1. 171–2)

> (This was not the people to be happy with quiet peace,
> or to be nourished by its freedom without wielding weapons.)

Roman historical writers worked with psychological and moral categories, rather than the impersonal forces through which modern historians tend to see events. So it is not surprising that restless Caesar is the Roman people writ large. But what is explained as an inevitable process in the case of the Roman people is simply gratuitous in the case of Caesar.

An epic of suicide

Lucan was not the only poet to have written a poem on the Roman civil wars, though none of the other poems survive. A trunk of such a composition appears in Petronius' novel, *Satyricon*. It is delivered by

Eumolpus, a comic figure of the stereotypical poet, always declaiming his work at inopportune moments, and taking a high moral tone that is quite out of keeping with his disgraceful behaviour. That his magnum opus should be a *Civil War* suggests that this is already a hackneyed topic. In the *Civil War* poem of Petronius' Eumolpus, Rome, having exhausted the possibilities of foreign conquest, turns on itself. Lucan compresses this idea into a single line, the third of his epic, in which he announces that he will sing of a powerful people 'turned with victorious arm against its own entrails':

in sua victrici conversum viscera dextra.   (1. 3)

It is a typical epic hexameter: the verb, the past participle *conversum* (turned), is planted in the middle, and the two adverbial phrases *in sua...viscera* (into its own entrails) and *victrici...dextra* (with victorious right hand) are interlaced on either side. Lucan's civil war is a parody of the noble Stoic suicide, which is itself a means by which the *vanquished* can reclaim freedom in voluntary death.

In some ways Lucan's *Civil War* is an epic of suicide. There are several scenes in which the vulnerable human body is turned into an offensive weapon in the frenzy of battle. For instance, one of Caesar's soldiers, by the name of Scaeva, rallies his troops by urging them to break the enemy's weapons on their chests and blunt the steel with their throats (6. 150–51). His own behaviour (196–246) verges on the territory of *Monty Python and the Holy Grail* ('What are you going to do, bleed on me?'). Transfixed by a forest of spears, he is on the point of choosing an enemy on whom to fall when he is shot through the eye with an arrow. Scaeva pulls out the arrow, along with his eye, and treads them both into the ground; then he caps this self-destruction in the only way possible—by suppressing his own rage. He claims that he wants to be carried into Pompey's camp, a deserter in death. But this is only a ruse, and the soldier who moves to lift him is run through by Scaeva's sword, as a just punishment for believing him to have been defeated. Die hard, indeed! In another passage, dying soldiers in a sea battle fall on the spiked prow of an enemy ship so that their body softens the blow of the ship as it rams one of their own. Lucan's epic of suicide plays endless variations on an act that is emblematic of civil war itself. Lucan can even make a joking pun on the vocabulary of suicide. When the crew of a ship that has been sunk in battle try to clamber on board a friendly ship, they are repelled by their own fellows, who fear that their ship will sink if they take their comrades on board. Some even have their arms chopped off as they grab the gunwales. *A manibus cecidere suis* (3. 667): 'they fell away from their own hands (i.e. leaving their hands behind)', says Lucan, with characteristically grotesque humour. But the same words also mean 'they fell (died) by their own hands'. The preposition *a* with the ablative can express either distance/separation or agency. So the same words express the abstract notion that this civil-war-within-a-civil-war is a form of suicide and they convey the physical dissolution of the body's integrity (they fell away from their own hands). There can be few poems that are as brutal to the human body as Lucan's, though Ovid's *Metamorphoses* would be a strong contender, as we shall see.

But not all these assaults on the agent's own body are suicidal, especially not where Caesar is concerned. The first episode of Lucan's poem is Caesar's crossing of the Rubicon, the act by which civil war is declared. How is this momentous action, in fact no more than the unopposed crossing of a minor river, to be made adequate to its historical significance? Lucan first confronts his Caesar with an apparition of Rome, in the person of a grieving woman who implores him to go no further, if he is indeed still a citizen. Caesar is horrified by the apparition, but he quickly recollects himself to make a speech in which, calling on deities associated with Rome's most sacred traditions, he protests that he is still *her* Caesar, if only she will allow him to be. Anyone who forces Caesar to become Rome's enemy, he claims, is himself the guilty one. Then he crosses the river. We switch suddenly to the parched fields of Libya in a simile that compares Caesar to a lion who catches sight of a human enemy; hesitating at first, he then whips himself up to such a pitch of frenzy that:

> torta levis si lancea Mauri
> haereat aut latum subeant venabula pectus
> per ferrum tanti securus volneris exit.   (1. 210–12)

> (If the light Moorish javelin
> is hurled and sticks, or the hunting spears enter its broad chest,
> it passes through the steel, untroubled by this great wound.)

The last line presents us with powerfully bifurcated sensations. It is both abstract and physical, simple and obscure. Syntactically it is quite straightforward, and formally it is constructed in a familiar way. The main statement, *per ferrum...exit* (he escapes through the steel), encloses the line. An adverbial phrase, *tanti securus volneris* (untroubled by such a wound), holds the centre, with a noun and adjective pair in the genitive (*tanti...volneris*) sandwiching an adjective in the nominative (*securus* = unconcerned [by such a great wound]). But how can you pass through steel, especially the steel of a spear? Clearly Lucan likes the paradox, but what are we to imagine? One translator has 'along the length of the spear', which is a viable understanding of *per* (through). The lion forces its way on so that the spear passes *through him* as he passes *along its length*. Lucan's horrific physical image, painful to imagine, has to be constructed from the abstract language, requiring the reader to do considerable imaginative work with the preposition *per*. Is this what it feels like for Caesar to make himself deaf to the plea of the *patria*? The lack of physical specificity in Lucan's language means that the same words could be understood in a different sense: 'he dies (*exit*) by (*per*) the steel, indifferent to such a wound'. And this brings us to the third of Lucan's protagonists, who did commit suicide in the wake of Caesar's victory in the civil war, namely Cato. Lucan's simile locates the lion in Libya (= Africa), which is where Cato fought a last-ditch battle, taking up leadership of the republican cause after the death of Pompey. If Cato had not been so in love with death, Lucan implies, he might have been a triumphant lion rather than a defeated republican suicide.

Cato is introduced in the second book of the *Civil War*. Up until now we readers have been spectators of events, but now we are presented with a choice. Book 2 raises the question of how Cato will handle a situation in which to commit oneself to either side is to commit a crime. After Caesar has crossed the Rubicon, Brutus, the man who will eventually assassinate him, visits Cato to ask his advice and to take his lead. Brutus suggests that merely to join this war is as good as to support Caesar, for Caesar counts a vote for civil war as a vote for himself. Cato, we know, is a figure of uncompromising virtue, but we can't be sure what slant he will give to the situation. How will he wrest a moral decision from this impossible dilemma? Quite as important to a Roman audience would be the related question of what rhetorical slant Lucan will give to the problem he has set himself. Displays of rhetoric had become a popular form of entertainment for the elite in Lucan's time. Crowds gathered to hear rhetoricians compete in the exercise known as *suasoria*, in which the rhetorician gives advice to a historical character at a particularly difficult moment of choice. For instance, suppose that Antony says that he will spare Cicero's life if Cicero burns his writings. What is Cicero to do? Competing rhetoricians would put a different *color* (literally, 'colour'; 'slant' or 'spin' would be our terms) on the situation.

Lucan's Cato gives a Stoic *color* to his dilemma. He replies that *virtus secura* (2. 287) will go wherever the fates drag it. *Securus* is a watchword of Stoic ethics, which aimed to produce a state of mental calm derived from the knowledge that nothing outside one's own control could influence one's happiness. Virtue alone is sufficient for happiness; it is a value incommensurable with all others. Virtue is *secura* (fearless, immune) because it cannot be touched by the world with which it engages, in so far as it is in tune with Fate, the divine mind that providentially governs all. So, in following Fate *virtus* operates at a higher level than Brutus' political considerations. 'Security' in this sense is good, but *securus* is an ambivalent word. Compounded of the prefix *se* (without) and *cura* (care, concern, worry), it has a range of meanings from 'untroubled' and 'confident' to 'careless' or 'negligent' via 'immune'. Ten lines after Cato has expressed confidence in the immunity of Stoic virtue from the taint that civil war confers on all participants, he makes another argument for joining in: 'Keep far away this madness, O gods, that Rome should fall, and by her fall rouse up | the Dahae and the Getae—and I remain unmoved' (*procul hunc arcete furorem,* | *o superi, motura Dahas ut clade Getasque* | *securo me Roma cadat,* 2. 297). The word for 'unmoved' is *securus*. 'Security' in this case is a bad thing, though once again it plays a crucial role in Cato's argument that he should participate in the war. Lucan's Cato is utterly selfless and devoted to the cause of liberty, but at the same time his contempt of life and transcendence of anything that smacks of a worldly motive make us ponder whether the two senses of *securus* are really so different. Is the ultimate liberty, for Cato, death? Less than a hundred lines before these two uses of the word *securus* there is another: Sulla, the murderous general who, back in the eighties BC, initiated the sequence of civil wars that is still being played out in Lucan's epic, is described watching the slaughter of Roman citizens that he has ordered:

> intrepidus tanti sedit securus ab alto
> spectator sceleris. (2. 207–8)
>
> (Unshaken, he sat above, without a qualm,
> spectator of a crime so great.)

Sulla is unshaken by the spectacle he has commanded. His 'security' might be the Stoic virtue of serene detachment from the turmoil of a benighted world. But of course, it is not. What he watches is what he has himself brought about. The paradox, that Sulla watches his own crime as though it were simply another event in the world, is artfully conveyed by the wording of this line and a half. The first line piles up words that emphasize Sulla's detachment: *intrepidus*, *sedit* (he sat), *securus*, *ab alto* (from on high). Only the adjective *tanti* tells us that there is more to come, and we have to wait until the last word of the sentence for the noun it modifies (*tanti ... sceleris*, of such ... a crime). Meanwhile we conjecture that the genitive case of the adjective (*tanti*) is governed by *securus* (careless **of** such a great ...), as in the phrase *securus tanti volneris* (careless of such a great wound) in Caesar's lion simile. But the noun *sceleris* (crime) turns out to have a more important connection with the emphatically enjambed *spectator* (spectator of such a great crime). Sulla is untroubled by what he has brought about because he is a spectator, engaged only in watching. His 'security', in this connection, comprises something of the English sense of 'safety', and it brings him uncomfortably close to us readers, who also watch monstrous crime from a safe distance. Matthew Leigh has argued that throughout his epic Lucan forces the reader to confront the distinction between two possible responses to his work, spectacle and engagement.[2] Will we engage with the moral issues that his poem raises or will we sit back and enjoy the very considerable spectacle with which Lucan regales us? Does our removal from the scene of action mean that only one of these options is open to us? What would it mean to us *now* to be engaged in that struggle? What would it have meant for Lucan at the court of the emperor Nero?

But to return to Cato. Suspecting that virtue cannot remain untainted by (*securus*) the moral quagmire into which he will step, Cato maintains his uncompromising persona in this potentially compromising choice by a breathtaking upping of the rhetorical ante:

> crimen erit superis et me fecisse nocentem.   (2. 288)
> (The gods will be accused of having made even me a criminal.)

Earlier Lucan had declared

> victrix causa deis placuit, sed victa Catoni.   (1. 128)
> (The victorious cause attracted the gods, but the defeated cause—Cato.)

Cato seems more than half in love with defeat. We remember the simile of the Numidian lion, with its undertones of suicide. Caesar's ruthless determination can assimilate the suicidal recklessness of Cato's virtue and come out the other end: the Numidian lion rushes onto the spear and through it. Would the republican cause have been in better hands if Cato had been more like Caesar?

---

[2] Matthew Leigh, *Lucan: Spectacle and Engagement* (Oxford, 1997).

When he introduced Pompey, Lucan suggested that the great general provides his followers with the comforting shade of a great name, not only *Pompey* but *libertas* and *respublica*. In Book 2, devotion to an empty name is given a positive slant by Cato:

> ceu morte parentem
> natorum orbatum longum producere funus
> ad tumulos iubet ipse dolor, iuvat ignibus atris
> inseruisse manus constructoque aggere busti
> ipsum atras tenuisse faces, non ante revellar,
> exanimem quam te conplectar, Roma, tuumque
> nomen libertas, et inanem persequar umbram.   (2. 297–303)

> (As a father, bereaved by the death
> of his sons, is compelled by grief to stretch
> out the funeral by the graveside, he finds pleasure
> in putting his hand to the black fire and holding the dark torch
> at the tomb's mound. So I will not be torn away
> before I embrace your corpse, Rome, and your
> name, liberty, and follow an empty shade.)

Cato's motive is simple piety. His devotion to liberty is such that he is compelled to follow even its name and empty shadow (*inanem...umbram*) to the grave. These words remind us of our introduction to Pompey as 'the shadow of a great name' (*magni nominis umbra*). Cato will follow Pompey not because he is duped by empty shadows and the comfort (shade) of mighty words, but because he wants to be present at the funeral of liberty and to pay respect to its shade (ghost) as it departs. Yes, all that is left is the shadow of a great name, but it *is* a great name, and respect must be paid to its shadow. Cato yearns to be in at the end, to experience and to participate in the obsequies. That is Lucan's need, too, for he must always regret that he lives under the shadow of an event in which he took no part. His own epic hovers over the decisive event, torn between the ruthless energy of Caesar, which will give birth to the future in which Lucan lives and breathes, and the pious devotions of Cato, squeezing the last drops out of an idea that history has rendered hollow.

Without the gods, without liberty and the Republic, we are left with personal charisma, that anti-republican quality. Of course, there were great men under the Republic, men who seemed to incarnate its values. One of them is alluded to when Cato describes the desire of the bereaved father to take part in the funeral of his son. Lighting the funeral pyre is one of the observances required of the male next of kin at a Roman funeral. But the words Lucan uses for this part of the ritual are extreme: *iuvat ignibus atris inseruisse manus* ([the father] wants to thrust his hands into the black fires). *Inseruisse manus* (to thrust his hands) is too strong an expression for what the father does when lighting his son's funeral pyre. It would immediately conjure up, in the Roman reader's mind, the action of Mucius Scaevola, who tried to assassinate an enemy king besieging Rome in the early days of the Republic. Captured by the king, Scaevola was threatened with torture if he did not reveal the details of any further plots against him. Scaevola defiantly thrust his hand into the fires that had been prepared for the torture and declared that there were many others at Rome who would be prepared to do the same thing. Unlike Scaevola, Cato can't point to others who wait in the wings. The scene that conjures up this memory of early republican virtue is a funeral, and at this funeral what should be a moment for mourning and grief has become the opportunity for a grandstanding claim to invulnerability. Cato, then, like Pompey, has his limitations as a representative of the cause that is lost.

We do not see anything more of Cato until Book 9. By then, Pompey has been defeated by Caesar, and what is left of the republican army has passed into the command of Cato. Book 9 is taken up by his campaign in Africa, or rather by a march, with no clear strategic value, which makes an astonishing display of endurance in the face of a hostile nature. Lucan left the epic incomplete at his death, halfway through Book 10. Some have speculated that he would have completed it in twelve books, ending with Cato's suicide. We will never know.

We last see Pompey, Lucan's nominal hero, as a headless trunk on the shore of Egypt, where he has met a sordid death at the hands of a pharaoh hoping to curry favour with Caesar. There his corpse is recovered from the sea by one of his solders, who hastily cremates it, buries the ashes in the sand, and plants a stone with the words 'Here lies Magnus' written with a charred stick. Lucan the narrator then takes over to wrench sublimity from the totality of this defeat. He castigates the soldier for burying Pompey at all, for that is to confine his soul:

> situs est, qua terra extrema refuso
> pendet in Oceano: Romanum nomen et *omne*
> imperium Magno tumuli est modus; obrue saxa
> crimine plena deorum. si *tota* est Herculis Oete
> et iuga *tota* vacant Bromio Nyseia, quare
> *unus* in Aegypto Magni lapis? *omnia* Lagi
> arva tenere potest, si *nullo* caespite nomen
> haeserit. erremus populi cinerumque tuorum,
> Magne, metu *nullas* Nili calcemus harenas.   (8. 797–805, my italics)

> (He is located where the ends of the earth
> loom over Ocean: the Roman name and all its empire
> is the limit of Pompey's tomb; overturn the headstone
> covered with accusation of the gods. If all of Oeta belongs to Hercules
> and the range of Nysa is all dedicated to Bacchus, why
> is there one stone in Egypt for Pompey? He could fill
> the whole kingdom of Lagus (Egypt) if his name were fixed
> on no stone. Mankind would be in doubt, and from fear of your ashes,
> Pompey, we would not tread on any of the Nile's sands.)

The very uncertainty and inadequacy of Pompey's grave would make his imaginary presence ubiquitous. 'Nothing' becomes 'everything' as the passage lurches between *omne* (all) or *tota* and *unus* (one) or *nullo* (none). I have italicized those words in the Latin text. If we look closer, we can see that the passage moves in three stages. First, a magnificent statement of the correlation between Pompey's presence and the Roman empire. Then the opposite: a protest that Hercules and Bacchus have whole mountain ranges associated with their name and Pompey only a stone. Finally, a renewed and more complex statement of Pompey's potential ubiquity: if his grave truly had no fixed location, we would avoid the whole of Egypt for fear of treading on his tomb. The nucleus of the passage is Lucan's doubly impious command: *obrue saxa crimine plena deorum* (overturn the stone covered with accusation of the gods). To deprive a grave of its identifying stone would be a terrible violation to a Roman mind. But any stone that reads 'Here lies Pompey' is not telling the truth, as the previous lines have made clear. The words on the stone are also an accusation of the gods, who have allowed this to happen to the champion of Roman liberty. Lucan adds that it is unjust that Hercules and Bacchus should have mountains dedicated to them and Pompey only a stone. (This is not quite as outrageous a comparison as it seems, since both these gods were originally mortals, and had been divinized for their services to men.)

Lucan's resonant equation between the bounds of the earth and the extent of the Roman empire is surely intended to recall the speech in Book 1 of the *Aeneid*, where Jupiter promises *imperium sine fine* for the Roman people. Jupiter goes on to prophesy the coming of a Caesar from the Julian family, which traces its descent from Aeneas' son, Iulus. In Vergil, Caesar's *imperium* (power, command) will be limited only by Ocean, and his fame only by the stars: **imperium Oceano,**

famam qui terminet astris (*Aeneid* 1. 287). Vergil's line is elegantly con-
densed, setting us the puzzle of how to relate the first two words
(command by Ocean), to solve it in the second half of the line by sup-
plying the verb that goes with both pairs of nouns (who will *bound*
his fame by the stars). The line then reads: 'who will bound his com-
mand by the Ocean and his fame by the stars'. If we look back to the
passage of Lucan I have just quoted, we see that *Oceano* and *imperium*
appear in consecutive lines at exactly the same metrical positions as
they take up at the beginning of Vergil's line. Hardly a coincidence.
Scholars are divided on whether Vergil's Caesar is Augustus or Julius
Caesar, but Lucan seems to have taken it as referring to Julius and to
have produced his own competing version of Vergil's prophecy, now
applied to the sublime fame of the civil war's *loser*. Loss itself, and
particularly the loss of Pompey's material remains, turns Pompey
into an idea, a memory of the Republic, all the more ubiquitous for
not having a location. In the next book Lucan attributes to Cato a
very similar thought, but with a slightly different attitude to Pompey:
now that Pompey is dead, Cato declares that he can be a whole-
hearted Pompeian, because the cause that bears his name is no longer
the cause of a living person. Republicanism is incompatible with
individualism.

Lucan's epic was left unfinished at his death, but the ending that we
now have is not inappropriate, for all its abruptness. Caesar, having
followed Pompey to Egypt, falls under the spell of Cleopatra, pre-
tender to a throne now occupied by her brother. Those Egyptians who
are opposed to her claim, including the architect of Pompey's murder,
Achillas, besiege him in the palace, and Caesar finds himself in a des-
perate situation. In the last lines of the poem, as he despairs of his life,
Caesar looks back and spots in the mêlée—Scaeva. We last saw him

stamping on his own eye in a rampage of suicidal battle lust. Like Caesar, Scaeva is a survivor!

Seneca's *Thyestes*: the ultimate thought

The civil wars were traumatic for the Romans, not only because they pitted brother against brother but because they could be seen as harking back to the foundation of Rome, when Romulus killed his brother Remus. That fratricide was the 'primal scene', the original sin, of Roman history, and it gave the civil wars a tragic status, as though they derived from a curse dating back to the very foundation of Rome. The theme of fratricide had another ancestry for Roman writers, namely Greek tragedy, which is rife with murderously dysfunctional families, and particularly brothers who kill each other. Seneca's *Thyestes* has its roots in Greek tragedy, but this story of fratricide and cannibalism had been popular with Roman tragedians before Seneca. Unfortunately, almost all Roman tragedy, with the exception of Seneca, is lost.

Seneca's plays are a fitting representative of their period, for theatricality has rightly been identified as a leading characteristic of Neronian culture. The emperor, after all, was a performer, both on stage and off. Whether Seneca's plays were meant to be staged or were to be read at a recital remains a subject of controversy. But, either way, they can be considered theatrical because of the self-conscious manner in which the main characters 'hold the stage', acknowledging the pressure to do something worthy of the resonant names they have inherited from Greek tragedy. Words rather than action are the focus of this drama. The Senecan protagonists command our attention, gear themselves up to action, and terrorize others by the sheer force of their rhetoric. The most famous of them are monsters: Atreus feeds his brother with his own children and Medea kills her children to spite her husband. They incarnate the indiscriminate competitiveness that is supposed to characterize 'Silver Latin' literature itself. Both are motivated by revenge, but the revenge they seek is absolute: the nullification of the person who has wronged them and whose wrong is felt as an intolerable challenge to their selfhood.

Seneca's *Thyestes* concerns the self-destructive royal house that provided the subject of many Greek tragedies; the family tree includes Tantalus and Pelops, in the previous two generations, and Agamemnon and Orestes in the following two. All these were involved, as perpetrators, victims, or both, in terrible crimes. Seneca's protagonist in this play is not the Thyestes of the title but his brother, Atreus, king of Argos when the play opens. Atreus rules, having expelled his brother, who had seduced Atreus' wife and, with her help, seized the throne. With Thyestes in exile and himself on the throne you would think that Atreus might be content to call it quits, but that is not to reckon with the psychology of Senecan revenge. As Atreus puts it, 'You do not avenge crimes unless you exceed them' (*Thyestes* 195–6). On his first entrance Atreus delivers a blast of withering rhetoric at—himself;

> Ignave, iners, enervis et (quod maximum
> probrum tyranno rebus in summis reor)
> inulte... (*Thyestes* 176–8)

> (Lazy, sluggish, gutless and (this I hold to be
> the greatest disgrace for a tyrant with something at stake)
> unavenged...))

The negative prefixes (*ignave*, *iners*, *enervis*, *inulte*) plunge us into the voracious hole that is Atreus' psyche. Whether he is goading himself into action or straining to conceive an act grand enough to compensate for the fact that it will come too late, Atreus' rhetoric serves to stave off an insatiable hunger. The pile-up of vocatives directed at himself both expresses a lack and tries to fill it. After three words that play with the same sounds (*ignave iners enervis*), Atreus indicates that the worst (*maximum*) is still to come. A rather pedantic parenthesis interrupts the tide of vocatives to allow Atreus to introduce himself to us, quite unapologetically, as a tyrant. Tyrants have their own code of behaviour, and Atreus' *probrum tyranno* (disgrace for a tyrant) is an oxymoron that takes us to the heart of his topsy-turvy world. The climax comes with another vocative, another negative, and this time it points not to a quality that he lacks, but to an act that is yet to be performed—vengeance.

Once Atreus has completed his opening tirade against himself, gearing up for revenge in a magnificent twenty-eight lines, on comes an adviser who tries to steady him. Seneca was himself the tutor and adviser of Nero, so these scenes have a peculiar resonance for their author. Dialogue in Seneca's plays is usually contest. A common scene pits the protagonist against an adviser, who tries in vain to moderate the protagonist's dire intentions with worthy sentiments. The cynical *Realpolitik* of the tyrant produces a more powerful rhetoric and a more penetrating wit, against which the commonplaces of the adviser are defenceless. In this case, the adviser leads off with a commonplace of ancient thought on tyranny: 'Does the people's adverse opinion strike no fear in you?' But his words are dealt out for maximum impact.

> Fama te populi nihil
> adversa terret? (204–5)

> (Does the voice of the people against you
> strike no fear?)

The adviser breaks in to complete the line of verse left incomplete at the end of Atreus' speech. In his opening half line the phrase *fama...populi* (the opinion of the people) encloses *te* (you, accusative) as the buzz of public opinion surrounds the tyrant. We wait to learn what verb has *te* as its object. Over the line break the words *adversa terret* (against [you] frightens [you]) deliver the threat of public opinion with maximum punch. Here the opinion of the people stands starkly against (*adversa*) the tyrant, rather than enclosing him (*fama te populi*). The unfolding of sense across the enjambement in a sequence of suspense and release is combined with a typically Latin spatial pattern: two three-word combinations are interwoven: *fama...populi...adversa* (the hostile opinion of the people) and *te...nihil...terret* (does it not scare you at all?). We can read the sentence either as a two-part sequence divided by the line break or as a series of alternations (fama *te* populi *nihil* adversa *terret)*.

Atreus dismisses the spectre of public opinion. For him, the greatest reward of power is that the people must not only put up with, but they must even *praise*, the acts of their master (*cogitur tam ferre quam laudare*: literally, 'is compelled as much to endure as to praise', 206–7). The adviser picks up Atreus's *cogitur* (is compelled) and spells out the nature of the compulsion: 'Those whom *fear* compels to praise are made enemies by fear' (207–8). Then he puts it in the positive: 'but whoever aspires to the glory of true goodwill will want to be praised from the heart rather than the tongue' (209–10). Atreus clinches the first round with breathtakingly brutal wit:

> Laus vera et humili contingit viro,
> non nisi potenti falsa. quod nolunt velint.   (210–11)

> (True praise is in the grasp of even the lowly,
> false praise is for the powerful alone. Let them want what
>   they don't.)

'True praise (*laus vera*) even (*et*) falls to the lowly man (*humili contingit viro*); only (*non nisi*) to the powerful (*potenti*) false (i.e. praise). What they don't want (*quod nolunt*), let them want it (*velint*).' Latin usage allows Seneca to omit the verb from the second half of his contrast between true and false praise, since it has already been expressed in the previous line, and this enables Atreus' stark and epigrammatic juxtaposition of false praise with power (*potenti falsa*). With the space and energy he has accumulated from this compression Atreus drives on to complete the second line with a command that expresses the final, impossible aspiration of power: *quod nolunt velint*. English cannot achieve the compression of the two juxtaposed Latin verbs, *nolo* (I do not want) and *volo* (I want); nor can it imitate the elegant chiasmus with which Atreus delivers his devastating theory of power: true praise (A) even falls to the lowly man (B) only to the powerful (B) false (A).

Always competitive, Atreus has not only outmanoeuvred his adviser but also outdone his earlier incarnation, in a lost tragedy called *Atreus* by the republican tragedian Accius. In that play Accius' Atreus declares, in an epigram that was repeated by the mad emperor Caligula, *oderint dum metuant* (let them hate provided they fear). The principle of Accius' Atreus is merely the starting point for Seneca's scene between tyrant and adviser. It is not just that Atreus doesn't care if he is hated, provided that he is feared, nor that he regards fear as the tyrant's essential weapon, but that tyranny for him is the opportunity, even the duty, to explore the ultimate reaches of power. Fear may secure power but, as Seneca put it in his treatise *De Clementia* (On Clemency), any paltry assassin can be feared (1. 5. 3). *De Clementia* was addressed to the young Nero, and in it Seneca tried to steer the new emperor in the direction of an enlightened attitude to power: anyone can kill, but only the truly powerful can exercise clemency. In *Thyestes*, the stage tyrant takes this structure of thought in an alarming direction: anyone can earn true praise, but only the powerful can elicit false. Is this to make his subjects 'want what they don't want', as Atreus goes on to declare? The ultimate power is to control the very subjectivity of your subjects, turning their will against them. Atreus is obsessed by the possibility of an act that will both avenge the insult thrown at him by his brother and express once and for all the true nature of power.

When his adviser realizes that resistance to Atreus is futile, he is drawn into a discussion about the best means of revenge. But it's hardly a discussion, for again the adviser finds himself playing the straight man to Atreus' ingenious rhetoric. As the adviser runs through the usual means of punishment (sword, fire, etc.), Atreus dismisses them, one by one, until he himself suggests 'Thyestes himself' (259). Puzzled, but overawed by the magnitude of what he senses behind this enigmatic phrase, the adviser protests 'This is more than anger' (259). Atreus agrees, and describes how his own internal disturbance at this thought is matched by rumbles in the earth, thunder from a bright sky, and movement from the household gods themselves. In a frenzy of excitement he cries out

> fiat hoc, fiat nefas
> quod, di, timetis.   (65–6)

> (Let it come about, that crime,
> O gods, which you fear.)

Fiat (let there be) is the ultimate word of command. *Fiat lux* (let there be light) is the command of the creator god in the Latin Bible. Atreus' repetition of *fiat* brings with it a shift in the metrical value of the word, whose second syllable is lengthened before the consonant with which *nefas* begins (the h of *hoc* doesn't count as a consonant). *Let* there be

light, let there *be* light, would be an equivalent of the effect, only it is
not light that Atreus invokes, but crime (*nefas*, cf. nefarious). *Nefas* is
'what cannot be spoken' (*ne-fas*). Its meaning shades from 'sacrilege'
to 'crime'. Here both meanings are appropriate, because what Atreus
wants is what the gods fear. We are some way beyond 'let them hate
provided they fear' but not quite as far as 'let them want what they
don't want'. Atreus wants what others don't *because* they don't, even if
'they' are the gods.

To make Thyestes the instrument of his own punishment would
take Atreus in the right direction ('let them want what they don't
want'), but when the adviser asks Atreus what specifically he has in
mind he responds:

> nescioquid animus maius et solito amplius
> supraque fines moris humani tumet
> instatque pigris manibus; haud quid sit scio
> sed grande quiddam est. ita sit. hoc, anime, occupa.   (267–70)

> (My mind swells with something greater, beyond the ordinary
> and above the limits of human custom,
> and it presses on my lazy hands; I don't know what it is,
> but it is something great. Let it be so. Take possession of it, O mind.)

Atreus' mind (*animus*) swells (*tumet*, cf. tumour). It swells in anger, in
presumption, in the pregnancy of thought and with the bloating of his
bombast. *Tumet* covers all those meanings. But the thought with
which his mind is pregnant is unknown to him: his mind swells with
an 'I know not what' (*nescio-quid*), something that is 'greater (*maius*),
larger than (*amplius*) the usual (*solito*), and *beyond* the bounds of
human ways (*supraque fines moris humani*)'. The three-part crescendo
is itself the swelling bombast indicated by one meaning of the word
'*tumet*'. Not only does Atreus' mind swell, but it 'presses on' (*instat*)

his lazy hands. *Instat* (literally, stands on) is the word from which we derive our 'instant', the moment that presses on us. But here Atreus' mind does not know what it insists upon, and so his hands are made to seem lazy by the mind's indecisive urgency. We might call *pigris* (lazy) here a proleptic use of the adjective, in which the attribute anticipates an effect, rather than describing a characteristic that is already there (prolepsis means 'taking in advance' in Greek). The example of prolepsis given in the *Shorter Oxford Dictionary* is Shakespeare's 'Hang his poison in the sick air' (*Timon of Athens* III. iv): the air is only sick because the poison has been hung there, but the adjective anticipates this effect. Prolepsis gives an adjective something of the dynamism of a verb. Atreus' proleptic 'lazy' ('my intention presses on my hands *so as to make them seem* lazy') here conjures up the physicality of an intention all dressed up with nowhere to go. Much of the drama of *Thyestes* is generated by Atreus' attempt to define what it is that will satisfy his consuming need, to give a name to what it is that obsesses him.

At the beginning of the lines I have just quoted, *nescioquid* is a pronoun: Atreus' thought is pregnant with an 'I know not what'. But in the third line it has dissolved into the indirect question *haud quid sit scio* (I hardly know what it is [but it is something big]). The 'something' has slipped out of his reach, just as it was coming into being. Now the 'something' is outside his mind, not inside, and he urges his mind to 'take possession of it' (*occupa*, cf. occupy). But the deed may be already 'occupied', as turns out to be the case when Atreus remembers the feast prepared by Procne for her husband, Tereus. The mythical Tereus had raped Procne's sister, Philomela, and attempted to cover his tracks by cutting out Philomela's tongue (more of this in the next chapter). When Procne discovered the outrage she killed her son by Tereus (Itys) and served him up to his father, who unwittingly ate him. This seems a promising model for Atreus' revenge, given that it turns the victim into his own punishment, as Atreus has already resolved. But no sooner has Atreus recalled this monstrous crime than he acknowledges in disappointment that it is already *occupatum*, repeating the same word from four lines earlier, but with a different shade of meaning. Is the absolute for which Atreus yearns, then, a competitive notion, or can it be defined in its own terms (*quod nolunt velint*)? Should he look inward to discover what he wants, or outward, at what has not yet been achieved?

Finally, Atreus is able to articulate the vengeance that would satisfy him:

> liberos avidus pater
> gaudensque laceret et suos artus edat.   (277–8)

> (Let the greedy father tear
> his children, rejoicing; let him eat his own limbs [i.e. 'flesh
> and blood'].)

We begin with the object (*liberos*, children) then proceed to the subject, *avidus pater* (greedy father), and then, before we are given the verb (*laceret*, tear), another adjective in emphatic enjambement gives a further turn to the screw (*gaudens*, rejoicing, cf. gaudy). This is certainly a revenge that goes beyond the feast of Tereus, and it fits Atreus' own definition of tyrannical power, 'Let them want what they don't want'. But is it possible? Can the father be made to eat his children (his 'own' flesh and blood) greedily and joyfully? That all depends on how you translate the adjectives *avidus* and *gaudens*. If we take them as equivalent to adverbs (eat them greedily and joyfully) then it's a tall order, but if we take them strictly as adjectives (the greedy, celebrating father), then perhaps something can be arranged...

Atreus' moment of revelation is now celebrated with an extraordinary pair of images in which the 'something' that has been haunting Atreus is transferred onto Thyestes:

> tota iam ante oculos meos
> imago caedis errat, ingesta orbitas
> in ora patris.   (281–3)

> (Before my eyes now the whole
> image of slaughter hovers, bereavement thrust
> into the father's face.)

The passage revolves around the juxtaposition of the two contrasting verbs, *errat* (wanders, cf. err, erratic) and *ingesta* (thrust upon or crammed in, cf. ingest), a juxtaposition brought about by a typically Latin chiasmus of parallel phrases in the two halves of the sentence (*abba*). The tormenting vagueness of the image of slaughter, the *nescioquid* that was haunting Atreus, now takes shape as the bereavement of Thyestes, which is thrust in his face (*ingesta in ora*), as clear for him to see as the wandering image of slaughter was not for Atreus. Atreus has projected his own tormented vision onto Thyestes. But the phrase *ingesta orbitas in ora patris* also admits of a crude physical meaning ('his bereavement crammed into the mouth of the father'). The physical meaning is supported by the metrical elision of the final vowel of *ingesta*, 'swallowed', before the opening vowel of *orbitas*, giving us *ingestorbitas*. The repetition of the *or-* sound (**or**bitas in **or**a) intensifies the oral effect. Atreus ends his speech by urging himself not to be frightened at what he has conceived but to press on. After all, whatever is unspeakable about the crime will be done by Thyestes, not himself.

And press on he does. Atreus invites Thyestes back from exile in a pretended gesture of reconciliation and, reluctantly, Thyestes comes. During his exile Thyestes has learned that the man who possesses little is spared the perils and cares of the rich and powerful. He is apprehensive about returning to the palace, and delivers a welter of commonplaces about the advantages of obscurity: 'crime doesn't enter the lowly hut; the cup drunk at the simple meal can be trusted, for poison is drunk from gold; the world is not plundered for my dinner, but my house needs no protection' (446–70). In short, 'to be able to do without a kingdom is itself a great kingship' (*immane regnum est sine regno pati*, 470). This paradox is the quintessence of Stoic ethical thought, which stresses the freedom of the mind to be its own master. It is the attitude that the Stoic Seneca recommends in his *Moral Epistles*, a series of letters urging a life of virtue, indifferent to worldly success, on his correspondent, Lucilius. Seneca had himself suffered exile because of his connections with the royal house. He had been recalled by Nero's mother, Agrippina, to tutor her son, for whom she had imperial ambitions. Seneca exerted a positive influence on the young emperor, but gradually Nero was seduced by less savoury companions. Seneca tried to retire, but his request was refused by Nero, and eventually he was implicated in a conspiracy and forced to commit suicide. Seneca may have seen himself, then, not only in the ineffectual adviser of the first act of his *Thyestes*, but also in the exiled Thyestes, recalled to the seat of power. Thyestes' Stoic convictions turn out to be weakly held, and it doesn't take much for his sons to persuade him, against his better judgement, to accept the offer of shared power. Seneca himself, who preached indifference to luxury and power, was an enormously rich man, and he knew that it was difficult to reconcile his wealth with Stoic principles. 'It is a great man who can eat from earthenware as though it were gold,' he said, 'but no less a man who can eat from gold as though it were earthenware,' (*Moral Epistles*, 5. 6).

The triumph of evil?

Both Thyestes and Atreus' adviser may reflect the uneasy conscience of Seneca the Stoic politician. But it may also be that Atreus himself is a perverse mirror image of Seneca the uncompromising Stoic sage. To overcome one's instincts, to display one's indifference to the standards of the herd with arresting paradoxes, to place all else beneath the single-minded pursuit of the supreme goal—all this Atreus has in common with the Stoic sage in his pursuit of virtue. We might say that Atreus expresses the emotions of the Stoic sage, but grafted onto a very different ethical content. The Stoic is always *under way* to virtue, which is an uncompromising task-master and an ever-receding goal. Atreus, by contrast, succeeds in *realizing* his monstrous ambition when he slaughters Thyestes' children and serves them up to his brother in a luxurious banquet. Or so it seems at first.

> Aequalis astris gradior et cuncta super,
> altum superbo vertice attingens polum.
> nunc decora regni teneo, nunc solium patris.
> dimitto superos; summa votorum attigi.
> bene est, abunde est, iam sat est etiam mihi—
> sed cur satis sit? pergam et implebo patrem
> funere suorum.   (885–91)

> (I walk as a rival to the stars and, above everything,
> I touch the highest pole with my proud head.

Now I possess the insignia of power and the throne of my father.
I dismiss the gods; I have attained my highest wish.
It is good, it is ample, it is enough even for me—
but why should it be enough? I will carry on and fill the father
with the death of his children.)

Atreus stands outside the house in which his brother is feasting. But in his imagination he is walking, with his head in the stars, or with the (divine) stars as his equals, in a proud procession. The image is both vertical and horizontal, capturing both the 'headiness' of power and the proud (*superbus*) gait of the Roman dignitary among his fellows. The first two lines make up a typical theme and variation: 'Equal to the stars I walk (*gradior*) and above all' places the verb in the middle of the line, with equivalent phrases on each side. But the order of the elements in these phrases has been reversed to stress the contrast between 'equal' and 'above' (**aequalis** *astris…cuncta* [all] **super**). The second line is enclosed by the phrase *altum…polum* (the high pole), with the adverbial phrase (*superbo vertice*, with a proud head) in the middle. In the third line, the dicolon has been compressed into a single line, with the verb (*teneo*, I hold) in the middle and an accusative phrase on each side. Paradoxically, only a status that removes Atreus from the human realm could confirm his kingship. Nero was said to have made a similar remark after the completion of his gargantuan and stupendously luxurious Golden House: 'Now at last I can live like a human' (Suetonius, *Life of Nero* 31. 2). Atreus dismisses the gods (*dimitto superos*) because he no longer needs to make any prayers. With the words *summa votorum attigi* he declares that he has reached (*attigi*, attained) the limits (*summa*) of his prayers (*votorum*, cf. vote). Here, the opening of his speech is recapitulated in more abstract form, for the primary meaning of *summus* is 'top' and *attigi*, a verb compounded from *tango* (I touch), repeats *attingens* from the second line. By *realizing* his prayers *in full* Atreus has *touched* the *highest* stars. He does not need the gods now because he is divine.

After a succession of bipartite structures, Seneca varies the pace with a tricolon crescendo which takes up the fifth line. But it is a paradoxical crescendo. *Bene* (well) is trumped by *abunde* (ample), but *sat* (enough) seems a poor climax to the sequence. Until we read on— enough *even for me*. What is enough for Atreus? To ask the question is to invite dissatisfaction: 'But why *should it be* enough?' *Sat* is cognate with *satur*, 'full', and Atreus goes on: 'I will fill the father with the death of his children'. With Thyestes full from the self-destructive appetite that Atreus has imposed on him, Atreus is himself satisfied. But even that, in itself, is not enough for Atreus. He needs to make Thyestes fully aware of what he has done, and to watch his brother's reactions as the full enormity of what has happened dawns on him. And so do we. It is here that the motives of the audience and those of Atreus fuse. Atreus commands the servants to open the doors of the house. In Greek tragedy, a wheeled platform would be used to bring a scene within the house onto the stage, and Seneca here alludes to that practice only to include this stage event within the drama of the play itself. It is a striking moment of metatheatre (where the drama reflects on the motives, pleasures, and mechanisms of theatre itself). Atreus acts as director and as playwright, setting up the scene of tragic recognition for his, and our, delectation:

> libet videre, capita natorum intuens,
> quos det colores, verba quae primus dolor
> effundat aut ut spiritu expulso stupens
> corpus rigescat. fructus hic operis mei est:
> miserum videre nolo, sed dum fit miser.   (903–7)

(I want to see, when he looks on the heads of his children,
how his colour changes, what words the first rush of grief
pours out, and how his body stiffens in awe
as he gasps. This is the fruit of my work.
I don't want to see him wretched but *becoming* wretched.)

Modern television audiences are well acquainted with the camera's
lust for the moment when someone breaks down in tears, or is caught
losing control in the face of an unexpected emotional confrontation
or piece of news ('And the winner is...'). Atreus' words here bring
home the full extent to which Seneca's drama of unhinged desire is a
tale for the consumer society, the society of the image.

The first line and a half zooms in on faces, gazing, gazed at, and
reacting: Atreus wants to see (*libet videre*), as Thyestes looks at the
faces of his children (*capita natorum intuens*), what changes of colour
pass across his face. From facial expression we move to the words he
will pour out (*effundat*) in the first onset of grief (*dolor*). The pouring
of words is followed by the expulsion of breath (*spiritu expulso*), and
the process terminates in petrifaction (*stupens, rigescat*). It is ironic
that the word *rigescat* (stiffens) is followed immediately, at the begin-
ning of the next sentence, by *fructus* (fruit). Atreus blossoms as
Thyestes withers. The passage is rounded off with a one-line Senecan
epigram, 'I don't want to see him wretched but (to see him) as he
becomes wretched'. *Miser* in its accusative (*miserum*) and nominative
forms respectively encloses the line: it is not enough for Atreus to turn
Thyestes into an object, he wants to stage-manage Thyestes' subjectiv-
ity ('let them want what they don't want'). Earlier in the play, Atreus
had said something very similar to the adviser when the latter lamely
suggested that he should kill his brother with a sword. 'You're talking
about the end of the punishment; I want the punishment itself' (*de*

fine poenae loqueris; ego poenam volo, 246). What is the punishment *itself*, and when precisely does Thyestes *become* wretched? As we shall see, the moment that Atreus desires has always passed. Thyestes' consciousness will always be out of step with the punishment that has been inflicted upon him, and Atreus' quest for the absolute act of power is doomed to frustration.

But, in the scene that ensues, Atreus enjoys playing cat and mouse with the apprehensive Thyestes, whose festive dinner has been accompanied by premonition and unease. Atreus gradually, and sadistically, brings his brother to the recognition of what he has done. He relishes the opportunities for irony when Atreus asks to have his children brought to him to complete the pleasure of the moment. Finally he presents Thyestes with the heads of his children, asking 'Do you recognize your children?' 'I recognize my brother,' Thyestes replies (1005–6). Or perhaps he says 'I recognize a brother,' for the Latin (*agnosco fratrem*) has no possessive adjective and no article, definite or indefinite. The possessive can be omitted in Latin when it is not needed, and articles, those 'fussy little words that blur our uninflected English', have no place in the language. Does Thyestes, then, see Atreus *for the brother he is*? We must remember that 'brotherhood' was not always a cosy word for a nation whose founding act was the fratricide of Romulus, and whose history was dogged by civil war. But no doubt we can find examples closer to home. We may understand Thyestes' two-word response, then, as 'I see the hand of my brother,' 'I see my brother finally in his true lights,' or 'I recognize the nature of brotherhood.' A Roman would not have had to choose between these nuances.

In his *Poetics* Aristotle had identified recognition as one of the crucial ingredients of a complex tragic plot, describing it as 'a change from ignorance to knowledge, tending either to affection or to enmity' (*Poetics* 1452ª). This certainly fits the scene before us, in which Thyestes is enlightened about the true nature of his bother's 'reconciliation'. Atreus sets up a recognition scene, and announces it as such. This is another example of metatheatricality, which here uncomfortably aligns the motives and desires of Atreus with those of the tragic audience. We savour Thyestes' unwittingly ironic words along with Atreus, and we anticipate the moment of recognition with excitement and curiosity. When Atreus says that he wants to see 'what colours Thyestes goes' as he looks on the faces of his children, the phrase he uses is *quos det colores* (literally, what colours he gives). *Color* is a word used in Roman rhetorical theory to mean either the figures an orator might use to ornament a speech or, more specifically, the slant or 'spin' he might give to a situation or argument. The verb *dare* (to give) can be used of involuntary actions, but it has a range of more active senses, including 'to utter'. For the audience, it is indeed of interest to see what 'complexion' Thyestes (and Seneca) will put on the situation when the recognition takes place. And we are not disappointed, for 'I recognize my brother' is a brilliant rhetorical coup that puts the situation in a quite unexpected light.

But, to return from the metatheatrical to the theatrical, we can now ask whether Atreus' revenge has been a success. In a sense, it has. The original crime of Thyestes had dishonoured Atreus, and now Thyestes is forced to 'recognize' him, and only him, even to the exclusion of his own children. But what of 'the punishment itself' and the ambition to make others 'want what they don't want'? One could say that Thyestes was 'greedy' and 'rejoicing' *when* he ate his children, in the sense that it happened at a luxurious celebratory feast, however clouded by anxiety. But did he eat them greedily and with joy? Atreus' triumph swiftly gives way to disappointment and regret:

> hoc quoque exiguum est mihi.
> ex vulnere ipso sanguinem calidum in tua
> defundere ora debui, ut viventium
> biberes cruorem; verba sunt irae data
> dum propero.   (1053–7)

> (Even this is paltry to me.
> I should have poured warm blood from the wound itself
> into your mouth, so you could have drunk
> the blood of the living. I have cheated my anger
> in my haste.)

Atreus complains that he has bypassed the punishment itself and left himself with 'the end of the punishment'. Now he wants to press the rewind button. Echoing sounds in exactly the same position of consecutive lines fuse the mouth of Thyestes (*ora*, cf. oral) with the blood (*cruorem*) of his children. The lines topple over into each other in a series of enjambements that seems to mirror the pouring of blood from living children into father's mouth, or perhaps the very hurry that has cheated Atreus of this satisfaction. 'Cheated' doesn't quite catch the full force of what Atreus says, for here he uses a colloquial idiom, rare in high poetry, that translates literally as 'Words were given to my anger' (*verba sunt data*, 1056). To 'give words' to someone is to deceive that person, and here it is especially appropriate, given the flood of rhetoric that Atreus has served up to his anger. Many of those words were devoted to gearing himself up for a revenge that Atreus felt was long overdue. But revenge is a dish best eaten cold, and now he castigates himself for having been in too much of a hurry. What follows is a description of his murder and cooking of the children that

is anything but hurried. It is a splendid example of the Senecan gro-
tesque and I quote it now, in Emily Wilson's translation:[3]

> Chopping up
> Their lifeless bodies, I pared their limbs
> To little scraps, which I plunged in the boiling pots,
> And had them simmered on a gentle heat.
> I cut the arms and legs and muscles off
> While they were still alive, and skewered them
> On nice slim spits. I saw them groan, and brought
> Fresh fires with my own hands.—But all of this
> Could have been better done by their own father.
> My vengeance is a failure. (1058–66)

The speech ends with a characteristically Senecan point, which sums
up Atreus' disappointment:

> scidit ore natos impio, sed nesciens,
> sed nescientes (1067–68).

> (He tore his children with impious mouth, but did not know it,
> and nor did they.)

Yes, Thyestes tore (*scidit*) his children (*natos*) with an impious mouth
(*ore...impio*), but he was unknowing (*nesciens*) and so were they
(*nescientes*). Where English has to add something like 'but he did it
(unknowing) to children who (did not know)', Latin allows us to omit
the verb that has already been expressed (*scidit*), leaving us with the
bare juxtaposition of subject (*nesciens*) and object (*nescientes*). What
Seneca does add is the repetition of *sed* (but), which makes a separate
item of the two points of view. *Sed nesciens* is bad enough (the father
ought to have eaten his children in full awareness of what he was
doing). But after the line break *sed nescientes* brings on something still

---

[3] Emily Wilson, *Seneca: Six Tragedies* (Oxford, 2010).

more horrifying—the children should have been aware that their father was eating them. We are not far from the horror of Goya's painting 'Saturn Eating His Children'.

So, Atreus has foundered on the impossibility of his visions of absolute power. The moment itself has passed into its aftermath and cannot be savoured. More importantly, the total domination of another's subjectivity implied by 'let them want what they don't want' is a contradiction, and cannot be realized. But Seneca leaves us with no comforting moral, no reflection on the incoherence of evil, for he gives Atreus the last words of the play.

> THYESTES   Vindices aderunt dei:
>   his puniendum vota te tradunt mea.
> ATREUS   Te puniendum liberis trado tuis.   (1110–13)
>
> THYESTES   Avenging gods will come;
>   my prayers hand you over to them for punishment.
> ATREUS   I consign you to your sons for punishment.

Thyestes must look to the future and to the gods, and he can act only through wishes or prayers (*vota*). Atreus needs no future, no gods, and he can make do with fewer words because he has turned Thyestes into his own hell. He repeats his brother's gerundive (*puniendum*, for punishing) and the main verb *tradunt* (hand over), both in the same position of the line. But where Thyestes flanks these words with a demonstrative pronoun referring to the gods (*his*, these) and a possessive adjective referring to himself (*mea*), Atreus' single line begins and ends with 'you': 'you for punishment I hand over to the children, yours'. And there the play ends.

In the interests of streamlining the action, I have omitted from my account of this play some significant elements. In the prologue a Fury

chases the ghost of Tantalus up from his punishments in the under-
world to inspire his descendants with the ancestral sin. Atreus' grand-
father, Tantalus, who had been granted the unique privilege of dining
with the gods, had served up his own son Pelops to the gods to test
whether they would detect the outrage. They did. In the underworld
his punishment is to stand in a pool of water that recedes every time
he tries to drink from it, while boughs of fruit trees dangle before his
eyes, but swing out of his reach when he tries to grasp them. He is
'tantalized'. Tantalus tells the Fury that he would rather return to the
tortures of hell than share the air of the upper world with Atreus, a
typical Senecan paradox. At first, he refuses to set the tragedy in
motion, but the Fury intensifies the torments of his hunger and thirst,
and he concedes. When Atreus comes on, then, he is already pos-
sessed by the spirit of his ancestor Tantalus, whose hunger can never
be satisfied. But this external aspect of Atreus' motivation does not
prevent Seneca from giving us an extraordinarily vivid and convincing
portrait of Atreus' deranged psychology, as we have seen.

The other element of this play that I have not touched on is the
chorus, which comments after each act on what has transpired. The
chorus's often naive moralizing, delivered in metres that recall Horace,
can get things quite wrong. After Thyestes welcomes Atreus back to
Thebes, for instance, the chorus breathe a huge sigh of relief that the
brothers are reconciled, and enlarge on the theme of change: 'even the
greatest storms subside; all great power finds itself subordinate to a
greater; no one should trust too much in good fortune or despair of
relief in bad' (a summary of 577–622). It is all very Horatian, and com-
pletely inappropriate to the world of Atreus' unrelenting fury. But, in
other places, the chorus seem very much in tune with the spirit of this
play. After they have heard a detailed account from a messenger of

Atreus' killing, butchering, and cooking of his nephews, the chorus express vividly the horrible frisson, the mixture of pride and shame that they, as witnesses of these events, share with the audience of the play.

> nos e tanto visi populo
> digni, premeret quos everso
> cardine mundus? in nos aetas
> ultima venit? o nos dura
> sorte creatos, seu perdidimus
> solem miseri, sive expulimus!
> abeant questus, discede, timor:
> vitae est avidus quisquis non vult
> mundo secum pereunte mori.   (875–83)

> (Have we of all peoples been judged
> worthy to be crushed by the world
> unhinged? Has the last of the ages
> come upon *us*? We have been born
> under a harsh fate, we who have lost
> the sun or expelled it.
> Away with mourning! Vanish, grief!
> He is greedy of life who does not want
> to die when the world is perishing with him.)

The horror of apocalypse is accompanied by an awe that verges on pride. Do we alone of all generations have the power to bring the world to an end? It is a question that haunted the Cold War generation, and now it passes to the generation threatened by global warming. Seneca's chorus begins with the most important word, *nos. We* have been picked out, of all the peoples of history (*e tanto...populo*, 'from so great a population'). Does the word *tanto* (so great) bring back memories of *Tant*alus, the man, of all men, chosen to dine with the gods, who chose to abuse the privilege? *Digni* (worthy), in enjambement, begins the next line. But the climactic sequence *nos ... visi ... digni* (we ... have seemed ... worthy) is overturned by the rest of the line, which converts the nominative *nos* into an accusative by means of the relative (*quos*), 'we ... whom ...' *Quos* is surrounded by two verbs of catastrophe: *premeret* (oppress) and *everso* (wrenched). So, we have been judged worthy (as the ones whom) *the world would obliterate*, the world wrenched (*everso*) from its hinge (*cardine*). I have translated these lines as a statement, but they are usually printed as a question, as in my quotation above. An ancient text would have had no such punctuation, and the decision whether to frame these lines as a bewildered question or a proud statement, or something in between, would have been an aspect of the text to be decided by a performer, whether reader or actor.

The chorus ends with a suicidal reflection that takes us back to the world of Lucan: 'He is greedy (*avidus*) for life who does not wish to die when the world perishes' (882–3). Can there be a *greed* for life? How different in spirit is this negative phrase from the 'lust for life' of the Hollywood-ized genius! Both *avidus* and *non vult* (does not want) need our participation if they are to have the emphatic sense they require: 'his desire to live is greed, whoever does not *want* to die'.

Coda: the death of a brother (Catullus)

Seneca and Lucan have taken us to some dark places and, more disturbingly, left us there. Neither of them allows us any hope that there is a world outside the fratricidal vortex of their poems. But there is one Latin poet for whom the word 'brother' was suffused with love rather than hate, though he wrote under the shadow of Caesar's rise and of the threat of civil war. It seems appropriate to end this chapter with the poem in which Catullus says farewell to a beloved brother. The poem unfolds in a single sentence reflecting the different facets of a complex emotion; its final words, *ave atque vale* (hail and farewell), are among the most often quoted and imitated in the Latin canon. It begins with a journey, for Catullus' brother, as the poet tells us in other poems, died somewhere near Troy, the home of Rome's ancestor Aeneas. Catullus' journey to his brother's grave recalls Odysseus' journey home from Troy to Ithaca, in which 'He saw many cities of men and knew their mind | and suffered many pains in his heart' (Homer, *Odyssey* 1. 3–4):

> Multas per gentes et multa per aequora vectus
>   advenio has miseras, frater, ad inferias
> ut te postremo donarem munere mortis
>   et mutam nequiquam alloquerer cinerem.
> quandoquidem fortuna mihi tete abstulit ipsum,
>   heu miser indigne frater adempte mihi,
> nunc tamen interea haec, prisco quae more parentum
>   tradita sunt tristi munere ad inferias,
> accipe fraterno multum manantia fletu,
>   atque in perpetuum, frater, ave atque vale.   (Poem 101)

> (Transported through many peoples and many seas
>   I come, brother, to these unhappy funeral rites,
> to present you with the last gift of death
>   and address in vain the mute ash.
> Because fortune has taken your person from me,
>   alas, poor brother, taken unjustly from me,
> now, for the meantime, receive what is given as a sad gift
>   at funerals, in accordance with the ancient custom
> of our fathers, wet with a brother's copious weeping,
>   and forever, brother, hail and farewell.)

6

·············

SCIENCE FICTION: LUCRETIUS' *DE RERUM NATURA* AND OVID'S *METAMORPHOSES*

We end with two epic poems that are, in their very different ways, startlingly modern. Each of them presents a distinctive vision of the way things are, but they do not do so, as did Lucan and Vergil, by telling us a story about how we got to be where we are. Neither do they focus on politics, institutions, heroes, or leaders. Instead, both these epics are intensely concerned with the physical world, and they see the fate of humans, in quite different ways, as embedded in nature. They also agree that everything is in constant change. But there the similarity ends, for the one poem takes the form of a philosophical argument, while the other is a compendium of stories and a virtuoso display of narrative technique. In the one, the gods play no role in the fate of humans, while the other presents humans as the prey of lustful, jealous, and vicious gods. Stylistically, too, they are completely different, as we shall see. The two works I am describing are Lucretius' *De Rerum Natura* and Ovid's *Metamorphoses*. The latter has been much translated, adapted, read, and appreciated in recent years, but Lucretius' poem does not enjoy anything like the reputation it deserves. The reasons are not hard to see: Lucretius' subject matter appears forbidding, and his poem is difficult to translate into an English that is anything like as urgent as the Latin. Lucretius is a missionary of the Epicurean philosophy, and his poem is one long struggle to bring his readers round to the only way of understanding the world that will allow them (us) to enjoy a human happiness.

Where Lucretius burns with conviction and urgency, Ovid is cool. In his *Metamorphoses*, a compendium of mythological tales, he tells us stories about the transformations undergone by humans; his narrative is a seamless chain of violent and extreme experiences, told with detached sophistication. Ovid's world is a world of wonder, of humans who are turned into trees, rocks, animals, flowers, water, and stars. But the reality that Lucretius would persuade us to accept is no less strange: everything that exists has come about through the chance collision of atoms falling through the void. The stupendous variety of the phenomenal world, and even the complexities of human behaviour can, and must, be understood in terms of the motion of atoms.

Poetry as conversion: Lucretius' *De Rerum Natura*

Lucretius' *De Rerum Natura* is a philosophical epic, but the modern understanding of philosophy does not prepare you for the passionate zeal with which Lucretius seeks to convert his readers to Epicureanism. Conversion and zeal we associate more with religion than with philosophy, which claims to be the dispassionate search for the truth. In the ancient world, however, philosophy was regarded as the art of living, and the central concerns were ethical. So, if Lucretius' poem deals mostly with physics, that is because a proper understanding of the physical substrate of our existence is essential to our happiness. That happiness is threatened by fear, and particularly fear of death and fear of the gods. From these fears stem all human ills. Once we accept that we are simply a combination of atoms that have come together to form a stable, but ever-changing, compound, and that eventually those atoms will go their separate ways, then we will cease to fear death. And once we know the atomic explanation for the occurrence of phenomena in the world, we will cease to attribute them to the gods and to fear their anger.

Epicureanism, a philosophy founded by the Greek Epicurus (341–270 BC) in Athens, has in modern times given its name to a refined hedonism, especially concerning the pleasures of the palate and the plate. Epicurus did make pleasure the main principle of life, but he was very clear that there is a limit beyond which pleasure cannot be increased, and that limit is the absence of pain—hardly a licence for wild indulgence! Epicureanism is an austere philosophy, austere both in its physics and in its ethics, so how does Lucretius' exposition of this philosophy amount to one of the greatest poems ever written? (Lovers of Lucretius, and I am one, tend to be almost as passionate in their advocacy of their poet as he is of Epicurus.) First of all, Lucretius' poem is a magnificent bifocal vision: we see the world we know in all its variety, colour, and, sometimes, terror, and we are also brought to imagine the invisible, colourless atoms bouncing off each other in the void to create the world of appearances in which we live. But connecting these two visions is a closely argued, combative, and urgent stream of philosophical reasoning. Brigid Brophy once described the experience of reading Lucretius as like playing chess with one hand while masturbating with the other. Not having tried this, I can't gauge its accuracy, but the attempt to imagine it helps to understand the sensation of reading Lucretius.

De Rerum Natura begins with one of the most exuberant and joyful first lines in Latin literature:

Aeneadum genetrix, hominum divumque voluptas

Metrically: dum da da / dum—da da / dum—da da / dum—dum / dum da—da / dum dum (the diagonal strokes mark the feet and the dashes the divisions of words).

Mother of the descendants of Aeneas, pleasure of men and gods

Lucretius (94–55 BC), a contemporary of Catullus, wrote in late republican Rome. Poets after him, such as Vergil, would have avoided the repeated endings in *-um*, marking the genitive plural (*of* the sons of Aeneas, *of* men, and *of* gods), but Lucretius loves alliteration and assonance, and here the repeated sounds are the beginning of a drumbeat that will resonate throughout his opening paean to Venus (the *-um* always falls at the beginning of a foot). She is invoked as the *genetrix* of the race that descends from Aeneas, and then, in a typical Latin dicolon, as the pleasure of men and gods. *Voluptas* (cf. voluptuous) is surely one of the most inviting words for pleasure in any language. Brophy spoke of its 'sexy glottal stop' (*-upt-*). The *-um* sounds move towards the *-upt-* of *voluptas*, which makes a climactic announcement of the principle of Epicurean ethics, pleasure.

Commentators have puzzled for centuries over why Lucretius, who believed that the gods existed, but had no concern for us, should begin his poem with a long-breathed invocation of Venus, as the goddess who leads all beings to propagate their kind in the stirrings of spring. The answer is that Lucretius starts from where his audience is; he does not plunge in with the first principles of atomic theory, but gradually takes us from the world as we see and 'know' it to the world as it really is. Venus, the goddess of love and ancestor of the Roman race (as the mother of Aeneas), is a good place from which to begin, and so are spring and the procreative urge. It is also appropriate to start a poem titled *De Rerum Natura* (*On the Nature of Things*—that difficult word '*res*' again) with the moment when Venus inspires the animal world to procreate, for the root of *natura* is the verb *nascor* (past participle passive, *natus*), 'I am born'. Nature is how things come to be born. After describing how Venus leads the animal world in its procreative dance, Lucretius announces that he will tell us how nature generates everything from the first elements and then dissolves everything back into them. The model for this process continues to be birth, for Lucretius calls his first elements *materies* (matter, derived from *mater* (mother)), *genitalia corpora* (generative bodies), and *semina* (seeds). The first two books will take us from these familiar versions of natural process to the forbidding world of atomic motion, in which invisible atoms, whose only qualities are size, weight, and shape, combine to form compounds and the patterns of movement from which everything we see derives. In the first book, Lucretius surveys the various views that have been held on the constituents of matter and argues that they fail to account for the phenomena.

It used to be thought that Lucretius was poetical only in his digressions from the gritty philosophical matter of his poem. There are a number of such purple passages in his epic, and the opening hymn to Venus is certainly one of them. Another is the extraordinarily intense denunciation of passionate love in Book 4, which contributed to the legend that Lucretius had been driven mad by a love potion (memorably celebrated in Tennyson's poem 'Lucretius'). But it would be wrong to dismiss the philosophical exposition as unpoetical. In the *De Rerum Natura* Lucretius makes poetry out of argument itself, as he goes about his mission of conversion. He will persuade us that the world must be as the Epicureans understand it, otherwise it would not be as we see it is. The argument is intense and relentless, and Lucretius describes this logical assault on the reader with violent metaphors. He will not let us off the hook. There is a more friendly version of this relationship, too, for the poem is addressed to a certain Memmius, a distinguished Roman politician. It is characteristic of Roman poetry to be cast in the form of an address to a particular (usually real) individual. Ancient didactic poetry is no exception, and Lucretius' *De Rerum Natura* is written to convert Memmius to the truth. Memmius is presented as a reluctant recipient of Epicurus' message, slow to accept such an extraordinary and unorthodox vision, apt to lose his concentration, and a bit lazy. Lucretius batters away at his reluctance, rallies his attention, and pours an inexhaustible stream of eloquent reasoning into his ears. Early on, concluding a series of arguments for the existence of void (without which bodies wouldn't be able to move), Lucretius says to Memmius:

> quapropter, quamvis causando multa moreris,
> esse in rebus inane tamen fateare necessest.
> (*De Rerum Natura* 1. 398–9)

(Therefore, although you may delay by citing many objections, nevertheless you must admit that there is void in matter.)

This is typical of the way Lucretius casts his recalcitrant reader. Memmius will bring up objections (*causando* is a legal term), but that is only delaying the inevitable moment when he will have to admit it, *esse in rebus inane* (that there is void in things). My translation is adequate only for the meaning of these words in the immediate argument. *Inane*, the neuter of an adjective meaning 'empty', is Lucretius' usual word for the void, a concept crucial to Epicurean physics, for without void matter could not move. But *inane* also means empty in a metaphorical sense, 'Having appearance without reality, false, illusory, hollow' as the *Oxford Latin Dictionary* puts it. And *res* (of which *rebus* is the ablative plural) we have already encountered in Vergil's *sunt lacrimae rerum*. It has an enormous range of meaning, including 'affairs' or 'public business'. So these words could (and, outside this work, would) mean 'there is a hollowness in human affairs'. This is not an inappropriate message to Memmius, the man of affairs. In the preface to his poem, Lucretius prays to Venus to bring peace to the world, for in these turbulent times Lucretius cannot write his poem in calm, nor can Memmius fail his country in its hour of need. Epicureanism recommended abstinence from public life in order to achieve the state of *ataraxia*, untroubledness, which was essential to happiness. One of Epicurus' most famous, and controversial, sayings was *lathe biosas*, 'Don't let them notice that you've lived'. The double meaning, physical and ethical, of the words *esse in rebus inane* links the two aspects of the Epicurean philosophy, and it is a good example of what it means to write Epicurean poetry.

One of the reasons why Lucretius wrote his *De Rerum Natura* as a poem is because it is not enough for us readers to throw our arms in the air and surrender, to acknowledge that he is right: we must also *see* the world as Lucretius wants us to see it. Lucretius must offer us a vision of the atomic world to which we can commit ourselves imaginatively, for without some kind of imaginative cooperation the argument will not have its ethical effect, and the whole purpose of the *De*

Rerum Natura is to make our happiness possible, to free us from fear. But how can we *see* the world of the atoms? There is something of a contradiction involved in Lucretius' insistence that only atomic theory will explain the phenomena, while this theory commits us to believing that the world we see is generated by the movement of unseen particles. In spite of this, Epicureanism insisted both on the reliability of the senses and on the reality of invisible atoms. And so Lucretius' poem takes a close look at the world as it is and at the same time asks us to look beyond that world to the atomic reality beneath. A double vision is required of us, and not only in what we see, but also in what we feel. Let us take a small example of this. In Book 3, Lucretius makes his most concerted attempt to argue us out of the fear of death. He argues, first, that the soul is mortal (otherwise we will be afraid of punishment in the afterlife) and, second, that death is nothing to us. Death is not an experience that we live through. In the course of this argument, Lucretius makes a distinction between the *animus* and the *anima*: the *anima* is life-spirit, suffused throughout the body, whereas the *animus* is (roughly) the mind, and it resides in a particular part of the body. We can lose a certain mount of *anima* without dying, provided that the *animus* is unharmed, but the opposite is not true. Lucretius compares the *animus* in this respect to the pupil of the eye: if the rest of the eye is damaged but the pupil remains sound, vision is not destroyed; but if the pupil is destroyed, darkness ensues:

> at si tantula pars oculi media illa peresa est,
> occidit extemplo lumen tenebraeque sequuntur,
> incolumis quamvis alioqui est splendidus orbis. (3. 413–15)
>
> (But if that diminutive middle part of the eye has been eaten away,
> light immediately falls, and darkness follows,
> even though the bright orb is intact otherwise.)

Light and eye are common metaphors for life in ancient literature, so it is appropriate to compare the loss of life to the eye's loss of sight. But there is another phenomenon that makes its appearance in these lines. The second line is a strikingly 'poetic' way of saying that the eye loses its vision, and the phrasing encourages us to read the event as a sunset: light falls (*occidit*, cf. occident) and darkness (*tenebrae*) ensues. The same words can also accommodate a third reading, as a description of death: *occidit* is a verb that is frequently used for death, and loss of light followed by darkness is a conventional way of speaking about death, especially violent death in epic. It is with the third line that the three systems of imagery (life, eye, sunset) meet and interact with one another. 'Brilliant orb' (*splendidus orbis*) is a poetic periphrasis for 'eye' that calls to mind the sun. But to say that the sun, having set, remains intact otherwise (*alioqui*) is to make a quite different point from saying that the light of the eye is lost if the pupil is damaged, though the eye is otherwise (*alioqui*) intact. Both meanings are conveyed by the same words. If we transfer these meanings back onto the subject of these lines, namely life itself, they have quite opposite implications. The fact that the sun sets in one place, but appears intact elsewhere, is hopeful, but the fact that the eye is blinded, even if part of it remains intact, does not offer much comfort. Throughout the poem, Lucretius tries to make us see familiar things from an atomic perspective: compounds form out of atoms moving randomly through the void, stabilize, dissolve into their constituent atoms, and then become part of new compounds; dissolution and creation form a continual cycle. In these lines we see double, as the pathos of death, viewed from an individual perspective, is subsumed into an overarching natural cycle: the sun that sets here rises elsewhere.

Like Epicurus, Lucretius insists that the senses are reliable guides to reality. He must then address the issue of optical illusions. How is it that we see (hear, feel) things that are not there? The answer is that the eyes do not deceive us, though the mind sometimes interprets what it sees in the wrong way. A vivid series of optical illusions illustrates this point, of which the most striking is an extraordinary description of the reflection of the sky in a puddle of water.

> at collectus aquai digitum non altior unum,
> qui lapides inter sistit per strata viarum,
> despectum praebet sub terras impete tanto
> a terris quantum caeli patet altus hiatus;
> nubila despicere et caelum videare videre et
> corpora mirando sub terras abdita caelo.   (4. 414–19)

> (But a puddle of water, no deeper than a finger,
> which collects between the stones on the paving of roads,
> furnishes a view beneath the earth with a plunge as great
> under the earth as the lofty gaping of the sky stretches above us;
> you would seem to be able to look down on the clouds and see the sky
> and bodies hidden under the earth in a miraculous sky.)

The sights and sounds of everyday Roman life have as vivid a presence in Lucretius' epic as the sublime expanses of the universe, but here both come together in a single image. Between the paving stones of a Roman road a vision opens up that reaches both down into the earth and up to the heaven in dizzying succession. The vision plunges downwards (*impete*, from *impetus*, conveys the motion) before we realize that what we are seeing is the gaping (*hiatus*) of the sky. The same sounds are associated with the plunge (*impete*) downwards as with the opening out (**patet**) of heaven. But the fact that we are seeing the sky reflected in the water below us is expressed in terms of the illusion that we are looking as (*tanto*) deep into the earth as (*quanto*) the sky stretches above us. While, in the next line, the jingle *videare videre* (you would seem to see) reminds us that we are getting confused. But who could resist the attraction of seeing heavenly bodies hidden beneath the earth in another sky? All this has been seen in a puddle no more than a finger deep! The tone is both wondering and mocking. Certainly, Lucretius is making fun of the grandiose interpretations that the mind puts on what the eye sees. And yet he is also describing the nature of the Epicurean vision that we must accustom ourselves to seeing, or at least imagining: the vast arena of atomic action beneath what is scarcely visible to us. The sky beneath the earth may be an optical illusion, but it is no more strange a marvel than the busy atomic action that is going on beneath our vision in the solidly stable objects that confront us.

In Lucretius' world the atoms 'wander' through the void, impelled by collision with other atoms, bouncing off each other. Occasionally, a group of atoms manages to create a stable pattern of motion within itself, forging a compound that is held together both by the connections between atoms of different shapes and by the continual bombardment of atoms from outside. The compounds are the phenomena that make up our daily experience: trees, people, air, stones, etc. Beneath their apparent stabilities lies a world of conflict and collision. Ironically, it is conflict and collision that are the creative forces in the Epicurean universe. Lucretius offers us, as both a manifestation and an analogy of this atomic motion, the movement of motes in a sunbeam.

> cuius uti memoro, rei simulacrum et imago
> ante oculos semper nobis versatur et instat.
> contemplator enim, cum solis lumina cumque
> inserti fundunt radii per opaca domorum:
> multa minuta modis multis per inane videbis
> corpora misceri radiorum lumine in ipso,

> et velut aeterno certamine proelia pugnas
> edere turmatim certantia nec dare pausam,
> conciliis et discidiis exercita crebris;
> conicere ut possis ex hoc, primordia rerum
> quale sit in magno iactari semper inani.   (2. 111–22)

In the excellent translation of Ronald Melville:[1]

> An image and similitude of this
> Is always moving present to our eyes.
> Consider sunbeams. When the sun's rays let in
> Pass through the darkness of a shuttered room,
> You will see a multitude of tiny bodies
> All mingling in a multitude of ways
> Inside the sunbeam, moving in the void,
> Seeming to be engaged in endless strife,
> Battle and warfare, troop attacking troop,
> And never a respite, harried constantly,
> With meetings and with partings everywhere.
> From this you can imagine what it is
> For atoms to be tossed perpetually
> In endless motion through the mighty void.

Again, Lucretius uses a closely observed image from everyday life. He describes this, in the first line of the passage, as a *simulacrum et imago*, a dicolon whose elements mean approximately the same thing (similitude). But the first sentence culminates in the verbs of the second line, *versatur et instat*, another dicolon. *Versari* means 'to be constantly before one', while *instare* means 'to thrust itself on us'. Not quite the same thing. The image is always there, and it demands our attention. The somewhat aggressive language (*instare* can mean 'to threaten' or 'bear down on') anticipates the battle imagery that is to come. Melville

---

[1] *Lucretius: On the Nature of the Universe*, trans. Ronald Melville (Oxford, 1997).

is right to use 'multitude' on two consecutive lines, but the effect is not the same as Lucretius' *multa minuta modis multis* (many small things in many ways) where the word *multus* (many) appears twice in quick succession, but in two different cases (*multa*, nominative plural; *multis*, ablative plural). The four words '*multa minuta modis multis*' (metrically, dum da, da / dum da, da / dum, dum / dum) are a typically Lucretian combination of similar sounds, a vibratory shimmer of sameness and difference, which results from the shuffling of similar sounds. The two forms of *multus*, at the beginning and end of the sequence, are metrically different (dum da; dum dum). Something similar happens a few lines down, where Lucretius juxtaposes words using the prepositional prefixes *con-* (= *cum*, together) and *dis-* (apart) to convey the 'meetings and partings' of the atoms (*con-ciliis et dis-cidiis*) and follows this up with a word beginning with the prepositional prefix *ex-* (from) in *exercita* (exercised). The jamming together of these prepositional prefixes makes the line a force-field of violent motion. But it doesn't stop there, because Lucretius goes on to say that 'you can conjecture' (*con-icere ut possis*) from this (*ex hoc*) what it is for the atoms to be tossed (*iactari*) in the void. Not only does he repeat the *con-* prefix from the beginning of the previous line and the *is* sound from *conciliis et discidiis* (in *possis*), but he also brings back the preposition *ex*. Finally, 'conjecture' (*conicere*) is compounded from the verb *iacio* (throw), which appears with a frequentative suffix in *iactari* (to be tossed). The effect of all this is to give us a very material feeling for the way in which meaning is constructed out of the basic building blocks of language. Lucretius' penchant for rearranging the same sounds, prefixes, or roots to produce different meanings has its doctrinal point too. One of the analogies he offers for how the same atoms combined in different arrangements produce different compounds is language itself. If we should wonder how atoms with no secondary characteristics except a limited variety of size, weight, and shape could combine to create the enormously varied world we see around us, then we need only consider language, which works with a limited repertoire of letters, sounds, and elements of meaning to create whole epic poems. When we read Lucretius we feel what it is to inhabit an atomic nature.

Lucretius claims that the behaviour of motes in a sunbeam is not only an analogy that helps us to imagine 'what it is for atoms to be tossed perpetually in endless motion through the mighty void', but also a symptom of the same, for the random and turbulent motion of the motes indicates that invisible bodies are moving those motes, and smaller bodies are moving them, and so on, until we reach the atoms. In the sixteen lines in which he makes this point about atomic motion the words *caecus* (blind), *plagae* (blows), and *turba* (crowd) recur, reinforcing the impression of violent and random atomic action. But this doesn't mean that the physical world is random. At the level of atomic compounds there is regularity in the laws of nature, even if at the level of the individual atoms there is not.

The simile of motes in a sunbeam comes a hundred or so lines into Book 2, which deals with atomic motion and shapes, and explains how secondary qualities are generated from these. The book begins with a famous, to some tastes infamous, introduction, in which Lucretius speaks of the pleasures of observing the troubles of others from a safe distance:

> A joy it is, when the strong winds of storm
> Stir up the waters of a mighty sea,
> To watch from shore the troubles of another.
> No pleasure this in any man's distress,
> But joy to see the ills from which you are spared,

And joy to see great armies locked in conflict
Across the plains, yourself free from the danger.
But nothing sweeter is than this: to dwell
In quiet halls and lofty sanctuaries
Well fortified by doctrines of the wise,
And look thence down on others wandering
And seeking all astray the path of life—
The clash of intellects, the fight for honours,
The lust for wealth, the efforts night and day
With toil and sweat to scale the heights of power.
O wretched minds of men! O hearts so blind!
How dark the life, how great the perils are
In which whatever time is given is passed!
Do you not see that Nature barks for this,
And only this, that pain from out the body
Shall be removed away, and mind enjoy
Sweet sense of pleasure, freed from care and fear.
(2. 1–19, trans. Melville, modified)

The opening lines of Book 2, quoted out of context, have often given the impression that there is a strain of *Schadenfreude* in the Epicurean outlook, or at any rate a bald acknowledgement of the human enjoyment of such voyeuristic pleasures. Even with Lucretius' disclaimer that it's more about seeing what you have avoided than about enjoying the suffering of others, this seems like an unattractive attitude. The language of fortification brings the ancient philosophical ideal of mental calm, *securitas* (being without care, *cura*), into the more dubious realm of the English word 'security' (the security of the gated community!). But this passage is cast in the form of a priamel (see Glossary). *Suave* and *suave etiam* (it's pleasant) are capped by the crucial point: *sed nil dulcius est* (but nothing is sweeter). The passage moves from natural disaster, through the human struggles of war, to the psychological motivations that cause turbulence in the human soul. What is sweetest is to look down on the ambitions and struggles of those who lack knowledge of what nature demands, and who pursue goals that will not make them happy. The heights become metaphorical; they are those of philosophy, which affords not only perspective on, but also detachment from, the rat-race that absorbs the unenlightened. When Lucretius calls the heights from which the philosopher looks down the '*templa serena*' (clear heavenly precincts) he implicitly compares the philosopher with the gods, and more specifically with the gods who, in Homer's *Iliad*, watch the deadly combats of mortals from the safety of their heavenly seats, as though they were the audience of a play. The Epicureans have often been cast as atheists, but they did not deny the existence of the gods, only their involvement in human affairs. For if the gods were to become wrapped up in human affairs they would no longer be the *makares*, the happy ones, as Homer calls them. We should not fear the gods, who have no interest in us, but should rather reverence them as models of a life that humans can attain. So here the gods are the model for the Epicurean sage.

The battles that Homer's gods observe on the plain of Troy are driven by the aristocratic warrior ethos of competition. The same ethos drove the politicians of the late Republic in Rome, as it plunged into the vortex of civil war. It is expressed in a ringing dicolon crescendo, *certare ingenio, contendere nobilitate* (to compete in intellect, to contend in nobility of birth); Lucretius' contempt for these mainstays of Roman political life is highly unorthodox. As in the later passage describing the motes in the sunbeam, the language here stresses violence, blindness, and randomness. Line 10 contains two words meaning 'wander' (*palantis, errare*). We must learn to look on the turbulence of human affairs with the same detachment as we do on the 'battles' of the motes in the sunbeam. But the pleasures of the sage are not exclusively those of a superior detachment from the errors and torments of others. We must listen to the demands of nature, which, like a dog, 'barks out' (*latrare*) its needs: that it be free of bodily pain and mentally free to enjoy the pleasure of the senses without fear or anxiety.

Though the Epicureans set great store by friendship, they did not approve of what we would call romantic love. But this was a more orthodox view than their outlook on politics. It was as ingrained in ancient thought that passionate love was a sickness, or madness, as it was that a citizen should engage in the public life of his city. Passion was clearly no more conducive to the *ataraxia* (calm) on which the Epicurean set his sights than was ambition. Lucretius saw the fear of death and consequent yearning for security as the driving forces behind ambition and the destructive desire for high position or power. Behind the violence of lovemaking he saw the same yearning for an impossible absolute:

> denique cum membris collatis flore fruuntur
> aetatis, iam cum praesagit gaudia corpus
> atque in eost Venus ut muliebria conserat arva,
> adfigunt avide corpus iunguntque salivas
> oris et inspirant pressantes dentibus ora,
> nequiquam, quoniam nil inde abradere possunt
> nec penetrare et abire in corpus corpore toto.   (4. 1105–11)

> (Finally, when, with limbs entangled, they enjoy the flower
> of youth, at the very point when the body can taste the coming joy,
> and intercourse has reached the point of sowing the woman's fields,
> they grind their bodies greedily, and mix their saliva,
> and breathe one into the other, pressing teeth against lips,
> in vain, for they can't scrape anything away with them,
> nor penetrate and sink into the other's body.)

The passage starts promisingly, with the bodies brought together to enjoy the flower of youth. The (male) body, on the point of orgasm 'tastes in advance' (*prae-sagit*) its joys, and the man is on the point of 'sowing the woman's fields'. But at this point the natural imagery is diverted into a grasping scramble, all the more intense because the lovers' goal, to penetrate and disappear into one another, is impossible. This is a much more violent version of Plato's description of what lovers want in his *Symposium*. There, lovers are said to be seeking their lost other halves, in order to become whole again, while in Lucretius they try to fuse through mutual interpenetration. Lucretius offers us an alarming psychological interpretation of sexual frenzy on the point of orgasm. Ultimately, it is the exclusive focus on an irreplaceable beloved that, in Lucretius' view, prompts this doomed yearning for what cannot be. His solution? Don't conserve your precious bodily fluids and store up for yourself pain and suffering, but ejaculate into whatever body presents itself:

> ulcus enim vivescit et inveterascit alendo
> inque dies gliscit furor atque aerumna gravescit,
> si non prima novis conturbes vulnera plagis
> vulgivagaque vagus Venere ante recentia cures.   (4. 1068–71)

> (For the sore thrives and digs itself in, feeding,
> and day by day the madness increases and the misery deepens,
> if you do not confuse the first wound with new blows,
> and, drifting into a wandering Venus, cure the recent hurt.)

Passionate love is an ever-deepening madness and disease, according to Lucretius. In the first two lines, he uses four verbs with the inceptive suffix (*-sc-*), which signifies a continuing process. The suffix picks up the *c* in *ulcus* and lets it suffuse the two lines: the sore (*ulcus*, cf. ulcer) *comes* to life (*vive**sc**it*) and *becomes* old (*inveterascit*, cf. inveterate). But this does not enfeeble it. Quite the contrary, for the frenzy grows (*gliscit*) and the misery becomes heavier (*gravescit*). In the third and fourth lines, Lucretius presents his solution. The third line is a 'Golden line', with the verb in the middle (*conturbes*, confuse), two adjectives on one side of it, and the corresponding nouns on the other (*prima...vulnera* = the first wounds; *novis...plagis* = new blows). To lay blow on top of wound (*vulnera plagis*) might seem paradoxical advice, guaranteed to compound the sore. But, as we have already seen, the random movement and collisions of the atoms in the universe are described by Lucretius without the negative weight attached to violence in the human sphere. Without atomic collision no world would come about. In the case of love, too, confusion is positive, because it deflects the lover's obsession with a single beloved. The final line of this passage is an extraordinary tongue-twister, which materializes in sound the confusion that has been recommended. *Vulgivaga... Venere* is a roundabout way of saying 'sex with a prostitute', using an adjective compounded of *vulgus* (crowd) and *vagus* (wandering). *Vagus* then reappears, applied to the lover himself. The line runs, literally, 'unless you, wandering, salve the recent (wounds) with a crowd-wandering Venus'. Both the prostitute and her potential customer are drifting like atoms that bump up against each other in the void, a corrective to the futile and destructive goal-directedness of the panting lovers. What is remarkable about the passage on love at the end of Book 4 is the way that ethical issues are conveyed by language that is associated with atomic physics. But this is only because the language of atomic physics in the *De Rerum Natura* has already been infused with metaphor. Lucretius' assault on love is compatible with his goal, throughout the work, to direct us from the narrow focus on an irreplaceable body (our own) towards the contemplation of an ever-shifting world, in which compounds form and then dissolve from the chance encounters of the eternal atoms.

Ovid's epic of sex...

By way of transition to Ovid's *Metamorphoses*, we can begin with a vision of sexual intercourse that is quite as intense and violent as Lucretius' lovers scrabbling to disappear into each other:

> 'I've won, he's mine!' she cried, and flung aside
> Her clothes, and plunged far out into the pool,
> And grappled him and, as he struggled, forced
> Her kisses, willy-nilly fondled him,
> Caressed him; now on one side, now the other,
> Clung to him as he fought to escape her hold:
> And so at last entwined him, like a snake
> Seized by the king of birds and borne aloft,
> Which, as it hangs, coils round his head and claws,
> And with its tail entwines his spreading wings;
> Or ivy wrapping round tall forest trees;
> Or, in the sea, a squid whose whipping arms
> Seize and from every side surround their prey.
> The youth fought back, denied the nymph her joy;
> She strained the more; her clinging body seems
> Fixed fast to his. 'Fool, fight me as you will',
> She cried, 'You'll not escape! Ye Gods ordain
> No day shall ever dawn to part us twain.'   *Metamorphoses* 4. 356–70.[2]

This is the climax of Ovid's story of Salmacis and Hermaphroditus. Hermaphroditus, son of Hermes and Aphrodite, is a beautiful boy who sets out to see the world. One day, tired from his travels, he strips off and bathes in the waters of a pool that is the home of the nymph

---

[2] *Ovid: Metamorphoses*, trans. A. D. Melville (Oxford, 1986).

Salmacis. She immediately desires Hermaphroditus, but he is virginal, shy, and reluctant, and so Salmacis dives in and forces him. The gods grant the prayer Salmacis makes at the end of this passage, and the two bodies become fused in a metamorphosis. Like many of the tales in Ovid's epic, this is also a just-so story, or to put it in technical language, an aetiology: this one is the story of how the Hermaphrodite came to be. Ovid's *Metamorphoses* has sometimes been called an epic of love, for that is the focus of most of the stories. But a good portion of Ovid's 'love' stories are stories of rape, and this is one of them. What is untypical, of course, is that here a woman is raping a man. The reversal is indicated by the simile, in which the tables are turned on the eagle by its own prey. The whole passage reads like a parody of the many male rapes in the *Metamorphoses*, for this is the victory of the weak. If water is yielding, it is also encompassing: Salmacis is 'poured around' Hermaphroditus (*circumfunditur*, omitted from Melville's translation); the ivy, which is so often in Latin literature a figure for the devotion and dependency of the weaker sex, has now become threatening, by association with the snake simile.

Not only, then, do Salmacis and Hermaphroditus metamorphose in this story, but so does one of the most common motifs of Ovid's poem, the motif of rape. Here, Ovid tries to imagine what it would be like for a woman to rape a man, and he comes up with a convincingly threatening image. One way to think of the form of Ovid's epic poem is as a series of variations on a number of story patterns and motifs. In the early books of the epic, to take an example, hunting appears as a figure of relations between different kinds of being: humans hunt animals, gods hunt humans, men 'hunt' women; everybody is, and has, a predator. Our predators are the gods. But, starting with the story of Apollo and Daphne in Book 1, the hunter can become the hunted, as he also does, for instance, in the stories of Actaeon and of Pentheus.

An important component of the hunting theme in the early books of the *Metamorphoses* is the association between hunting and love. On the one hand, ancient culture tended to make hunting and love mutually exclusive activities: young men or women who dedicated themselves to the virginal goddess of hunting, Diana (Greek Artemis), usually foreswore the pleasures of Aphrodite. On the other hand, ancient erotic literature frequently represented love as a pursuit, or hunt. So, hunting is the avoidance of love, but love is a form of hunting. Ovid's stories in the first few books of the *Metamorphoses* play with this ambiguous relation. In one of the first stories of the *Metamorphoses*, Apollo the hunter tells Cupid, boasting of the power of his bow, to leave hunting to real men. Cupid then shoots Apollo, who falls in love with the nymph Daphne. The hunter is hunted; the hunter is overcome by love. By the time we are introduced to Salmacis in Book 4, we are curious to see what will be made of the fact that she refuses to join her coevals in the hunt. In fact, Salmacis reverses the trend of all those followers of Diana in the *Metamorphoses* who reject love for hunting, for she stays behind to attend to her toilette. But Salmacis is not simply a lover who rejects hunting, for she exchanges one kind of hunting for another, her aggressive pursuit and 'rape' of Hermaphroditus.

The *Metamorphoses* has a permutational structure: it's as though Ovid were rolling the dice to see what combinations could be made of a restricted number of themes and motifs. The poem has no progression or narrative thrust, though its texture is continuous (*perpetuum*, as Ovid calls it) and its flow unstoppable. One story simply turns into another. Although Ovid announces at the beginning of the *Metamorphoses* that his poem will stretch from the beginning of the world to his own times, the chronological structure is only superficial. Ovid does indeed start with the emergence of the world out of chaos, and he ends with the empire flourishing under Augustus, but between those two points chronology is more or less abandoned, and he moves from one story to another with complete freedom and conspicuous randomness.

The story of Salmacis is one of a series of stories told by a group of Theban sisters (the daughters of Minyas) to pass the time while the rest of Thebes celebrates a festival of Bacchus. The Minyads do not recognize the godhead of Bacchus, and so they themselves will be punished and transformed when they have finished telling their tales; they will supply one of the many stories of humans punished by gods whom they have insulted, deliberately or not. Salmacis and Hermaphroditus, then, is a story within a story, and Ovid plays with Chinese boxes of stories nested within stories, sometimes to dizzying effect. At one point in the *Metamorphoses* we have four layers of narration (A tells a story about B, in which B tells a story about C, in which C tells a story about D). In some respects the main theme of the *Metamorphoses* is narration itself.

But the most obvious theme of the epic is, of course, metamorphosis. Almost always a story ends with a transformation when one of the characters has reached a point of intolerable extremity. The most famous of metamorphoses, much favoured of painters, is that of Daphne, in the first book. Daphne is the nymph whom Apollo desires when Cupid transfixes him with one of his arrows. She is also a follower of Diana, and so she has dedicated herself to perpetual virginity. Apollo chases her and she flees, but as he gains on her and is about to have his way she prays to the river god to change and destroy the beauty that is causing her persecution:

> vix prece finita, torpor gravis occupat artus:
> mollia cinguntur tenui praecordia libro,
> in frondem crines, in ramos bracchia crescunt,

pes, modo tam velox, pigris radicibus haeret,
ora cacumen habet: remanet nitor unus in illa.   (1. 548–52)

(Her prayer scarcely finished, a heavy sluggishness overcomes
    her limbs:
her soft breast is circled by thin bark,
her hair becomes leaves, her arms stretch into branches,
her foot, once so swift, sticks in lifeless roots,
the tree-top covers her face: her beauty alone remains.)

In Bernini's magnificent sculpture of this scene, the motion of
Daphne's flight is continued by the metamorphosis of her upheld
arm, sprouting with leaves, as though the transformation were itself
part of her straining to escape from Apollo. In Ovid, by contrast,
the speed of the chase suddenly evanesces. As Daphne's limbs are
overtaken by sluggishness the verse itself slows down, and her
transformation is described in five end-stopped lines, whereas the
excitement of the chase had been characterized by enjambement.
In the second line of this passage, Ovid rejuvenates a typical Latin
poetic structure, in which two sets of noun and adjective are inter-
woven with each other, by having it enact the wonder of metamor-
phosis. *Mollia...praecordia* (soft heart) is gradually infiltrated by
tenui...libro (with thin bark) in a line that captures the languorous
quality of this transformation, as though lovemaking had been
transmuted into another key. Then Ovid ticks off the various cor-
respondences that allow us to make a tree out of a human, or vice
versa: foliage is hair, limbs are branches, feet are roots. Since the
natural world has already been metamorphosed by our anthropo-
morphic metaphors, it's not a big stretch to reverse the process. In
other metamorphoses, Ovid condenses transformation to a number
of familiar processes to which all human bodies are subject: this

grows longer, that grows shorter, this hardens, that softens, one thing curves, another straightens, until we get from human to animal, vegetable, or mineral.

Although Ovid's epic is not a story, nor even a chronological sequence of stories, there are some signs of an order that will allow us to orientate ourselves in this epic of transformation and change. There are, for instance, points where clusters of stories share a common theme. After the early books, in which gods indulge themselves with mortal women, usually with disastrous consequences for the women, there are a number of stories of humans who succumb to forbidden desires. Love of sister for brother, daughter for father, husband for sister-in-law, and girl for girl come thick and fast in the middle books. If this is an epic of love, it is a love that seldom has a happy outcome. Ovid is a powerful psychologist, and he traces the onset of these passions with subtlety and wit. Let us take the story of Byblis, who falls in love with her own twin brother, Caunus.

At first, Byblis does not recognize her passion, and finds nothing unusual in hugging and kissing her brother. It is right, after all, for a sister to love her brother, and her passion grows under the shelter of *pietas*:

> mendacique diu pietatis fallitur umbra. (9. 460)
>
> (And for long she is deceived by the shadow of dutifulness.)

Gradually her love swerves (*declinat*) from dutifulness (*pietas*) and she finds herself taking special care with her appearance when she is about to see her brother. But still she does not know her own mind, and her passion has not formed any clear wish, though she calls her brother 'master' and wants him to call her 'Byblis', rather than 'sister'. When she is awake she harbours no untoward hopes, but when she is asleep she dreams of intercourse with her brother, and on waking tries to conjure up the image of her dream again. Ovid's narrative has so far traced the metamorphosis of Byblis' feelings up to the point where their nature cannot be disguised, and she is confronted with a clear image of her own desire. At this point, on waking from her dream, Byblis conducts an internal monologue that begins with a sharp recoil from the implications of her dream, but ends with the decision to reveal her love. In her monologue, Byblis returns to her dream repeatedly, but each time from a different angle; she makes a number of specious arguments that draw her nearer to accepting her love, but then she backs away. In a final decisive sally, she resolves to declare her love, but then, retreating, settles for entrusting her hidden passion to a letter. The letter, which will declare an unspeakable passion in indirect form, is an analogue of her dream, in which her desires were satisfied in fantasy. Byblis' speech is a masterpiece of psychology that can be appreciated even in translation. Here is the second half, in Melville's version:

> What do my dreams portend? What weight have dreams?
> Do dreams have weight at all? The gods forbid!
> Yet gods have loved their sisters; yes, indeed!
> Why, Saturn married Ops, his kin by blood,
> And Ocean Tethys, and Olympus' lord,
> Jove, married Juno. But the gods above
> Are laws unto themselves. Why try to fit
> The different rules of heaven to modes of men?
> This flame I'll force, forbidden, from my breast,
> Or, if I fail, oh, let me perish first,
> And as I'm laid dead on my bier, then let
> My brother kiss me. Yet for what I want
> Two minds must meet: suppose it brings delight
> To me, it must be sinful in his sight.
> But then no scruples held the fabled sons
> Of Aeolus from their six sisters' beds!
> How do I know these stories? Why so pat

> These precedents? What will become of me?
> Away, perverted passion! Let me love
> My brother with a proper sister's love!
> Yet if his love had first been fired by me,
> Maybe his madness would have found me willing.
> Well then, if I were willing had he wooed
> I'll woo myself. Can I speak out? Can I
> Confess? Love will compel me! Yes, I can.
> Or if shame locks my lips, then I'll reveal
> By private letter love my lips conceal.   (9. 496–516)

We know that the young Ovid studied for a career in law, which required him to master the demanding art of rhetoric. Byblis' speech is full of ingenious arguments, striking epigrams, and paradoxes of the kind that were cultivated in the exercise speeches through which students of rhetoric honed their skills. But Byblis shows a critical awareness of her own rhetorical cleverness ('Why so pat these precedents?'), and her final decision is desperately grasped rather than settled upon. Her letter to her brother, however, is an accomplished piece of sophistry, twisting an appeal to the careless abandon of young love to suit her incestuous desire:

> Let old men know the law,
> Examine what's allowed, what's right or wrong.
> Study the statutes. Love that heeds no rules
> Suits our young years. As yet we have not learnt
> What is allowed, think everything allowed,
> And follow the example of the gods.   (9. 551–6)

Ovid probably has at the back of his mind Catullus' famous invitation to reckless, life-affirming love:

> Vivamus mea Lesbia atque amemus
> rumoresque senum severiorum
> omnes unius aestimemus assis.   (Poem 5, 1–3)

(Let us live, my Lesbia, and love,
and set the value of old men's tongues,
all of them, at a penny's worth.)

But Byblis has applied this sentiment in a perverse way, to disguise the horror of a monstrous desire. Ovid's Byblis is a brilliant portrait of willed self-deception, in which the ingenious logic of the rhetorical school has been incorporated into a story where its very ingenuity performs a dramatic function. From his earliest poetry on, Ovid represented love as the site of deception and self-deception, sometimes unwitting but sometimes quite self-conscious. In the story of Byblis he runs the gamut of love's deceptions.

Caunus is appalled by his sister's revelation, as we knew he would be. Byblis reacts to his horror and disgust by thinking up reasons why her approach was unsuccessful: she should have been more circumspect, and should have sounded him out first; face to face she could have been more persuasive; the bearer of the letter should have waited for a more opportune moment to deliver it; and so on. But finally, acknowledging that what's done is done, she tells herself that she must continue with her suit because, as she plausibly argues, 'If I don't persevere he'll think it was merely lust' (9. 622). So, for the sake of appearances she must press her incestuous suit. Caunus flees the country with Byblis in pursuit. Eventually, exhausted by her search, Byblis lies down and weeps until, consumed by her own tears, she turns into a stream.

…and violence

The world of Ovid's *Metamorphoses* is often a violent one, and Ovid does not shy away from the horror, gore, and monstrosity that accompany his scenes of violence. These were as influential as any aspect of this hugely influential book. From Seneca's tragedies and Lucan's epic to Shakespeare's *Titus Andronicus* and on to the gore fests of contemporary film, Ovid's influence, direct or indirect, can be felt whenever violence tips over into the gruesome and the macabre. One of the most famous examples of this occurs in the story of Tereus and Philomela, in which Tereus rapes his sister-in-law Philomela and then cuts out her tongue so that she cannot accuse him:

> radix micat ultima linguae,
> ipsa iacet terraeque tremens inmurmurat atrae.
> utque salire solet mutilatae cauda colubrae,
> palpitat et moriens dominae vestigia quaerit.
>   (*Metamorphoses* 6. 557–60)

> (The remaining stump of the tongue flickers
> while the tongue itself lies trembling on the ground and
>   murmurs to the dark earth,
> and, as the tail of a mutilated snake will wriggle around,
> it throbs and, dying, looks for the foot of its mistress.)

The stump of the severed tongue flickers (*micat*), like the tongue of a snake, in Philomela's mouth. By contrast with the two short syllables of *micat* the next line brings on the four syllable *inmurmurat*, a darker word for the mumbling of the severed tongue to the dark earth (*terrae...atrae*). This is followed by the grotesque simile that introduces the snake, suggested by the word '*micat*', in a line that plays subtle variations on repeated sounds (utque *salire solet* mutilatae cauda colubrae). The animation of the tongue climaxes with the absurd, and much criticized, image of the severed tongue seeking out its mistress. Black humour is a feature of Ovid's poem, and many have found it a characteristically juvenile trait of a poet too pleased with his own wit, unable to leave well alone. But we must read on before making up our minds on this. Philomela overcomes her muteness by weaving her story into a tapestry and sending it to her sister, Procne, whose stupefied reaction is—silence:

> silet: dolor ora repressit,
> verbaque quaerenti satis indignantia linguae
> defuerunt...   (9. 583–5)

(She is silent: pain closed her mouth,
and words outraged enough failed her searching tongue...)

The second and third lines go, literally: '*words* **to her searching** *outraged enough* **tongue** | failed'. *Quaerenti...linguae*, 'to her searching tongue'. We remember the severed tongue of Procne's sister, which searched (*quaerit*) for its mistress twenty-five lines earlier: the gruesome passage can now be seen as a figurative cliché (the searching tongue) made literal, and in fact many of Ovid's transformations take the form of literalizing a metaphor. There is plenty of gore in Ovid's *Metamorphoses*, but it is not always pure gore.

Though the *Metamorphoses* doesn't trace the history of the world continuously from the beginnings to his own times, Ovid does begin with the origin of the cosmos and he ends with the rule of Augustus. The creation of the cosmos is described, as in most ancient cosmogonies, as a process of separation. Originally there was chaos, an indiscriminate lump, and this became order when earth was separated from heaven and sea from earth. The chaotic mass is arranged into 'limbs' (*membra*) in what amounts to the first metamorphosis of the epic. But most of the poem after that will tell of limbs that *lose* their human articulation in the process of metamorphosis, and it will also tell of the transgressing of the boundaries between the separate orders of being, which reverses the separations that created order in the first place.

Gods will copulate with humans, and occasionally transform themselves into animals for this purpose, and humans will become animals, vegetables, and minerals, or vice versa. It is a vision that has something in common with Lucretius' *De Rerum Natura*, in which compounds come together out of the floating atoms and then resolve back into their constituents in a ceaseless process of change. But where Lucretius dissolves the human into the motions and processes of the atoms, Ovid saturates the natural world with human stories, for each of his narratives ends with the origin of a new natural species as a human is transformed. The transformations perpetuate some moment of human extremity, which becomes the explanation for the characteristic, repetitive activity of the natural being into which the human has been transformed. One of the most poignant examples of this is the story of Aesacus, a young man who fell in love with Hesperie. As often in Ovid, this 'love' prompts a chase, during the course of which Hesperie is bitten by a poisonous snake and dies. In suicidal despair, Aesacus throws himself off a cliff. But the sea goddess Tethys takes pity on him, and turns him into a bird. Thwarted in his desire for death, Aesacus repeatedly tries to commit suicide by plunging into the sea, but is continually frustrated by his new nature. And this is the origin of the bird known as the 'Diver' (11. 749–95).

The nearest Ovid comes to a Lucretian didacticism in his epic is where, towards the end, he introduces the Greek philosopher Pythagoras to give a lecture on the theme of metempsychosis, the transmigration of the soul from one body to another. Pythagoras was by reputation the first vegetarian, a position dictated by his belief that the soul of your grandfather may have inhabited the cow from which that steak you're eating was sliced. Like Lucretius, Ovid's Pythagoras argues that we needn't fear death, but for an opposite reason—our souls are immortal, and simply change their habitation on death. That there is change instead of death Lucretius would have agreed, and there are many reminiscences of Lucretius in the lengthy speech on mutability that Pythagoras delivers. But if everything is subject to change, what about the Roman empire? Ovid doesn't say. In the final lines of the *Metamorphoses* he ties the survival of his book to the longevity of the empire. The transformation of Ovid, after his death, into this indestructible book we are reading is the last metamorphosis of the epic, which brings it to a close:

> iamque opus exegi, quod nec Iovis ira nec ignis
> nec poterit ferrum nec edax abolere vetustas.
> cum volet illa dies, quae nil nisi corporis huius
> ius habet, incerti spatium mihi finiat aevi:
> parte tamen meliore mei super alta perennis
> astra ferar, nomenque erit indelebile nostrum.
> quaque patet domitis Romana potentia terris,
> ore legar populi, perque omnia saecula fama,
> si quid habent veri vatum praesagia, vivam.   (15. 871–9)

> (And now I have accomplished a work which neither the anger of
>   Jove, nor fire,
> nor steel, nor corrosive time can demolish.
> Let that day, which has rights over nothing more than this body,
> bring to an end the uncertain span of my life:
> still the greater part of me will be borne, flourishing,
> above the lofty stars, and my name will be inextinguishable,
> and wherever Roman power spreads over the vanquished nations
> I will be on the lips of the people, and throughout the generations
>   my fame,
> if there is any truth in the prophecy of poets, will keep me alive.)

It is a confident boast, and not untypical of Roman poets, for whom humility was no virtue. The basic claim is made in the first sentence, which has a rhythm that is peculiarly Latin. In English we must say 'a work which neither x nor y nor z will be able to destroy'. Ovid's Latin distributes the words 'will be able ... to destroy' (*poterit... abolere*) between the last two negative phrases (*nec ferrum... nec... vetustas*). In other words, instead of first listing the impotent forces (neither...nor...nor...) and then naming what they will not be able to do, as we must in English, Ovid allows the latter to assemble within the negative phrases. The effect is polyphonic, as one melody comes to completion within the other or, to change the metaphor, it is like a wave rising up and breaking through the repetitive phrases (*nec...nec...nec...*).

We are reading Ovid's prediction because it has come true in ways he could not have imagined. The Roman empire is long gone, but its language lives on while there are still those who read it, and with every reading of his epic Ovid himself comes alive. *Vivam*, 'I will live', is the last word of this poem of change. It is striking that Ovid heads the list of natural forces that might threaten human works (fire, steel, decay) with 'the anger of Jupiter' (*Iovis ira*), a periphrasis for the thunderbolt. Ovid finished his *Metamorphoses* on the Black Sea, where he would end his life. He had been exiled there in AD 8 by Augustus, for reasons that are not entirely clear. But one cause was certainly his book *The Art of Love*, which Augustus thought (with some reason) preached adultery. This did not fit with the moral regeneration that was the linchpin of Augustus' 'restoration of the Republic'. In the poems Ovid wrote from exile, bewailing his plight and trying to persuade the emperor to recall him, he refers to his fate as a thunderbolt from Jupiter. So, in these final lines, as Ovid metamorphoses into his book and rises above the stars, embarking on his enduring posthumous career, he pauses to give Augustus the finger.

EPILOGUE

When does Latin poetry end? With the triumph of Christianity (some-where in the fourth century)? With the last verses written in Latin (not yet)? With the shift from classical quantitative to accentual metres (from the middle of the third century)? It is notoriously hard to draw the line under classical literature, but the little poem reputed to have been writ-ten by the emperor Hadrian (AD 117–38) on his deathbed seems to belong to a different world from that of the poetry we have read so far.

> Animula vagula blandula,
> hospes comesque corporis,
> quae nunc abibis in loca,
> pallidula rigida nudula,
> nec ut soles dabis iocos?

> (My charming little wandering soul,
> guest and companion of the body,
> what places will you go to now?
> Darkling, harsh, all bare,
> forgetting your usual jokes?)

Hadrian, who spent a great deal of his reign travelling the vast extent of the Roman empire, has been called 'the restless emperor', so this address to his soul, about to set out on the ultimate, most unknown journey, seems an appropriate form of last words. Hadrian addresses his soul as it is on the point of leaving his body, or maybe after it has departed. That the soul is a guest, companion, or even prisoner of the mortal body is a common ancient philosophical idea, but Hadrian invests the idea with a pathos that is hard to parallel. It is not uncommon in ancient poetry for speakers to address themselves, or a part of themselves, with encouraging words or reprimands, but here the pathos produces an unusual separation between Hadrian and the soul he addresses. Is Hadrian addressing his *anima* (psyche, life-spirit) as a part of himself, distinct, perhaps, from his *nous* (intelligence)? Or is he addressing himself under this designation? Will the soul go on its journey without 'him' (whatever that may be), or is Hadrian girding himself for the unknown? Perhaps the *anima* is thought of as whatever is left of him after he has been separated from his body, and the disembodied Hadrian-to-be is alien enough to become an object of address.

What strikes any reader of this poem immediately is the tone of Hadrian's words. The first and fourth lines are almost entirely made up of diminutives (marked by the -*ul*-, which only the word *rigida* lacks). This makes it very difficult to translate these lines into English, which has no diminutive form—hence all those 'Little Thises and Thats' (Little Red Riding Hood for the German *Rotkäppchen*, for instance). Hadrian's poem is difficult to translate into English because the diminutive form supplies a tone of voice rather than a meaning. If we translate *animula* as 'little soul (*anima*)', what do we do with the four adjectives '*vagula*', '*blandula*', '*pallidula*', and '*nudula*'? The first two belong to the soul and the other two attach to the places to which it will go. In the case of the soul, the diminutives are affectionate, but one 'little' or 'dear' is quite enough for one line of poetry in English. The diminutives in the fourth line are more difficult to characterize, since they describe the unknown and unpleasing places to which the soul will travel on its wanderings. For this reason some have wanted to take these adjectives with the soul (*animula*), as their grammatical form could be either neuter plural (attaching to *loca*, places) or feminine singular, like *animula*. All three adjectives (pale, stiff, and naked) might work with 'soul'; the first and fourth lines would then create a kind of chant addressed to the soul. Perhaps we can have it both ways if we read the adjectives as applying to the 'places' but having a causative force ('places which make you pale', etc.), a relatively common usage in Latin. Another way of taking the line, and I prefer this one, is to understand the diminutives as applying to the *loca* (places), but conveying the tone of voice one uses to speak reassuringly to a child: 'those places where you'll be going are a wee bit scary'. Hadrian talks to his soul as if he were talking to a child for whom he has an amused concern. The soul is described as *blandula*, 'endearing', or 'wheedling', 'coaxing', 'flattering'. (An interesting shift in sense and values has taken this word from its positive ancient meaning to give it the negative associations of our 'bland'.) The playful, childlike soul is fond of jokes, but these will have to cease when it goes on its journey (*nec ut soles dabis iocos*).

The nearest parallel to Hadrian's poem in earlier Latin poetry is Catullus' requiem for his mistress's sparrow (Poem 3). Catullus strikes a (mock) sentimental tone and describes the sparrow, which was his mistress's constant companion, as going 'on that dark journey from which they say no one returns'. He ends his poem with a string of diminutives, berating the wretched little (*miselle*, dim. of *miser*) sparrow because it has caused Lesbia's 'little eyes' (*ocelli*, dim. of *oculi*) to be 'all swollen' (*turgiduli*, dim. of *turgidi*). Catullus' requiem for Lesbia's dead sparrow would have been well known to Hadrian and his readers. Does this connection bring Hadrian's poem closer to Catullus' elegant facetiousness, or does it emphasize the difference between them?

It is not only the diminutives that are unusual in this poem. The rhythm too, is very distinctive. The poem is written in iambic dimeter. So, in a perfectly regular line, like the final one, you would have four iambic feet (short long: da dum), as follows:

da dum	da dum	da dum	da dum
nec ut	soles	dabis	iocos (pronounced yocose)

However, since two short syllables can be substituted for a long, in theory one could have a run of short syllables, and this is what the diminutive forms produce in the first and fourth lines. The first line runs:

da da da da, da da da, dum da da (the commas mark off the words).

This is very hard to articulate, unless you emphasize the stress accent: aniMula vaGula BLANdula. And similarly, in the fourth line: pallIDula RIgida NUdula. This produces a line of three stresses, instead of the regular four iambs that you would expect for this metre. The rhythm morphs from accentual to quantitative and back.

With Hadrian's poem, then, we come close to the accentual verse familiar from Christian hymns, with their heavy emphases and rhymes. The most well known of these is the anonymous thirteenth-century poem *Dies Irae* (Day of Anger), a terrifying vision of the Last Judgement. As part of the Catholic Requiem Mass, the *Dies Irae* was set by many composers, including Mozart and Verdi. *Dies Irae* is written in a four-stress line, with heavy stresses on the first, third, fifth, and seventh syllables:

Dies irae, dies illa
solvet saeclum in favilla
teste David cum Sibylla.

quantus tremor est futurus
quando iudex est venturus
cuncta stricte discussurus

And so on, for eighteen stanzas. The rather loose version of William Irons (1849) gives a good impression of the metre and rhyme.

> Day of wrath! O day of mourning!
> See fulfilled the prophets' warning
> Heaven and earth in ashes burning!
>
> Oh, what fear man's bosom rendeth,
> When from heaven the judge descendeth,
> On whose sentence all dependeth.

The rhyme is produced mainly by using words of the same grammatical form, which, in an inflected language, tend to have similar endings. In Hadrian's poem, three out of the five lines rhyme because they have nominative feminine nouns or adjectives at the end. That is an effect that would have been avoided in earlier Latin poetry, for which rhyme was not a significant structuring principle.

There is quite a gap between Hadrian's fond farewell to his soul and the thunderous terrors of the Last Judgement. Hadrian is as terse about what awaits the soul as the author of the *Dies Irae* is loquacious. But the Christian author does not characterize himself by the tone in which he speaks, for he speaks in a voice that can be adopted by the whole Christian community in the presence of its god. Hadrian's little poem, as we have seen, has a very particular tone of voice, and its quiet intimacy in the face of death's separation is an appropriate place to bring our exploration of the Latin poets to an end.

GUIDE TO FURTHER READING

The Oxford Classical Dictionary, fourth edition, edited by Simon Horn-blower, Esther Eidinow, and Anthony Spawforth (Oxford, 2012), is an invaluable reference work for all matters pertaining to the ancient world, and the literary entries are excellent.

On the fortunes of the Latin language, Nicholas Ostler's *Ad Infini-tum: A Biography of Latin and the World It Created* (London, 2007) is a very readable history of Latin from the beginnings to the present. Françoise Waquet's *Latin, or the Empire of a Sign* (2001) covers similar ground.

On the sounds of Latin and Latin poetry, Clive Brooks's *Reading Latin Poetry Aloud: A Practical Guide to Two Thousand Years of Verse* comes with two CDs and is a reliable guide to the sounds and metres of Latin poetry. There are several online sites where you can hear Latin poetry read aloud.

An excellent history of Latin literature is provided by *Literature in the Roman World,* edited by Oliver Taplin (Oxford, 2000); it is lively, up to date, and stimulating. Much fuller and more traditional in approach is Gian Biagio Conte's *Latin Literature: A History* (Baltimore, 1994). Susanna Morton Braund's *Latin Literature* (London and New York, 2002) is organized thematically and is a thought-provoking sur-vey of Latin literature, though it is not a history. Gordon Williams's study *The Nature of Roman Poetry* (Oxford, 1970), though not currently in print, lives up to its title and is well worth reading.

On individual authors, Bristol Classical Press's Ancients in Action series can be recommended (especially Philip Hills's *Horace*). More specialized, but still approachable, is the Cambridge Companion series, from Cambridge University Press, which includes thoughtful collections of essays on Horace, Vergil, Lucretius, and Roman Satire, with other authors and genres to come.

For the more adventurous, the series Latin Literature and its Contexts, from Cambridge University Press, features short, provocative books on aspects of Latin literature. Particularly important is Stephen Hinds's *Allusion and Intertext,* which provides a brilliant discussion of how Latin authors allude to each other.

All the above books can be read without a knowledge of Latin.

GLOSSARY

Accent   In Latin there is one accented syllable in each word. The accent falls on the penultimate syllable if that syllable is long or the ante-penultimate (last but two) if the penultimate is short. So, *merCAtor* (a merchant) and *eGREgius* (excellent). Latin verse does not depend on accent, as English verse does, but on quantity (see below).

Agreement   Latin is an inflected language (see **Inflection**). Nouns and adjectives are inflected to indicate number (singular or plural), gender (masculine, feminine, or neuter) and case. Adjectives must 'agree' with their nouns, i.e. their inflections must accord in number, gender, and case. Since Latin word order is very flexible, and nouns need not be placed next to their adjectives, inflection helps to show which words belong together.

Asyndeton   Greek for 'not bound together'. The rhetorical device of omitting conjunctions.

Case   Nouns, adjectives, and pronouns in Latin are inflected according to their case. In Latin there are six cases: nominative, vocative, accusative, genitive, dative, and ablative. The cases are associated with syntactical functions. The simplest are the nominative, for the subject, and the accusative, for the direct object. The dative indicates an indirect object. So 'He (subject, nominative) gave it (direct object, accusative) to me (indirect object, dative)'. The vocative is the 'calling' case: 'John (vocative), come here!' The genitive is the case of possession: 'The student's (genitive) book'. The ablative is more complex and can indicate separation, accompaniment, location, or time.

Chiasmus   A figure of word order in which two pairs of words (or larger units) are arranged so that the second pair reverses the order of the first (*abba*). For instance, the sequence noun–adjective may be followed by the sequence adjective–noun.

Dactyl   Greek for 'finger'. A metrical foot consisting of a long syllable followed by two shorts ($- \cup \cup$). It is the basic foot of dactylic hexameter.

Dicolon   'Two limb'. A sequence of two elements, often expressing the same idea. A common ancient way to achieve abundance (*copia*). For instance, 'I won't put up with this. I won't endure it.'

Diminutive   A suffix (in Latin usually *-ulus*) either conveying affection or diminishing the thing or person in question. *Gladiolus* is the diminutive of *gladius*, a sword, hence the name of the flower. In English, 'starlet' is a diminutive of 'star'.

Elegiac couplet   A common metrical form, used mainly by the love poets Catullus, Propertius, Ovid, and Tibullus. It is also common in epigram (e.g. Martial). The elegiac couplet consists of a dactylic hexameter followed by a dactylic pentameter (see the schema on p. 58).

Elision   'Rubbing out'. A term for the disappearance, for metrical purposes, of an open vowel at the end of a word when it is followed by a word beginning with a vowel, e.g. *Odi et amo* ('I love and I hate', Catullus) counts metrically as four syllables: *Od(i) et amo*. The same thing happens to a word ending in a vowel followed by an -m before a word beginning with a vowel: *O quant(um) est in rebus inane* ('what emptiness there is in human affairs', Persius).

Enjambement   In poetry, the carrying over of the sense from one line, or stanza, to another. The opposite of an enjambed line is an end-stopped line, in which the sense of a line is complete in itself. In Latin poetry, for instance, enjambement between the hexameter and pentameter of an elegiac couplet is common, but the couplets themselves are almost invariably end-stopped.

Foot   The basic, repeated unit of a metrical line (e.g. spondee, dactyl, iamb).

Gerund, gerundive   A gerund is a verbal noun (*walking* is good for you), and a gerundive is a verbal adjective (these tasks are *to be done*). In Latin these forms characteristically feature *-nd* at the end of their stem, so the gerund of *amare* (to love) is *amandum* (which inflects like a noun) and the gerundive is *amandus* (which inflects like an adjective).

Hexameter   Dactylic hexameter, the metre of epic, consists of six dactylic feet. A spondee may be sustituted for a dactyl in all but the last two feet. The final foot is either a spondee or a trochee ($-\cup$). See the schema on p. 57.

Hendecasyllable   An 11-syllable metrical line used by Catullus, Martial, and others. The schema is $--/-\cup\cup-/\cup-\cup--$. See pp. 67–8.

Hendiadys   'One by means of two'. Two nouns joined by a conjunction in place of a noun plus modifier. For instance 'The house was guarded by lock and door' instead of the 'The house was guarded by a locked door'.

Hyperbaton   An effect of word order: the exaggerated separation of a noun from its adjective.

Iamb   A metrical foot consisting of a short syllable followed by a long ($\cup-$, da dum). One of the conventional associations of iambic metre is invective (insult). But it is also the metre of dramatic dialogue.

Inflection   The changes in the endings of nouns, adjectives, pronouns, and verbs which indicate case, number (singular or plural), and gender, or, in the case of verbs, person, number, tense, voice, and mood. So, the *-orum* at the end of *bonorum* indicates that the adjective *bonus* (good) is in the genitive plural masculine (of the good men). The *-etur* at the end of *laudetur* indicates that the verb *laudo* (I praise) is in the third person singular of the passive subjunctive (let him be praised). The inflection of nouns is called 'declension' and of verbs 'conjugation'.

Molossus   A metrical foot consisting of three long syllables ($---$).

Polyptoton   'Many casedness': a succession of nouns in different cases.

Priamel   The modern term for a rhetorical structure consisting of foil and cap. In a common form of priamel the foil takes the form 'Other people say (or like) a or b or c,' and the cap 'but I say (or like) d.' Horace's first ode is cast in this form.

Quantity   Latin verse is quantitative rather than (like English) accentual. Metrical feet are made up of different combinations of long and short syllables. There are some rules for determining the quantity of syllables (diphthongs are long; a vowel followed by two consonants, of which at least one is in the same word, is long), but most quantities must be learned individually.

Spondee   A metrical foot that consists of two long syllables ($--$).

Topos   (pl. *topoi*) A Greek word meaning 'place'. A *topos* is a conventional thought or commonplace (*koinos topos* in Greek), such as 'It is the highest trees that are struck by lightning'.

Tricolon (crescendo)   A sequence of three 'limbs' (*kola* in Greek). The limb can be anything from a word to a sentence. Caesar's 'I came, I saw, I conquered' (*Veni, vidi, vici*) is a tricolon. If the limbs become progressively longer we have a tricolon crescendo: 'The truth, the whole truth, and nothing but the truth'.

Zeugma   'Yoking'. The use of one verb with two nouns when it applies to each of them in a different sense: 'He took his coat and his leave'.

INDEX

INDEX OF POEMS DISCUSSED